THE ILLUSTRATED HISTORY ENCYCLOPEDIA
THE ANCIENT WORLD

D0800590

THE ILLUSTRATED HISTORY ENCYCLOPEDIA
THE ANCIENT WORLD

Discover what it was like to live in the Stone Age,
ancient Egypt, Greece and Rome

CHARLOTTE HURDMAN • PHILIP STEELE • RICHARD TAMES

southwater

This edition is published by Southwater

Southwater is an imprint of
Anness Publishing Limited
Hermes House
88–89 Blackfriars Road
London SE1 8HA
tel. 020 7401 2077
fax 020 7633 9499

Distributed in the UK by
The Manning Partnership
251–253 London Road East
Batheaston
Bath BA1 7RL
tel. 01225 852 727
fax 01225 852 852

Published in the USA by
Anness Publishing Inc.
27 West 20th Street
Suite 504
New York
NY 10011
fax 212 807 6813

Distributed in Australia by
Sandstone Publishing
Unit 1, 360 Norton Street
Leichhardt
New South Wales 2040
tel. 02 9560 7888
fax 02 9560 7488

10 9 8 7 6 5 4 3 2 1

Publisher: Joanna Lorenz
Managing Editor, Children's Books: Gilly Cameron Cooper
Editor: Joy Wotton
Designer: Julie Francis

Previously published as four separate books: *Step Into the Stone
Age*, *Step Into Ancient Egypt*, *Step Into Ancient Greece* and *Step Into
the Roman Empire*.

Printed and bound in Singapore

CONTENTS

INTRODUCTION
The Birth of Civilization

THIS BOOK COVERS over two million years of human history, beginning with our early human ancestors in Africa and ending with the mighty Roman Empire. This vast period of time—and the nature of daily life for our ancestors—is hard to imagine. In the modern world, our way of life is constantly changing. Every year there are new fashions in clothes, games and music, and hundreds of scientific discoveries. For most of human history, however, change has been very slow.

IMAGE FROM LIFE
Early humans lived by hunting wild animals and collecting edible wild plants. The importance of hunting was expressed in early art, like this 15,000-year-old painting of a bison from a cave at Altamira in Spain.

Hunters and Gatherers

Until as recently as 11,000 years ago, all humans lived a simple way of life. People lived in small family groups, gathering edible wild plants and hunting wild animals. They never stayed in one place for long but moved constantly, in search of new food sources or following herds of wild animals. These early hunting and gathering people used the same kind of tools for very long periods of time.

BLADES AND POINTS
A few tools made of wood and stone such as these arrow heads and knife blades, a fire, clothes made from animal skins and a shelter were all our early ancestors needed to survive.

Settling Down

The first fully modern human beings, whose brains and physical appearance were similar to ours, evolved in tropical Africa about 100,000 years ago. They were much better at learning how to live in new environments than earlier species.

MAMMOTH BONE HOME
This is a reconstruction of a mammoth-hunter's house. It was built in about 13,000 B.C. in the Ukraine. Three thousand years later, humans were living in almost every part of the world, even the icy Arctic.

Growing Crops

These early humans quickly spread out of Africa and replaced earlier species, such as the Neanderthals, who lived in Europe and Asia. Gradually, their numbers increased, until they could no longer survive just by hunting animals and gathering wild plants. People began to settle into a farming way of life. The first farmers settled in the Middle East about 11,000 years ago. A few thousand years later, farming had begun in Egypt, India and China. By Roman times (2,000 years ago), most people in Asia, Africa and Europe depended on farming for their food.

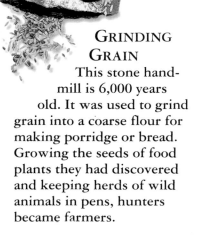

GRINDING GRAIN
This stone hand-mill is 6,000 years old. It was used to grind grain into a coarse flour for making porridge or bread. Growing the seeds of food plants they had discovered and keeping herds of wild animals in pens, hunters became farmers.

New Ways to Live

Farming led to huge changes in the way most people lived. It meant that they could live in one place all the time. They began to build long-lasting buildings of wood, brick and stone. People learned to bake clay to make pottery jars for storing and cooking food. Later they learned to heat certain rocks to create metals, such as gold, silver and copper. Metal tools were even better than stone ones.

Population Explosion

Farming led to important social changes. Because they had better land or worked harder, some farmers were more successful than others and grew more food than they needed to support their families. These farmers could exchange their surplus food for luxuries, such as fine jewelry and weapons, or they could use it to win power and influence over other people. As a result, inequalities of wealth and power began to develop between people in farming communities. Powerful individuals were able to become chiefs, ruling over people and controlling their land. Because farming increased the food supply, the human population began to rise more and more quickly.

MAKING LIFE EASY
A terra-cotta figure from Thebes shows a farmer plowing with two oxen. All sorts of new tools were invented to make farming easier, such as axes for cutting down trees, hoes for tilling the soil and, later, plows, and wheeled vehicles for carrying heavy loads.

LUCKY BRACELET
Craftworkers were supported by rulers so that they could develop their skills and make amazing objects, such as this Egyptian bracelet with the *udjat* eye.

When farming first began, there were only about twelve million people in the whole world. Today there are more than five billion people, most of whom still depend on farming for their food.

Cities, God-kings and Civilization

The population rose fastest in the places that had the most fertile soils, such as on the flood plains of great rivers. These included the Nile in Egypt, the Tigris and Euphrates in Iraq, the Indus in Pakistan and the Yellow River in China. The first civilizations (large communities with governments) arose in these areas between 5,500 and 3,500 years ago. Chiefs were not powerful enough to control such large communities as cities, so a new kind of ruler emerged: the king. To strengthen their power, kings issued codes of laws.

WRITING IT DOWN
An ancient Greek writes a letter on a wax tablet. The skill of writing was first used only for sending official messages, keeping government records of taxes and spending, and law codes. Only later was it used for recording history, legends, drama and ideas.

THE GOD-KING
When Akhenaten came to power in Egypt, he introduced worship of one god, the Sun disc Aten. To strengthen their power, ancient kings often claimed to rule with the support of the gods. Some, like the pharaohs of ancient Egypt, even claimed that they actually were gods.

The Invention of Writing

Farmers brought their surplus food to the cities to pay it to the king as taxes. The king then used this food to support people who had full-time specialized jobs, such as administrators, soldiers, builders and other craftsmen and women. All of these specialized workers depended totally on the ability of farmers to grow surplus food to feed them. Ruling these large communities was a complicated business. Systems of writing were invented to help rulers and administrators remember everything that they needed to know to do their jobs properly.

THE PYRAMIDS AT GIZA
The pyramids are a sign of the great power of the Egyptian pharaohs. The pharaohs controlled all the wealth and surplus food of Egypt, and used it to feed thousands of workers while they built these huge tombs.

The First Nation

The first civilization was founded by the Sumerians in the Middle East about 5,500 years ago. About four hundred years later, a second civilization developed in Egypt. The ancient Egyptian civilization was one of the most successful in history. It lasted over 3,000 years. While the Sumerians lived in dozens of cities, each with its own king, the Egyptians were all united in a single kingdom. They were the world's first nation. In time, new civilizations arose in the Middle East, Africa and Europe.

CLASSICAL STYLE
The ancient Greeks built some of the most beautiful buildings ever, such as the Parthenon temple in Athens (447-438 B.C.). Greek architectural styles were widely copied throughout the ancient world, and they are still influential today.

The Birth of European Civilization

The most important of these new civilizations was in Greece, across the Mediterranean Sea from Egypt. The ancient Greek civilization became one of the most inventive in history. Ancient Greek states were the first to allow citizens to govern themselves. They called this democracy. The ancient Greeks had some of the first scientists, philosophers and historians. They invented the theater. Their art and building styles are still copied today.

Growth of an Empire

The ancient Greeks were great travelers and colonizers. They founded cities all around the Mediterranean and throughout the Middle East. The Romans were strongly influenced by the Greeks. By the time of Christ, they had built one of the largest empires in history. Both Greece and Egypt came under Roman rule. Even though the Roman empire ended over 1,500 years ago, it still has an influence on our lives. The languages of modern Italy, Portugal, Spain, Romania and France are descended from Latin, the Roman language. Our alphabet was invented by the Romans. Germany and France have laws that are based on Roman laws. London and Paris were founded by the Romans.

LOVE OF MONEY
The ancient Greeks were among the first people in the world to use money.

LEGIONARY
A Roman legionary in full armor. War was important to all early civilizations, but it was the Romans who were most successful, thanks to their efficient, highly trained and well paid professional army.

9

THE STONE AGE

CHARLOTTE HURDMAN

CONSULTANT:
DR ROBIN HOLGATE, LUTON MUSEUM

The Stone Age spans over two million years—which is most of the history of humankind. It is called the Stone Age because most of the tools and weapons used in everyday life were made from stones and flints. It was a time when people lived in small family groups. Early Stone Age people gathered wild plants and hunted wild animals for food. They did not have permanent homes, but were constantly on the move, in search of new hunting grounds. Over a very long period, they gradually started to stay longer in one place as they learned to farm the land and domesticate animals. They began to build homes and villages, and make pottery and plows.

The Dawn of Humankind

THE FIRST PERIOD in human history is called the Stone Age. Stone was used to make tools and other objects. Some of these objects survive today. Wood, bone and plant fibers were also used, but they rotted, leaving little trace.

Our earliest human ancestors were making tools from stone at least two million years ago, but our story really starts with the arrival of modern humans, called *Homo sapiens sapiens,* about 100,000 years ago. The Stone Age is part of human prehistory, which means that it took place before there were any written records. Archaeologists have to be detectives, piecing together what might have happened. Special techniques, such as radiocarbon dating, help experts to figure out what life was like thousands of years ago. We can also look at modern-day hunter-gatherer cultures for clues as to how Stone Age people lived.

SKELETONS AND BURIALS
This is the skeleton of a Neanderthal man who was buried about 60,000 years ago. Human remains and the objects buried with them can tell experts a lot about early people.

CAVE PAINTINGS
This beautiful painting of a bison is from the caves at Altamira in Spain. It was painted in about 13,000 B.C. by prehistoric hunters. Cave paintings often show animals that were hunted at the time.

TIMELINE 120,000–10,000 B.C.

The huge periods over which human prehistory has taken place mean that even with scientific dating, timings can only be approximate.

120,000 B.C. Neanderthal people, or *Homo sapiens neanderthalensis*, are living in Europe and western Asia. There is evidence in Iraq that they are burying their dead.

Neanderthal woman

100,000 B.C. Modern humans, or *Homo sapiens sapiens,* are living in eastern and southern Africa.

skull of Homo sapiens neanderthalensis

skull of Homo sapiens sapiens

50,000 B.C. Humans settle in Australia from southeastern Asia.

42,000 B.C. Red ocher earth is mined in Swaziland in Africa.

38,000 B.C. Modern humans are living at Cro-Magnon in France.

| 120,000 B.C. | 100,000 B.C. | 80,000 B.C. | 60,000 B.C. | 30,000 B.C. |

SCENES FROM LIFE

This rock engraving, or carving, from Namibia shows two giraffes. It was carved by hunters in southern Africa around 6000 B.C. The North American continent is the only one where early prehistoric art like this has not yet been found.

SCULPTURES

Small carvings of prehistoric women are called Venus figurines. This one was made around 23,000 B.C. The many sculptures that have been found can give clues to Stone Age people's ideas and beliefs.

TOOLS

Looking at stone tools can tell us how they may have been made and used. Tools such as this hand-axe and these scrapers were used for preparing meat and hides.

CLUES IN CAVES

Many rock shelters and natural caves, like this one in Malta, have been lived in for thousands of years. Much of our knowledge about prehistoric people has been found by carefully digging through layers of rock and soil in sites like this. Many rock homes seem to have been lived in for thousands of years before being abandoned.

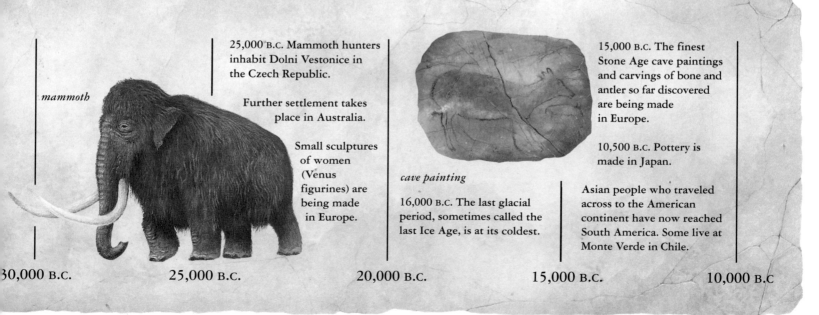

mammoth

25,000 B.C. Mammoth hunters inhabit Dolni Vestonice in the Czech Republic.

Further settlement takes place in Australia.

Small sculptures of women (Venus figurines) are being made in Europe.

cave painting

16,000 B.C. The last glacial period, sometimes called the last Ice Age, is at its coldest.

15,000 B.C. The finest Stone Age cave paintings and carvings of bone and antler so far discovered are being made in Europe.

10,500 B.C. Pottery is made in Japan.

Asian people who traveled across to the American continent have now reached South America. Some live at Monte Verde in Chile.

30,000 B.C.   25,000 B.C.   20,000 B.C.   15,000 B.C.   10,000 B.C

The Stone Age World

THE STONE AGE is the longest period of human history. It covers such a vast time period that it is often divided into stages, according to the type of tools people were using. The first and by far the longest stage was the Palaeolithic period, or Old Stone Age, which began more than two million years ago. During this time, people made the first stone tools. It was followed by the Mesolithic period, or Middle Stone Age, around 10,000 B.C. During this period people began to use new tools, such as bows and arrows, to hunt deer and wild pigs. From about 8000 B.C., the Neolithic period, or New Stone Age, began with the start of farming. However, the Stone Age has lasted for different periods of time in different parts of the world, so these distinctions are not always helpful. The Stone Age came to an end when people began to work metals on a large scale.

Modern human beings now live all over the earth, but views vary about how this happened. Some experts think we evolved, or developed, in Africa before spreading out into Asia and Europe. Others think we evolved separately in different parts of the world. The first people to reach America probably crossed from Siberia in Russia when the Bering Strait was dry land. This may have been around 13,000 B.C. or even earlier. By about 10,000 B.C., however, people had reached right to the tip of South America.

mastodon, Canada
20,000BC

bisons,
North America
9000BC

NORTH AMERICA

CENTRAL AMERICA

agriculture, South America
7000

Origins of agriculture

cave art, Argentina
8500BC

TIMELINE 10,000 B.C.–5000 B.C.

10,000 B.C. The last glacial period ends and the climate becomes warmer.

By this date, humans have reached Patagonia at the tip of South America.

Grindstones for making flour are used in Egypt and Nubia in northern Africa.

Mammoths and woolly rhinoceroses are now extinct in central and western Europe.

einkorn wheat

9000 B.C. The Clovis culture is flourishing in North America.

Einkhorn wheat is harvested in Syria.

Many large mammals have become extinct in America.

8500 B.C. Sheep and goats are now domesticated in Mesopotamia (modern Iraq).

Squash, peppers and beans are being grown in Peru.

Squash, peppers and beans

8000 B.C. Grains are cultivated in the Near East.

A lasting settlement is built at Jericho in Jordan and begins to grow to become the first town.

Mesolithic tools

10,000 B.C.   9000 B.C.   8000 B.C.   7000 B.C.

migrating reindeer, Russia
15,000BC

EUROPE

clay figurine,
Czech Republic
24,000BC

cave art, France
15,000BC

ASIA

pottery, Japan
10,500BC

settlement,
Turkey
6,500BC

rock art,
Sahara
6000BC

Peking Man, China
460,0000BC

Homo habilis *skull, Kenya*
2.5 million years ago

Homo erectus *skull,*
Java, 120,000BC

AFRICA

SOUTH AMERICA

N

cave art, Namibia
8000BC

AUSTRALIA

THE STONE AGE WORLD
This map shows places of
importance during the Stone Age.

indigenous peoples,
Australia
50,000BC

7000 B.C. Pottery is made in China and the Near East.

The town of Çatal Hüyük in Turkey is established.

The Bering Strait separates North America from Asia.

6300 B.C. Potatoes are cultivated in Peru.

Dugout canoes are used at Pesse in the Netherlands.

dugout canoe
being paddled

6000 B.C. Cattle
herding,
farming and
rock art are all
taking place in
the Sahara.

Copper and gold are first
used in Mesopotamia.

Farming begins in Greece
and southeastern Europe.

Crops and sheep are introduced
into Egypt from the Near East.

sheep

Britain is cut
off from the
continent of
Europe by
rising sea levels.

5500 B.C. Irrigation
is practiced in
Mesopotamia.

5300 B.C. Farming
is taking place and pottery is
made in central Europe.

0 B.C.   6000 B.C.   5000 B.C.

People from the Past

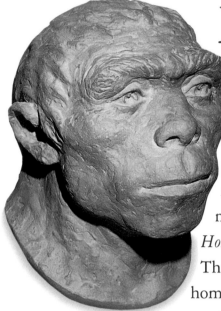

MODERN HUMANS and their most recent ancestors are called hominids. The first hominids formed two main groups—*Australopithecus* and *Homo. Australopithecus* first appeared about four million years ago and died out about one million years ago. *Homo habilis* appeared about two and a half million years ago and, like *Australopithecus,* lived in southern and eastern Africa.

About two million years ago, a new kind of hominid, *Homo erectus,* appeared. This was the first hominid to leave Africa, moving into Asia and later Europe. Eventually, *Homo erectus* evolved, or developed, into *Homo sapiens,* which evolved into *Homo sapiens sapiens,* or modern humans. By 10,000 B.C. *Homo sapiens sapiens* had settled on every continent except Antarctica.

PEKING MAN
This reconstruction is of a type of *Homo erectus* whose remains were found in China. These early people lived from about 460,000 to 230,000 years ago. Experts believe they may have been the first people to make regular use of fire.

CRO-MAGNON PEOPLE
The burial of a young Cro-Magnon man, whose remains were found in a Welsh cave, is shown in this picture. The body was sprinkled with red ochre and wore bracelets and a necklace of animal teeth. The Cro-Magnons were the first modern people to live in Europe, about 40,000 years ago.

TIMELINE 5000 B.C. – 2000 B.C.

5000 B.C. Rice farming is being carried out in waterlogged fields in eastern China.

Large areas of southeastern Asia are isolated by rising sea levels.

New Guinea and Tasmania have become separated from Australia.

wild rice

4500 B.C. Rice farming begins in India.

Farming begins in northwestern Europe.

4400 B.C. Wild horses are domesticated on the steppes, or plains, of Russia.

4200 B.C. Megalithic tombs, made of huge stones, are built in western Europe.

4100 B.C. Sorghum and rice are cultivated in the Sudan in Africa.

4000 B.C. Bronze casting begins in the Near East.

Flint mining in northern and western Europe increases.

early domesticated horse

3500 B.C. The llama is domesticated in Peru.

The first cities are built in Sumer, Mesopotamia.

The plough and wheel are invented in the Near East and spread to Europe.

3400 B.C. Walled towns are built in Egypt.

3200 B.C. Egyptians use sailing ships on the river Nile.

5000 B.C.	4500 B.C.	4000 B.C.	3500 B.C.	3200 B.C.

AUSTRALOPITHECUS
4.5 to 2 million years ago

HOMO HABILIS
2 to 1.6 million years ago

HOMO ERECTUS
1.6 million to 400,000 years ago

BROKEN HILL MAN

NEANDERTHAL MAN
120,000 to 33,000 years ago

MODERN MAN
100,000 years ago

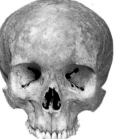

Archaeologists believe that our earliest ancestors came from Africa. One group, Australopithecus Africanus, walked upright.

Homo habilis *walked upright but had long arms.* Habilis *was probably the first hominid to make stone tools and to hunt.*

This hominid had a bigger brain than Habilis *and may have been as tall and heavy as modern people.* Erecutus *was a skillful hunter.*

This hominid was another Homo erectus. Erectus *invented new kinds of tools, used fire, lived in rock shelters and built huts.*

Homo sapiens neanderthalis *(Neanderthals) made flint tools. Neanderthals are thought to have been the first people to bury their dead.*

Our own subspecies, Homo sapiens sapiens *(modern man), developed over 100,000 years ago.*

NEANDERTHAL PEOPLE

The Neanderthals were a subspecies of *Homo sapiens* who flourished in Europe and western Asia from about 120,000 to 33,000 years ago, during the last glacial, or cold, period. They had larger brains than modern humans, with sloping foreheads and heavy brows.

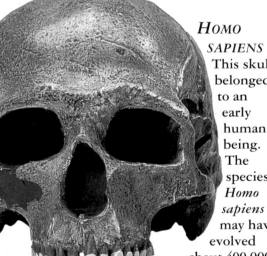

HOMO SAPIENS

This skull belonged to an early human being. The species *Homo sapiens* may have evolved about 400,000 years ago.

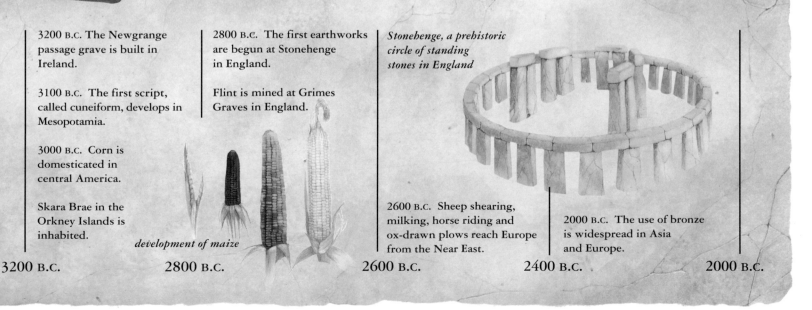

3200 B.C. The Newgrange passage grave is built in Ireland.

3100 B.C. The first script, called cuneiform, develops in Mesopotamia.

3000 B.C. Corn is domesticated in central America.

Skara Brae in the Orkney Islands is inhabited.

development of maize

2800 B.C. The first earthworks are begun at Stonehenge in England.

Flint is mined at Grimes Graves in England.

Stonehenge, a prehistoric circle of standing stones in England

2600 B.C. Sheep shearing, milking, horse riding and ox-drawn plows reach Europe from the Near East.

2000 B.C. The use of bronze is widespread in Asia and Europe.

3200 B.C.   2800 B.C.   2600 B.C.   2400 B.C.   2000 B.C.

Climate and Survival

COVERED BY ICE
Ancient ice still forms this Alaskan glacier. The height of the last glacial period was reached about 18,000 years ago. At this time, almost 30 percent of the earth was covered by ice, including large parts of North America, Europe and Asia, as well as New Zealand and southern Argentina. Temperatures dropped, and sea levels fell by over 100 yards.

ONE CHANGING ASPECT of our earth affected Stone Age people more than anything else—the climate. Over many thousands of years, the climate gradually grew cooler and then just as slowly warmed up again. This cycle happened many times, changing the landscape and the plants and animals that lived in it.

During cool periods, called glacials, sea levels dropped, exposing more land. Herds of animals grazed vast grasslands and the cold, bare tundra farther north. When temperatures rose, so did sealevels, isolating people on newly formed islands. Woodlands gradually covered the plains.

DEER HUNTER
In warmer periods, forest animals like this red deer replaced bison, mammoths and reindeer, which moved north. Humans followed the grazing herds or began to hunt forest game.

ANIMALS OF THE COLD
Mammoths were the largest mammals adapted to a colder climate, grazing the northern plains. The related mastodon was found in North America. Reindeer, horses, musk oxen, woolly rhinoceroses and bison were common, too.

ANIMAL EXTINCTIONS

This painting of a mammoth is from a cave in southwestern France. By 10,000 B.C., mammoths and woolly rhinoceroses were extinct in central and western Europe, as were bison and reindeer. In North America, mammoths, mastodons, camelids and many other large animal species vanished abruptly by 9000 B.C. Even in tropical Africa, the rich variety of animals of the savanna was reduced at the end of the last glacial period.

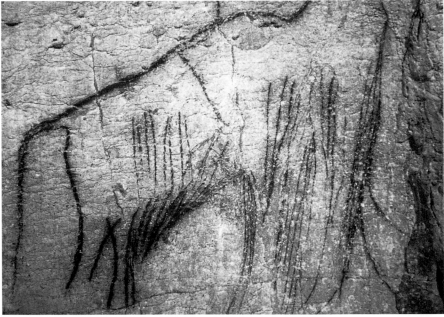

WILD BOAR

Pigs, such as wild boar, are adapted to living in a forest habitat. They use their snouts and feet to root for food on the forest floor. Pigs were one of the first animals to be domesticated because they will eat almost anything.

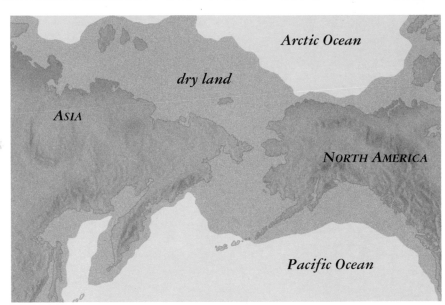

LAND BRIDGES

This illustration shows how two continents were joined by tundra during the last glacial period. Early man could migrate across the dry land that had been created over the Bering Straits and cross from Asia to North America. When the ice melted, the crossing was no longer possible and the continents were once again separated by sea. There were many land bridges during the glacial periods, including one that connected Great Britain to continental Europe.

ISOLATED ISLANDS

The White Cliffs of Dover are a famous landmark on England's southeastern coast, but this was not always so. During the last glacial period, Ireland, Great Britain and France were linked. When the ice began to melt, areas of low-lying land were gradually flooded, causing Britain to became an island by 6000 B.C.

Migration and Nomads

THE FIRST HUMANS did not lead a settled life, living in the same place all the time. Instead, they were nomads, moving around throughout the year. They did this in order to find food. Early people did not grow crops or keep animals. They hunted wild animals and collected berries, nuts and other plants. This is called a hunter-gatherer way of life. Moving from one place to another is called migration. Some Stone Age migrations were seasonal, following the herds of game. Others were caused by natural disasters, such as forest fires or volcanic eruptions. Changes in the climate and rising populations also forced people to move in search of new territory. After humans learned how to farm, many settled down in permanent homes to raise their crops.

MIGRATING HERDS
A huge herd of reindeer begins its spring migration across northern Norway. The Sami, or Lapp people, have lived in the Arctic regions of Sweden and Norway since ancient times. They herd reindeer for their meat and milk, following the herds north in the spring and camping in tents called *lavos*.

ANTLER HARPOON
This antler harpoon was found at Star Carr, in North Yorkshire, England. Antlers were easily carved into barbed points to make harpoons. The points were tied to spears and used for fishing and hunting.

SEASONAL CAMPS
In mesolithic times, the hunter-gatherers moved camp at different times of year. In late spring and summer, inland and coastal camps were used. Red and roe deer were hunted in the woods. Fish, shellfish, seals and wild birds were caught or gathered. Meat, hides and antlers were cut up and prepared, then taken to a more sheltered winter settlement.

hunting camp

hunting camp

hunting camp

hunting camp

winter base camp

coastal fishing camp

NATIVE AMERICANS

The Plains Indians of North America were nomads, living in cone-shaped buffalo-hide tents called tepees. Native Americans of the eastern plains, such as the Dakota shown above, lived mainly in permanent settlements, using their tepees for summer and autumn hunts. In the 1800s, the Plains Indians were forced by the United States government to live on reservations. They took their tepees with them and tried to preserve part of their traditional way of life.

TREES

The changing climate caused changes in vegetation. Heather, mosses and lichens grew on the cold tundra that covered much of the land during glacial periods. On the edge of the tundra were forests of pine, larch and spruce. As the climate warmed, the first trees to colonize open areas were silver birches. Gradually, the birches were replaced by oaks, hazels and elms. As forests grew larger, people found there was enough food to hunt and gather in one area without the need to migrate.

moss   *pine*

NOMADS IN THE DESERT

Although their numbers are dwindling, the Bedouin still live as nomadic herders in the dry regions of the Near East and Africa. They keep camels, sheep and goats to provide milk and meat. Their animals are also sold for other foods, such as flour, dates and coffee. Bedouins live in tents made from woven goat hair. They move from place to place in search of grazing land for their animals, just as people have done for thousands of years.

Social Structure

IN STONE AGE TIMES, there were very few people in the world. Experts estimate that the world's population in 13,000 B.C. was only about eight million. Today it is nearer six billion (six thousand million). We can make guesses about how Stone Age people lived together by looking at hunter-gatherer societies of today.

Although people lived in families as we do, these families lived together in groups called clans. All the members of a clan were related to each other, usually through their mother's family or by marriage. Clans were large enough to protect and feed everyone, but not so large that they were unmanageable. All the members of a clan, including children, were involved in finding and gathering food for everyone. Clans were probably also part of larger tribes, which may have met up at certain times of year, such as for the summer hunt. The members of a tribe shared a language and a way of life. When people learned how to farm, populations increased and societies began to be organized in more complicated ways.

MOTHER GODDESSES
This baked-clay sculpture from Turkey was made around 6000 B.C. She may have been worshipped as a goddess of motherhood. Families were often traced through the female line because mothers give birth, while fathers may remain unknown.

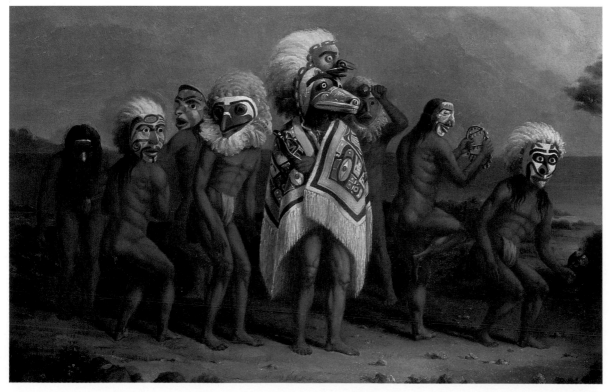

SHAMAN LEADERS
This painting from the 1800s shows Native American shamans performing a ritual dance. Shamans were the spiritual leaders of their tribes. They knew the dances, chants, prayers and ceremonies that would bring good luck and please the spirits. Shamanism is found in hunter-gatherer societies around the world today and was practiced in prehistoric times.

TRIBAL CHIEF

This man is a Zulu chief from South Africa. His higher rank is shown by what he wears. In prehistoric times, tribes might have been ruled by chiefs or councils of elders. An old man buried at Sungir in Russia around 23,000 B.C. was probably a chief. His body was found richly decorated with fox teeth and beads made of mammoth ivory.

SCENES FROM LONG AGO

Paintings on cliff walls in the Sahara Desert show hippopotamuses being hunted and herders tending cattle. Other images show a woman pounding flour, as well as wedding ceremonies and a family with a dog. They show that in 6000 B.C., the Sahara was a fertile area with organized communities.

A CYCLADIC FIGURINE

Between 3000 and 2000 B.C., some of the finest prehistoric sculpture was made on the Greek islands known as the Cyclades. This figurine is made of ground marble and shows a slender woman with her arms folded above her waist. Figurines showing musicians with harps and flutes have also been found. Such sculptures come from complex societies.

A TRADITIONAL WAY OF LIFE

The man on the left is helping a boy prepare for his coming-of-age ceremony in Papua New Guinea. Traditional ways of life are still strong in that country, where there are many remote tribes. In some villages, all the men live together, rather than with their wives and children. This allows them to organize their work, such as hunting, more easily.

Communication and Counting

OUR EARLY HUMAN ANCESTORS were communicating with each other using words and gestures as long ago as 300,000 B.C. Eventually, complex languages began to develop to pass on skills and knowledge. Hunters may have used a special sign language when tracking game, leaving markers to signal the route and imitating animal and bird sounds.

From about 37,000 B.C., people began to carve marks on bones and to use pebbles as simple counting devices. Days may have been counted on calendar sticks. In some cave paintings, experts have noticed dots and symbols that may be counting tallies or the beginnings of a writing system.

TALLY STICK
Notches carved on wooden sticks, or in this case on the leg bone of a baboon, may have been used as counting devices or as simple calendars. This one dates from about 35,000 B.C. Similar sticks are used by some groups of people living in southern Africa today.

By about 7000 B.C., tokens with symbols to represent numbers and objects were being used by traders in the Near East. They may have led to the first written script. This developed about 3100 B.C. and was a kind of picture-writing called cuneiform.

PICTURES AND SYMBOLS
This cave painting of a wild horse comes from Lascaux in southwestern France. It was painted in about 15,000 B.C. The horse is surrounded by symbols that, along with dots and notches, may have been a way of keeping track of migrating animals.

HAND ART
You will need: self-drying clay, rolling pin and board, modeling tool, sandpaper, yellow and red acrylic paints, water, two spray bottles.

1 Roll out the clay, giving it a lumpy surface like a cave wall. Trim the edges with a modeling tool to make a stone tablet.

2 Leave the clay to dry. When it is hard, rub the tablet with sandpaper to get rid of sharp edges and make a smooth surface.

3 Mix the paint with water and fill the spray bottles. Put one hand on the tablet and spray plenty of yellow paint around it.

WRITING DEVELOPMENT

This Sumerian clay tablet was made around 3100 B.C. It uses characters based on picture symbols to give an account of a year's harvest. As cuneiform writing developed, people wanted to express abstract ideas, such as good or bad, so they changed symbols already in use, often by adding marks.

SMOKE SIGNALS

This engraving from the late 1800s shows Native Americans using smoke signals to communicate with each other. Human beings have spent most of their history without written language, but this does not mean they were always unable to communicate or record important information.

HANDS ON

These hand stencils are from a cave in Argentina. They are similar to those found on rock walls in Europe, Africa and Australia. They may have been a way for prehistoric artists to sign their work.

4 Keeping your hand in exactly the same place, spray on the red paint so that you are left with a clear, sharp outline.

5 When you have finished spraying, remove your hand. Be careful not to smudge the paint, and leave the tablet to dry.

The artist of the original Argentine hand-painting sprayed paint around his or her hand. This was done either by blowing through a reed, or by spitting paint onto the cave wall!

25

Shelter

PEOPLE HAVE always needed protection from the weather. During most of the last 100,000 years, the earth's climate was much colder than it is today. People lived in huts in the open during summer, but when harsh weather came, families moved into caves. They built stone windbreaks across the entrances and put up huts inside to give further protection from the storms and cold. In summer, as they followed the herds of game, hunters built shelters of branches and leaves. Families lived in camps of huts made of branches and animal skins. Farther north, where there were no caves and few trees, people built huts from mammoths' leg bones and tusks. Wherever they settled, however, it was very important to be near a supply of fresh water.

CAVES AND ROCK SHELTERS
This is the entrance to a rock shelter in southwestern France. Neanderthal people were the first to occupy this site, in about 100,000 B.C. People usually lived close to the entrance of a cave, where the light was best and the sun's warmth could reach them.

MAMMOTH-BONE HOME
This is a reconstruction of a mammoth-hunter's house. It was built in about 13,000 B.C. in Ukraine. The gaps between the bones were filled with moss and shrubs. The entire structure was then covered with mammoth hide or turf.

A HUNTER'S HOME
You will need: self-drying clay, board, modeling tool, cardboard, brown-green acrylic paint, paintbrush, scissors, twigs, ruler, white glue, jar of water, fake grass or green fabric.

1 Roll out lengths of clay to form long and short mammoth bones and tusks. Then make some stones in different sizes.

2 Use the modeling tool to shape the ends of the bones and make the stones uneven. Leave the pieces, carefully separated, to dry.

3 Spread some modeling clay roughly over a piece of cardboard. Paint the clay a brown-green color and leave to dry.

MOBILE HOME

This model tepee was made in 1904 by the Cheyenne people of the Great Plains in the United States. Prehistoric people may have lived in tents or huts like this, made from branches covered with animal hides. They were quick to put up and take down, and could be folded for carrying. Portable homes were essential for people following migrating herds of animals.

SHELTERS OF TURF AND STONE

This is the outside of a Neolithic house in the village of Skara Brae in the Orkney Islands. It was built around 3000 B.C. The buildings were sunk into the ground and surrounded with turf to protect them from bad storms. Covered passages linked the houses.

A BURIED SITE

The village of Skara Brae in the Orkney Islands was built of stone because there were no local trees for building. Even the furniture inside was made of stone. In about 2000 B.C., the whole village was buried by a sandstorm, preserving the site until it was exposed by another great storm in 1850.

Where wood was scarce, heavy mammoth bones were used to weight down grass and animal hides covering a hunter's house.

4 Use a pair of scissors to cut the twigs so that they are 6 inches long. You will need about eight evenly sized twigs in all.

5 Push the twigs into the modeling clay to form a cone-shaped frame. Glue a few stones onto the clay at the base of the twigs.

6 Cover the twigs with pieces of fake grass or fabric glued in place. Be sure not to cover up the stones around the base.

7 Neatly glue the long mammoth bones and tusks all over the outside. Fill in gaps with smaller bones. Leave it all to dry.

Fire and Light

OUR ANCESTOR *Homo erectus* learned to use fire at least 700,000 years ago. This early human ate cooked food and had warmth and light at night. Fire was useful to keep wild animals away and to harden the tips of wooden spears. Hunters waving flaming branches could scare large animals into ambushes. *Homo erectus* probably did not know how to make fire, but found smoldering logs after natural forest fires. Campfires were carefully kept lit, and hot ashes may have been carried to each new camp. Eventually, people learned to make fire by rubbing two dry sticks together. Then they found that striking a stone against a kind of rock called pyrite made a spark. By 4000 B.C., the bow drill had been invented. This made lighting a fire much easier.

STONE LAMP
Prehistoric artists used simple stone lamps like this as they decorated the walls of caves 17,000 years ago. A lighted wick of moss, twine or fur was put in a stone bowl filled with animal fat. Wooden splinters or rushes dipped in beeswax or resin were also used.

AROUND THE HEARTH
This is the inside of a Neolithic house at Skara Brae in the Orkney Islands. In the center is a stone hearth, surrounded by beds, chairs and a dresser, also all made from stone. The smoke from the fire escaped through a hole in the turf roof. The large stones surrounding the hearth helped to protect the fire from being put out by drafts.

A MODEL BOW DRILL
You will need: thick piece of dowel, craft knife, sandpaper, wood stain, jar of water, balsa wood, brush, modeling tool, clay, rolling pin, scissors, chamois leather, raffia or straw.

1 Ask an adult to shape one end of the dowel into a point with a craft knife. The blade should always angle away from the body.

2 Lightly sand down the stick and paint it with wood stain. Ask an adult to cut out a balsa-wood base. Paint the base, too.

3 Use the modeling tool to gouge a small hole in the center of the balsa-wood base. The dowel should fit in this hole.

BUSH FIRES

Before people learned to make fire, they made use of accidental fires like this one in Africa, perhaps set off by lightning or the sun's heat. Early people learned to use fire for cooking. Many vegetable plants are poisonous when raw but harmless when cooked. Fire was also used for hunting. A line of fire was lit, and then the hunters would catch animals as they fled.

FIRE STARTER

A Kalahari bushman uses a modern bow drill to start a fire. The string of a bow is used to twist a wooden drill round and round as the bow is moved backward and forward. The drill's point rests on a wooden base. The rubbing of the drill on the base creates heat, which is used to set fire to a small heap of tinder, such as moss. The tinder is then added to a pile of dry grass and small sticks.

To hold the drill upright, prehistoric people used a stone or piece of wood at the top. Some had a wooden mouthpiece to hold the drill upright and free the other hand to hold the base.

4 Roll out the clay and cut out a bone shape. Make a hole in each end and smooth the sides with your fingers. Let it harden.

5 Use a pair of scissors to cut a thin strip of leather about twice as long as the bone. This is the thong used to twist the drill.

6 Tie the strip of leather to the bone. Thread the strip through both holes, tying a knot at each end to secure the leather.

7 Scatter straw or raffia around the base. Wrap the leather thong around the drill and place the point in the central hole.

Food for Gathering

MATTOCK
This mattock, or digging tool, was made from an antler. It dates from between 8000 B.C. and 4000 B.C. It has a hole drilled through it, in which a wooden handle would have been fitted.

STONE AGE hunter-gatherers had a very varied diet. They gradually discovered which plants they could eat and where they grew. From spring to autumn, women and children foraged for seeds, berries, nuts and roots. They found birds' eggs and the shoots and leaves of vegetable plants. In summer, plants such as peas, beans, squash and cucumbers were picked, and the seeds of wild grasses were collected. The summer sun also ripened wild dates, grapes, figs, blueberries and cranberries. In autumn, there were nuts such as almonds, pine nuts, walnuts, hazelnuts and acorns. These were stored underground; fruits and berries were dried to preserve them.

Insects, caterpillars and snails were food, too! Wild honeycomb and herbs added flavor. The foragers used digging sticks to unearth roots, while leather bags and woven baskets held food safely.

INSECT GRUB
This is a witchetty grub, the large white larva of a goat moth. These grubs are eaten as a delicacy by Australian Aborigines. Insects such as ants, grasshoppers, beetles and termites were healthy, high-protein food for Stone Age people.

BIRDS' EGGS
Prehistoric people ate many kinds of birds' eggs, from tiny quail eggs to huge ostrich eggs. These eggs were laid by a pheasant, a bird native to Asia. Eggs are rich in protein, vitamins and minerals, which make them a valuable food. Eggshells were also used to make beads for jewelry.

STEWED FRUIT
You will need: a large saucepan, 2 cups blueberries, 2 cups blackberries, 2 cups hazelnuts, wooden spoon, honeycomb, tablespoon, ladle, serving bowl.

1 Always choose firm, fresh fruit and wash it and your hands before you begin. First pour the blueberries into the pan.

2 Next pour in the blackberries. Use a wooden spoon to stir them gently into the blueberries, without crushing the fruit.

3 Shake in the whole hazelnuts and carefully stir the fruit and nuts once again until they are all thoroughly mixed.

WEAR AND TEAR

This Neanderthal skull is around 60,000 years old. From remains like this, experts can tell a lot about prehistoric people's diets. Stone Age people ate very few sweet things, so their teeth are rarely decayed, but people who ate a lot of grain often have very worn teeth from the hard outer cases of the seeds. Later, grain ground into flour contained a lot of grit, which also wore down teeth.

AUTUMN'S BOUNTY

The food that prehistoric people ate came mostly from plants. Each clan (tribe) had its own well-defined territory, over which it roamed, and each may have followed a seasonal route to visit favorite food plants. Dandelion leaves and nettle leaves could be gathered in the open countryside. Woodlands in autumn were a particularly rich source of food, with plenty of fruits and nuts. Many kinds of edible fungi, too, flourish in damp woodlands, especially during autumn.

nettle leaves

dandelion leaves *woodland fungus*

LOOKING FOR HONEY

This Mbuti man in the Democratic Republic of the Congo is smoking out bees from their nest in order to collect the honey. Prehistoric people may also have used fire to rob bees of their store. Collecting honey was worth the danger as it is rich in energy-giving carbohydrates, and its sweetness made foods tasty.

4 Add six tablespoons of honey from the comb. Now ask an adult to put the pan on the stove and bring it slowly to a boil.

5 Simmer the fruit and nuts very gently for 20 minutes. Leave to cool. Use a ladle to transfer your dessert to a serving bowl.

Prehistoric people would have cooked fruit in a similar way to preserve it as jam. Clay pots, rather than metal saucepans, were used for cooking and storing.

31

Fish and Shells

Toward the end of the last glacial period, about 12,000 years ago, the world's climate began to warm up. Melting ice flooded low-lying plains and fed many lakes, marshes and rivers. Trees grew across the grasslands and tundra, and bands of hunters started to settle down in campsites, some of which were permanent, beside seashores, lakes and rivers. Fishing and gathering shellfish became increasingly important sources of food for many people. Along the seashore, people foraged for seaweed and shellfish such as mussels, whelks, clams and crabs. They also hunted many kinds of fish, seals and seabirds. Rivers and lakes were full of fish such as salmon and pike, as well as crayfish, turtles, ducks and other waterbirds. Fishing was done from boats or the shore, using hooks, harpoons and nets. Traps made of woven willow were put at one end of a dam built across a stream. As fish swam through, they were caught in the trap.

SEAL HUNTER
The traditional way of life of the Inuit is probably very similar to that of prehistoric hunter-fishers. The Inuit have lived along Arctic coasts for thousands of years.

BONE HARPOONS
These bone harpoon heads from southwestern France date from around 12,000 B.C. They would have had wooden shafts and been attached to strips of leather or sinew.

A MODEL HARPOON
You will need: dowel, craft knife, wood stain, self-drying clay, wooden board, ruler, pencil, white cardboard, scissors, modeling tool, white glue, paintbrush, paint, jar of water, leather laces or strong string.

1 Ask an adult to cut down one end of a long thick dowel, using a craft knife. Cuts should be made away from the body.

2 Paint the dowel with wood stain and leave it to dry. The stain will darken the wood to make it look older and stronger.

3 Roll out a piece of white clay to make a shaft about 6 inches long. Shape one end of the clay to a rounded point.

FOOD FROM THE SEASHORE

The seashore provided a plentiful source of food all year round. Mussels, cockles, whelks, oysters, scallops, periwinkles, razors clams, crabs and lobsters could be found along sandy beaches and in rock pools. Seaweed and the fleshy leaves of rock samphire were also collected from rocks and cliffs.

edible crab

mussel   *rock samphire*

A SHELLFISH MIDDEN

These are the remains of a pile of triton shells found in Australia. Heaps of discarded shells and fish and animal bones are called middens. Archaeologists can learn a lot from middens. Besides giving clues as to what people ate, the shells often contain broken tools, thrown out with the rest of the rubbish.

FEARSOME FIGHTER

The pike lives in lakes and rivers. It is a powerful fish and a terrifying predator. Prehistoric people fished for pike from dugout canoes in late spring and early summer.

FISHING TACKLE

Fish hooks, made from carved bone, wood, antler, flint or shell, were attached to a strong line. A caught fish was stunned with a club before being hauled into the canoe.

Prehistoric hunters used harpoons for catching fish and for hunting reindeer and bison.

4 Draw out a serrated edge for a row of barbs on a strip of cardboard about 1 inch by 4 inches. Carefully cut out the barbs.

5 Use a modeling tool to make a slot down one side of the clay harpoon. Leave the clay to dry, then glue the barbs into the slot.

6 When the glue has dried, paint the head of the harpoon a suitable stone color, such as grayish brown.

7 Using a leather lace or strong string, tightly bind the harpoon head to the cut-down end of the wooden shaft.

Hunting Animals

DURING THE LAST GLACIAL PERIOD, clans hunted great herds of bison, horses, reindeer and mammoths that roamed the tundra and grasslands. At first they used stone axes and wooden spears. Later, spears with bone or flint barbs were developed, and spear-throwers were used to propel the spears farther and harder. Animals were attacked directly or caught in pitfall traps and snares. An entire herd might be chased over a cliff or into an ambush—this was a good way to build up a large supply of meat. As forests spread over the land, forest animals were hunted with bows and arrows. By about 12,000 B.C., hunters were using tame dogs to help in the chase. Every part of a kill was used. The meat was cooked for food or dried to preserve it. Hides were made into clothes, and animal fat was used in lamps. Bones and antlers were made into tools and weapons.

ANIMAL CARVINGS

This figure of a bison licking its back was carved from a reindeer's antler in about 12,000 B.C. It may have been part of a spear-thrower. Hunters often decorated their weapons with carvings of the animals they hunted.

BISON CAVE PAINTING

These two bison were painted on a cave wall in France around 16,000 B.C. The walls of caves in southwestern France and northern Spain are covered with almost life-size paintings of animals that were hunted at that time. Early hunters knew the regular migration routes of large animals such as bison and reindeer. They looked for sick or weak animals, or attacked at vulnerable moments, such as when the animals were crossing a river.

The circular illustration shows animals arranged around a ring of months: JANUARY FEBRUARY MARCH APRIL MAY JUNE JULY AUGUST SEPTEMBER OCTOBER NOVEMBER DECEMBER

THE GAME CYCLE

This illustration shows the animals people hunted in southwestern France between about 33,000 B.C. and 10,000 B.C. There was plenty of game to choose from. The hunters intercepted the animals at different times of the year as they followed their regular migration routes.

MAMMOTH HUNTERS

This woolly mammoth was carved from an animal's shoulder blade. Hunters worked in groups to kill these large mammals, one of which could feed a family for several months.

LEAP OF DEATH

In the engraving below hunters are stampeding a herd of horses over a cliff in France. The hunters probably crept up to the animals, then, at a signal, jumped to their feet, yelling to startle the herd. Skeletons of 10,000 wild horses have been found at this site.

MUSK OXEN

Today, one of the few large mammals that can survive the harsh winters of the tundra is the musk ox. Their thickset bodies have a dense covering of fur with a shaggy outer coat. During the last glacial period, musk oxen were hunted in Europe, Asia and North America.

The First Crops

I N ABOUT 8000 B.C., people in the Near East began growing their own food for the first time. Instead of simply gathering the seed of wild grasses such as wheat and barley, they saved some of it. Then, the following year, they planted it to produce a crop. As they began to control their food sources, the first farmers found that a small area of land could now feed a much larger population. People began living in permanent settlements in order to tend their crops and guard their harvest. Over the next 5000 years, farming spread from the Near East to western Asia, Europe and Africa. Farming also developed separately in other parts of Asia around 6500 B.C. and in America by about 7000 B.C.

The first farms were in hill country, where wheat and barley grew naturally, and there was enough rain for crops to grow. As populations increased, villages began to appear along river valleys, where farmers could water their crops at dry times of the year.

STONE TOOLS
This chipped flint is the blade of a hoe. It was used in North America between about A.D. 900 and A.D. 1200, but it is very similar to the hoes used by the first farmers to break up the soil. Rakes made of deer antlers were used to cover over the seeds. Ripe corn was harvested with sharp flint sickle blades.

SICKLE BLADE
This flint sickle blade has been hafted, or inserted, into a modern wooden handle. Ears of ripe corn would either have been plucked by hand or harvested with sickles such as this.

WILD RICE
Rice is a type of grass that grows in hot, damp areas such as swamps. It was a good food source for early hunter-gatherers along rivers and coasts in southern Asia. The seeds were collected when ripe and stored for use when little other food was available. The grain could be kept for many months.

WORLD CROPS

The first plants to be domesticated, or farmed, were those that grew naturally in an area. Wheat and barley grew wild in the Near East. In India, China and southeastern Asia, rice was domesticated around 5000 B.C. and soon became the main food crop. Around 3000 B.C. in Mexico, farmers grew corn, beans and squash. Farther south in the Andes mountains, the chief crops were potatoes, sweet potatoes and corn.

corn　　　*butternut squash*

GRINDING GRAIN

This stone quern, or hand mill, is 6000 years old. It was used to grind grain into a coarse flour for making porridge or bread. The grain was placed on the flat stone and ground into flour with the smooth, heavy rubbing stone. Flour made in this way often contained quite a lot of grit. To make bread, water was added to the flour. The mixture was then shaped into flat loaves, which were baked in a clay oven.

STRAIGHT TRACK

Several tracks were built across marshes between 4000 B.C. and 2000 B.C. in southern England. In some cases these were to link settlements to nearby fields of crops. The long, thin rods used to build the track above tell us a lot about the surrounding woodlands. The trees were coppiced, which means that thin shoots growing from cut hazel trees were harvested every few years.

A STEP UP

These terraced hillsides are in the Andes mountains of Peru. In mountainous areas where rainfall was high, some early farmers began cutting terraces, or steps, into the steep hillsides. The terraces meant that every scrap of soil could be used for planting. They prevented soil from eroding, or washing away. Farmers also used terracing to control the irrigation, or watering, of their crops. One of the first crops to be cultivated in Peru was the potato, which can be successfully grown high above sea level.

Taming Animals

ABOUT THE SAME time that people began to grow crops, they also started to domesticate (tame) wild animals. Wild sheep, goats, pigs and cattle had been hunted for thousands of years before people started to round them up into pens. Hunters may have done this to make the animals easier to catch. These animals gradually got used to people and became tamer. The first animals to be kept like this were probably sheep and goats around 8500 B.C. in the Near East.

Herders soon noticed that larger animals often had larger young. They began to allow only the finest animals to breed, so that domestic animals gradually became much stronger and larger than wild ones. Besides four-legged livestock, chickens were domesticated for their meat and also their eggs. In South America, the llama was kept for its meat and wool, along with ducks and guinea pigs. In Southeast Asia, pigs were the most important domestic animals.

WILD CATTLE
This bull is an aurochs, or wild ox. The aurochs was the ancestor of today's domestic cattle. Taming these huge, fierce animals was harder than keeping sheep and goats. Wild cattle were probably not tamed until about 7000 B.C. The aurochs became extinct in A.D. 1627. In the 1930s, a German biologist re-created the animal by crossing domesticated breeds such as Holsteins and Highland cattle.

WILD HORSES
Horses were a favorite food for prehistoric hunter-gatherers. This sculpture of a wild horse was found in Germany. It was made around 4000 B.C. Horses also often appear in cave art. They were probably first domesticated in Russia around 4400 B.C. In America, horses had become extinct through over-hunting by 9000 B.C. They were reintroduced by European explorers in the sixteenth century A.D.

DINGOES AND DOGS

The dingo is the wild dog of Australia. It is the descendant of tame dogs that were brought to the country more than 10,000 years ago by Aboriginal Australians. Dogs were the first animals to be domesticated. Their wolf ancestors were tamed to help with hunting and, later, with herding and guarding. In North America, dogs were used as pack animals and dragged a *travois* (a kind of sled) behind them.

DESERT HERDERS

Small herds of wild cattle were probably first domesticated in the Sahara and the Near East. This rock painting comes from the Tassili n'Ajjer area of the Sahara desert. It was painted in about 6000 B.C. at a time when much of the Sahara was covered by grassland and shallow lakes. The painting shows a group of herders with their cattle outside a plan of their house.

LLAMAS

The llama was domesticated in central Peru by at least 3500 B.C. It was kept first for its meat and wool, but later it was also used for carrying food and goods long distances. A relative of the llama, the alpaca, was also domesticated for its wool.

GOATS AND SHEEP

Rock paintings in the Sahara show goats and sheep, among the first animals to be domesticated. They were kept for their meat, milk, hides and wool, and are still some of the most common farmed animals.

Stone Technology

EARLY TOOLS

These chipped pebbles from Tanzania in Africa are some of the oldest tools ever found. They were made by *Homo habilis,* an early human ancestor, almost two million years ago.

STONE AGE PEOPLE were skilled toolmakers. They used flakes of stone to make knives, spearheads, arrowheads, engraving tools (burins), piercing tools and scrapers. About two and a half million years ago, our ancestors first learned that chipping stones could give them a sharp edge. Later, they found that flint was the best stone for this. A hammerstone was used to chip off flakes of flint until the desired shape and sharpness were reached. Early tools included hand-axes, which were used for digging and cutting up animals. As people became more skillful, they made smaller tools from flakes that had been chipped off, such as chisel-like burins. These in turn were used to carve harpoons, spearheads, needles and spear-throwers from antler and bone.

FLAKING

Neanderthals and Homosapiens were far better toolmakers than earlier people. They chipped flakes off pieces of flint to produce hand-axes (*left and middle*) and chopping tools (*right*). Pointed or oval-shaped hand-axes were used for many different tasks.

FLINT MINES

The Grimes Graves flint mine in Norfolk, England, where flint was mined from 2800 B.C. The miners traded flint with people in areas where it could not be found.

MAKE A MODEL AXE

You will need: self-drying clay, board, modeling tool, sandpaper, gray acrylic paint, dowel, craft knife, wood stain, jar of water, paintbrush, ruler, chamois leather, scissors.

1 Pull out the clay into a thick block. With a modeling tool, shape the block into an axe head with a point at one end.

2 When the clay is completely dry, lightly rub down the axe head with sandpaper to remove any rough surfaces.

3 Paint the axe head a stone color, such as gray. You could use more than one shade if you like. Leave the axe head to dry.

SPEAR POINT

The Cro-Magnons used long, thin flakes of flint to make their tools. This leaf-shaped spear point was made by highly skilled toolmakers about 20,000 years ago. Its finely flaked shape was made by delicately chipping over the entire surface.

STONES FOR TOOLS

Nodules of flint are often found in limestone rock, especially chalk, so they were reasonably easy to obtain. But other kinds of rock were used for toolmaking, too. Obsidian, a rock formed from cooled lava, was widely used in the Near East and Mexico. It fractured easily, leaving sharp edges. In parts of Africa, quartz was made into beautiful, hard-wearing hand-axes and choppers. A rock called diorite was used for making polished axe heads in Neolithic times.

quartz *chert (a type of flint)*

STONE AXES

These polished stone battle axes became the most important weapon in Scandinavia by the late Neolithic period. They date from about 1800 B.C.

TOOLMAKING LESSON

Stone Age people came to depend more and more on the quality of their tools. In this reconstruction, a father is passing on his skill in toolmaking to his son.

Prehistoric people used axes for chopping wood and cutting meat. They shaped a stone blade, then attached it to a wooden shaft.

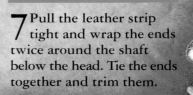

4 Ask an adult to trim one end of a piece of thick dowel using a craft knife. Paint the piece with wood stain and leave to dry.

5 To bind the axe head to the wooden shaft, first carefully cut a long strip of leather about an inch wide from a chamois cloth.

6 Place the axe head on the trimmed end of the shaft. Wrap the strip of leather around the head and shaft in a crisscross pattern.

7 Pull the leather strip tight and wrap the ends twice around the shaft below the head. Tie the ends together and trim them.

Carving Wood and Bone

ALTHOUGH THIS PERIOD is called the Stone Age, wood, bone, antler and ivory were just as important for making tools and other implements. Not only could these materials be carved and shaped by stone tools, but bone and antler hammers and punches were used to shape the stone tools themselves. By using these implements, better cutting edges and finer flakes of stone could be achieved.

Antler, bone, wood and ivory had many different uses. Antler picks were used to dig up roots and chip out lumps of stone. Antlers and bones were carved into spear-throwers and, along with ivory, were used to make needles, fish hooks, harpoon heads and knives. Wood was used to make the handles and mounts for spears, harpoons, axes, sickles and adzes, which were tools used for shaping wood, as well as to make bows and arrows. The shoulder blades of cattle were made into shovels, while smaller bones were used to make awls to punch small holes. Smaller bones were also used to make fine whistles and little paint holders. All these materials were often beautifully carved with animals and fine decorative patterns.

SPEAR-THROWER
This carving of a reindeer's head is probably part of a spear-thrower. Wood, bone and antler all have natural cracks and flaws in them. Prehistoric carvers often incorporated these into the design to suggest the animal's outline, as well as particular features, such as eyes, mouth and nostrils. Engraved, or carved, pictures in caves also often make use of the natural form of the rock.

ADZE
An adze was a bit like an axe, except that its blade was at right angles to the handle. The flint blade on this adze dates from about 4000 B.C. to 2000 B.C. Its wooden handle and binding are modern replacements for the originals, which have rotted away. Adzes were swung in an up-and-down movement and were used for jobs such as hollowing out tree trunks and shaping them to make dugout canoes.

AXE
Early farmers needed axes to clear land for their crops. An experiment in Denmark using a 5,000-year-old axe showed that a man could clear about $2^{1}/_{2}$ acres of woodland in about five weeks. This axe head, dating from between 4000 B.C. and 2000 B.C., has been given a modern wooden handle.

ANTLER PICK

Antlers were as useful to prehistoric humans as they were to their original owners! This tool comes from a Neolithic site near Avebury in England. Antler picks were used for digging and quarrying. Antler was a versatile material. It could be made into spear and harpoon points, needles and spear-throwers.

CRAFTSPEOPLE

This engraving shows Stone Age life as imagined by an artist from the 1800s. It shows tools being used and great care being taken over the work. Even everyday items were often finely carved and decorated by the craftspeople who made them.

CARVED BATON

This ivory object is known as a *bâton de commandment*. Several of these batons have been found, especially in France. But no one is sure what they were used for. Some experts think they were status symbols, showing the importance of the person carrying them. Others think that the holes were used to straighten arrows. Whatever their use, the batons are often decorated with fine animal carvings and geometric designs.

ANTLERS AT WORK

Two stags (male deer), fight. Only male deer have large antlers, which they use to battle with each other to win territory and females. The stags shed and grow a new set of antlers each year, so prehistoric hunters and artists had a ready supply of material.

Crafts

THE VERY FIRST HANDICRAFT was probably basketmaking, using river reeds and twigs woven together. Baskets were quick to make and easy to carry but not very durable. Pottery was harder-wearing. The discovery that baking clay made it stronger may have happened by accident, perhaps when a clay-lined basket fell into the fire. Baked clay figures were made from about 24,000 B.C., but it took thousands of years for people to realize that pottery could be useful for cooking and for storing food and drink. The first pots were made in Japan around 10,500 B.C. Pots were shaped from coils or lumps of clay. Their sides were smoothed and decorated before being fired in an open hearth or kiln.

Another Neolithic invention was the loom, around 6000 B.C. The first cloth was probably made of wool, cotton or flax (which could be made into linen).

BAKED-CLAY FIGURINE

This is one of the oldest fired-clay objects in the world. It is one of many similar figurines made around 24,000 B.C. at Dolni Vestonice in the Czech Republic. Here, people hunted mammoths, woolly rhinoceroses and horses. They built homes with small, oval-shaped ovens, in which they fired their figurines.

CHINESE JAR

It is amazing to think that this elegant pot was for everyday use in 4500 B.C. It was made in Banpo, near Shanghai. The people of Banpo were some of China's earliest farmers. They grew millet and kept pigs and dogs for meat. The potters made a high-quality black pottery for important occasions, and this cheaper gray pottery for everyday use.

MAKE A CLAY POT

You will need: terra-cotta modeling clay, wooden board, modeling tool, plastic flower pot, decorating tool, varnish, brush, sandpaper.

1 Roll out a long, thick sausage of clay on a wooden board. It should be at least 1/2 inch in diameter.

2 Form the roll of clay into a coil to make the base of your pot. A fairly small base can be made into a pot, a larger one into a bowl.

3 Now make a fatter roll of clay . Carefully coil this around the base to make the sides of your pot.

HOUSEHOLD POTS

Many early pots were decorated with basket-like patterns. This one has a simple geometric design and was made in Thailand around 3500 B.C. Clay pots like this were used for storing food, carrying water or cooking.

STEATITE IDOL

Steatite, or soapstone, has been used to make this carving from the Cycladic Island of Greece. Soapstone is very soft and easy to carve. Figurines like this one were often used in funeral ceremonies. They could also be used either as the object of worship itself or as a ritual offering to a god. This figure has a cross around its neck. Although the symbol certainly has no Christian significance, no one really knows what it means.

WOVEN THREADS

The earliest woven objects may have looked like this rope and cane mat from Nazca in Peru. It was made around A.D. 1000. Prehistoric people used plant-fiber rope to weave baskets and bags. The oldest known fabric dates from about 6500 B.C. and was found at Çatal Hüyük in Turkey. Few woven objects have survived, as they rot quickly.

Fired-clay pots could only be made where there were natural deposits of clay, so some areas seem to have specialized in baked-clay pottery and sculpture. The patterns used to decorate the pots vary from area to area.

4 With a modeling tool, smooth down the edges of the coil to make it flat and smooth. Make sure there are no air spaces.

5 Place your pot over a flower pot to support it. Keep adding more rolls of clay to build up the sides of your pot.

6 Smooth down the sides as you add more rolls. Then use a decorating tool with a serrated end to make different patterns.

7 Leave your pot to dry out. When the clay is dry, varnish the outside. Use sandpaper to smooth the inside of your pot.

Clothing

THE HUNTERS of the last glacial period were probably the first people to wear clothes. They needed them for protection from the cold. Clothes were made of animal hides sewn together with strips of leather. The first clothes included simple trousers, tunics and cloaks, decorated with beads of colored rock, teeth and shells. Fur boots were also worn, tied on with leather laces.

Furs were prepared by stretching out the hides and scraping them clean. The clothes were cut out and holes were made around the edges of the pieces with a sharp, pointed stone called an awl. The holes made it much easier to pass a bone needle through the hide. Cleaned hides were also used to make tents, bags and bedding.

Sometime after sheep farming began in the Near East, wool was used to weave cloth. In other parts of the world, plant fibers such as flax, cotton, bark and cactus were used. The cloth was colored and decorated with plant dyes.

PREPARING HIDES
An Inuit woman uses her teeth to soften a sealskin. Prehistoric hunter-gatherers probably also softened hides like this. Animal hides were first pegged out and scraped clean. Then they were washed and stretched taut on a wooden frame to keep them from shrinking as they dried. The stiff, dry hide was then softened and cut to shape for clothing.

PINS AND NEEDLES
These are 5000-year-old bone pins from Skara Brae in the Orkney Islands. Prehistoric people made pins and needles from slivers of bone or antler; their sides were then smoothed by rubbing them on a stone.

DYEING CLOTH
You will need: natural dyes such as walnuts, elderberries and safflower, saucepan, water, tablespoon, sieve, bowl, chamois leather, white cardboard, white T-shirt, wooden spoon. (Dyes can be found in health food shops.)

1 Choose your first dye and put approximately 8-12 tablespoons of it into an old pan. You may need to crush or shred it first.

2 Ask an adult to boil the dye, and then simmer it for one hour. Leave to cool. Pour the dye through a sieve to remove lumps.

3 Test a patch of chamois leather by dipping it in the dye for a few minutes. You can wear rubber gloves for protection.

NATURE'S COLORS

Stone Age people used the flowers, stems and leaves of many plants to make dyes. The flowers of dyer's broom and dyer's chamomile gave a range of colors from bright yellow to khaki. Plants such as woad and indigo gave a rich blue dye, while the bark, leaves and husks of the walnut made a deep brown. Plants were also used to prepare hides. Skins were then softened by being soaked with oak bark in water.

dyer's broom

birch bark

oak bark

RAW MATERIALS

This engraving shows an Inuit man hunting a seal in the Arctic. Animals provided skin for cloth, sinews for thread and bones for needles. Clothes made of animal skin kept out the cold and rain, and allowed early people to live farther north.

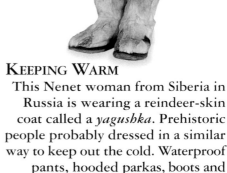

KEEPING WARM

This Nenet woman from Siberia in Russia is wearing a reindeer-skin coat called a *yagushka*. Prehistoric people probably dressed in a similar way to keep out the cold. Waterproof pants, hooded parkas, boots and mittens would have been worn.

GRASS SOCKS

Until recently the Inuit of North America gathered grasses in summer and braided them into socks like these. The socks were shaped to fit the foot snugly and were worn under sealskin boots.

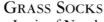

Safflower flowers for dyeing were picked when first open, then dried.

4 Lay the patch on a piece of white cardboard and leave it to dry. Be careful not to drip the dye over clothes as you work.

5 Make up the other two dyes and test them out in the same way. Compare the patches and choose your favorite color.

6 Dye a white T-shirt by soaking it in your chosen dye. Try to make sure that the T-shirt is dyed evenly all over.

Ornament and Decoration

CEREMONIAL DRESS
The amazing headdress, face painting and jewelry still seen at ceremonies in Papua New Guinea may echo the richness of decoration in Stone Age times.

BOTH MEN AND WOMEN wore jewelry in the Stone Age. Necklaces and pendants were made from all sorts of natural objects. Brightly colored pebbles, snail shells, fish bones, animal teeth, seashells, eggshells, nuts and seeds were all used. Later, semiprecious amber and jade, fossilized jet and handmade clay beads were also used. The beads were threaded onto thin strips of leather or twine made from plant fibers.

Other jewelry included bracelets made of slices of elephant or mammoth tusk. Strings of shells and teeth were made into beautiful headbands. Women braided their hair and put it up with combs and pins. People probably decorated their bodies and outlined their eyes with pigments such as red ochre. They may have tattooed and pierced their bodies, too.

BODY PAINT
These Australian Aboriginal children have painted their bodies with clay. They have used patterns that are thousands of years old.

BONES AND TEETH
This necklace is made from the bones and teeth of a walrus. It comes from Skara Brae in the Orkney Islands. A hole was made in each bead with a stone tool, or with a wooden stick spun by a bow drill. The beads were then strung onto a strip of leather or twine.

MAKE A NECKLACE
You will need: self-drying clay, rolling pin and board, modeling tool, sandpaper, ivory and black acrylic paint, paintbrush, water, ruler, scissors, chamois leather, cardboard, double-sided tape, white glue, leather laces.

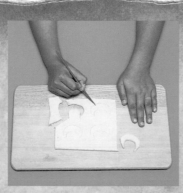

1 Roll out the clay on a board and cut out four crescent shapes with the modeling tool. Leave them on the board to dry.

2 Rub the crescents lightly with sandpaper and paint them an ivory color. You could varnish them later to make them shiny.

3 Cut four strips of leather 4 inches by 1 1/2 inches. Use the edge of a piece of cardboard to make a black crisscross pattern on the strips.

NATURAL DECORATION

We know about the wide variety of materials used in Stone Age jewelry from cave paintings and ornaments discovered in graves. Shells were highly prized and some were traded over long distances. Other materials included deers' teeth, mammoth and walrus ivory, fish bones and birds' feathers.

a selection of seashells

BANGLES AND EAR STUDS

This jewelry comes from Harappa in Pakistan. It dates from between 2300 B.C. and 1750 B.C. and is made from shells and coloured pottery. Archaeologists in Harappa have found the remains of dozens of shops that sold jewelry.

A WARRIOR'S HEADDRESS

This Yali warrior from Indonesia has a headdress of wild boars' teeth and a necklace made of shells and bone. Headdresses and necklaces made of animals' teeth may have had a spiritual meaning for Stone Age people. The wearer may have believed that the teeth brought the strength or courage of the animal from which they came.

Stone Age people believed that wearing a leopard-claw necklace brought them magical powers.

4 When they are dry, fold back the edges of each strip and hold in place with double-sided sticky tape.

5 Brush the middle of each crescent with glue and wrap the leather around, forming a loop at the top, as shown.

6 Braid together three leather laces to make a thong. Make the thong long enough to go around your neck and be tied.

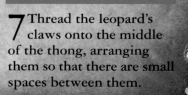

7 Thread the leopard's claws onto the middle of the thong, arranging them so that there are small spaces between them.

The Arts

STONE AGE ARTISTS were wonderfully skilled, working in stone, antler, bone, ivory and clay. They painted rock walls, engraved stone and ivory and carved musical instruments. They created images of the animals they hunted, as well as human figures and abstract designs. No one knows for sure why they were so creative.

The earliest works of art date from around 40,000 B.C. and were etched onto rocks in Australia. In Europe, the oldest works of art are cave paintings from about 28,000 B.C. Most cave paintings, however, date from around 16,000 B.C. The walls of caves in northern Spain and southwestern France are covered with paintings and engravings of animals. Stone Age artists also carved female figures, called Venus figurines, and decorated their tools and weapons. This explosion in art ended around 10,000 B.C.

VENUS FIGURINES
This small figure, called the Venus of Lespugue, was found in France. It dates from about 20,000 B.C. Her full figure probably represents the fertility of a goddess. She may have been carried as a good luck charm.

MUSIC AND DANCE
Stone Age rock paintings in Europe and Africa show people moving in dance-like patterns. This engraving from a cave on the island of Sicily dates from about 9000 B.C. Ceremonies in the Stone Age almost certainly included music and dancing, perhaps with drums and whistles, too.

MAKE A CAVE PAINTING
You will need: self-drying craft clay, rolling pin and board, modeling tool, sandpaper, acrylic paints, paintbrush, jar of water.

1 First roll out the craft clay, giving it a slightly bumpy surface like a cave wall. Cut it into a neat shape with a modeling tool.

2 When the clay has dried, lightly rub down the surface with sandpaper to make it smooth and give a good surface to paint on.

3 Paint the outline of your chosen animal in black. This painting shows a reindeer similar to those in Stone Age cave paintings.

EARLY POTTERY

These two female figures are some of the earliest surviving South American ceramics (baked pottery). They date from about 4000 B.C. to 1800 B.C. Their distinctive shape and fringed hair means they were made by people of the Valdivia culture. It seems that in some parts of the world, pottery was shaped into statuettes long before it was used to make storage vessels and cooking pots for food.

AN ARTIST'S MATERIALS

Prehistoric artists made their paints from soft rocks and minerals such as charcoal and clay. They ground these to a powder and mixed them with water or animal fat. Charcoal from the fire was used for black outlines and shading. Colored earth, called ocher, gave browns, reds and yellows. A clay called kaolin was used for white paint. The paint was stored in hollow bones. Brushes were made from animal hair, moss or frayed twigs.

ocher   *charcoal*

SPIRAL DESIGNS

These carved stones are from the temple at Tarxien on the island of Malta and date from around 2500 B.C. Many large stone monuments that were built in Europe around 4200 B.C. are decorated with geometric patterns.

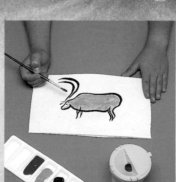

Stone Age artists painted in black, white and earthy colors.

4 Draw the most obvious features of your animal by exaggerating their size. The sweeping horns of this deer make it very striking.

5 When the outline is dry, mix yellow, red and black to make a warm color with which to fill in the outline of your animal.

6 Finish off your picture by highlighting some parts of the body with reddish brown paint mixed to resemble red ochre.

Trade and Distribution

S TONE AGE PEOPLE did not use bills and coins for money, as we do. Instead they bartered, or exchanged, things. When one person wanted a bowl, for example, he or she had to offer something in exchange to the owner of the bowl—perhaps a tool or ornament. Toward the end of the Stone Age, however, people began to use shells or stone rings as a kind of currency.

Even isolated hunter-gatherer groups came into contact with each other and exchanged things, such as seashells for tools or hides. With the beginning of farming around 8000 B.C. in the Near East, however, long-distance exchange and a more organized trading system began. New activities, such as farming, pottery and weaving, needed specialized tools, so a high value was put on suitable rocks. In western Europe, flint quarries produced axe blades that were prized and traded over enormous distances. Sometimes goods were traded thousands of miles from where they were made.

COWRIE SHELLS
Small, highly polished cowrie shells were popular as decoration for clothes and jewelry in prehistoric times. The shells have been found scattered around skeletons in burial sites, many of which are hundreds of miles from the coast. Later, cowrie shells were used as money in Africa and parts of Asia.

AXES
A good, strong axe was a valuable commodity. It was particularly important for early farmers, who used it to chop down trees and clear land for crops. Axe heads made of special stone were traded over wide distances.

BURIED WITH WEALTH
This communal burial on the Solomon Islands in the Pacific Ocean shows the deceased surrounded by shells and ornaments. Shells have been used for money for thousands of years—in fact, for longer and over a wider area than any currency, including coins. One hoard of shells, found in Iraq, was dated before 18,000 B.C.

STONE TRADE

During the neolithic period there was a widespread trade in stone for axes. At Graig Llywd in Wales (*left*), stone was quarried from the scree slopes and taken all over Britain. The blades were roughed out on site, then transported to other parts of the country, where they were ground and polished into axe heads. Rough, unfinished axes have been found lying on the ground at Graig.

FUR TRAPPER

A modern Cree trapper from the Canadian Arctic is surrounded by his catch of pine marten pelts. Furs were almost certainly a valuable commodity for prehistoric people, especially for hunter-gatherers trading with more settled farmers. They could be traded for food or precious items such as amber or tools.

SKINS AND PELTS

White Arctic fox skins are left to dry in the cold air. In winter, Arctic foxes grow a thick white coat so that they are well camouflaged against the snow. Furs like these have traditionally been particularly valuable to Arctic people, both for the clothing that makes Arctic life possible and for trading.

Transport on Land and Sea

THE EARLIEST MEANS of transport, besides traveling on foot, was by boat. The first people to reach Australia, perhaps as early as 50,000 B.C., must have used log or bamboo rafts to cross open water. Later, skin-covered coracles and kayaks (canoes hollowed from tree trunks) and boats made from reeds were used. On land, people dragged goods on wooden sledges or *travois* (triangular platforms of poles lashed together). Logs were used as rollers to move heavy loads. The taming of horses, donkeys and camels in about 4000 B.C. revolutionized land transport. The first roads and causeways in Europe were built around the same time. Around 3500 B.C., the wheel was invented by metal-using people in Mesopotamia. It quickly spread to Stone Age people in Europe.

HORSE'S HEAD
This rock engraving of a horse's head comes from a cave in France. Some experts think that horses may have been tamed as early as 12,000 B.C. There are carvings that appear to show bridles around the heads of horses, but the marks may indicate manes.

CORACLE
A man fishes from a coracle, one of the oldest boat designs. Made of animal hide stretched over a wooden frame, the coracle may have been used since around 7600 B.C.

MAKE A MODEL CANOE
You will need: cardboard, pencil, ruler, scissors, white glue, glue brush, masking tape, self-drying clay, double-sided tape, chamois leather, compass, thread, needle.

canoe top
— 8in —

canoe top
— 4in —

canoe base
— 8in —

canoe base
— 4in —

1 Cut cardboard to the size of the templates shown. Remember to cut semicircles from the long edge of both top pieces.

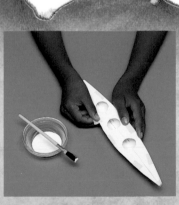

2 Glue the bases and the tops together, using masking tape to secure them as they dry. Join the top to the base in this way.

STONE BRIDGE

Walla Brook bridge on Dartmoor is one of the oldest stone bridges in Britain. Bridges make traveling easier, safer and more direct. The first bridges were made by placing tree trunks across rivers, or by laying flat stones in shallow streams.

SAILING BOATS

This is a model of a skin-covered boat called an *umiak,* which was used by the Inuit of North America. The figure at the back is the helmsman, whose job is to steer the boat. The other figures are rowing the oars. The ancient Egyptians seem to have been the first people to use sailing ships, around 3200 B.C.

KAYAK FRAME

This wooden frame for a kayak was made by an Inuit fisherman. It has been built without any nails; the joints are lashed together with strips of leather. Canoes such as this have been in use for thousands of years.

Inuit kayaks give clues about how Stone Age boats may have looked. The outsides were covered with skin.

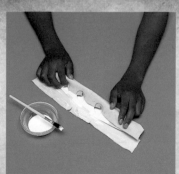

3 Draw 3 circles the size of the holes in the top, with a small circle inside. Cut them out and make rings the same size from clay.

4 Cover the modeling-clay and the cardboard rings with double-sided tape. These rings form the seats where the paddlers sit.

5 Cover your canoe with chamois leather, leaving holes for the seats. Glue the leather tightly in place so that all cardboard is covered.

6 Use a needle and thread to sew up the edges of the leather on the top of the canoe. Position and attach the seats and the oars.

Warfare and Weapons

WARFARE AND FIGHTING were certainly a part of Stone Age life. Prehistoric skeletons often reveal wounds received during a fight. For example, in a cemetery in Egypt dating from about 12,000 B.C., the skeletons of 58 men, women and children have been found, many with the flint flakes that killed them still stuck in their bones. In South Africa, a rare rock engraving, dating from between 8000 B.C. and 3000 B.C., shows two groups of people fighting each other with bows and arrows. No one knows exactly why these people fought each other. After 8000 B.C., as the population of farmers grew, conflict between farming groups competing for land increased. Early farming villages were often encircled by earthworks, mud-brick walls or high wooden fences for protection.

AMERICAN POINT
This type of stone weapon was used by hunter-gatherers in North America to hunt bison. It is called a Folsom point and dates from around 8000 B.C.

DEADLY ARROWHEADS
The first arrowheads may have been made of wood, hardened over a fire. Yet flint could be given a much sharper edge. This hoard was found in Brittany, France. Sharp weapons could mean the difference between life and death, so they were very valuable.

A BOW AND ARROW

You will need: self-drying clay, rolling pin and board, modeling tool, sandpaper, acrylic paint, paintbrush, two lengths of thin dowel (16 inches and 24 inches), craft knife, double-sided tape, scissors, string.

1 Roll out the craft clay and use a modeling tool to cut out an arrowhead shape. When dry, smooth with sandpaper and paint gray.

2 Ask an adult to trim down one end of the shorter length of dowel with a craft knife. This is the arrow shaft.

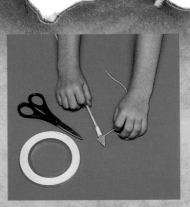

3 Tape the arrowhead to the shaft with double-sided tape. Wrap string around the tape to imitate leather binding.

VIOLENT DEATH

Many people in Stone Age times met with violent deaths. This skull contains an arrow point that entered through the unlucky victim's nostrils, presumably during a fight.

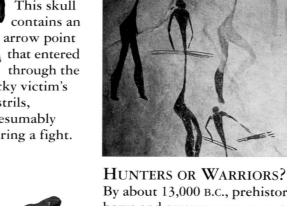

HUNTERS OR WARRIORS?

By about 13,000 B.C., prehistoric hunters had learned that bows and arrows were more powerful and accurate than spears. This rock painting, dating from around 6000 B.C., shows hunters or warriors with bows and arrows out on a raid.

BLADES AND POINTS

A selection of flint arrowheads and knife blades from Egypt shows fine workmanship. Flakes of flint about 8 inches long were used as lance heads. Shorter ones were made into javelins, knives and arrows. The heads were mounted onto wooden shafts with tree-resin glue and strips of leather.

Prehistoric hunter-gatherers carried small, lightweight bows from which they could fire many arrows quickly.

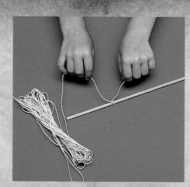

4 Use the longer length of dowel to make the bow. Tie a long length of string securely to one end of the bow.

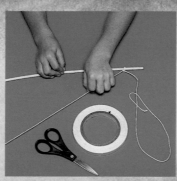

5 Ask an adult to help you carefully bend back the bow and tie the string to the other end. Tape will help to secure the string.

6 To tighten and secure the bowstring further, wind the string around each end several time. Then tie it and cut off the end.

7 Using double-sided tape, wrap another piece of string around the middle of the bow as a rest for the arrow.

Religion and Magic

WE CAN ONLY GUESS at the beliefs of Stone Age people. The first people we know of who buried their dead were the Neanderthals. This suggests that they believed in a spirit world. Early people probably worshipped the spirits of the animals they hunted and other natural things. Some paintings and engravings on rocks and in caves may have a magical or religious purpose. Small statues, called Venus figurines, were probably worshipped as goddesses of fertility or plenty. Prehistoric people probably thought illnesses and accidents were caused by evil spirits. It may have been the job of one person, called a shaman, to speak to the spirits and interpret what should be done.

As farming spread and settlements grew into towns, more organized religions began. Shrines decorated with religious pictures have been found at Çatal Hüyük in Turkey, the site of a well-preserved town dating from around 7000 B.C.

ANCIENT BURIAL
The skull of the skeleton from this burial found in France has been scattered with red ocher earth. Red may have represented blood or life for Stone Age people. Bodies were often buried on their sides, with their knees pulled up to their chins. Tools, ornaments, food and weapons were put in the graves. Later Stone Age people built elaborate tombs for their dead.

RITUAL ANTLERS
These antlers are from a red stag and were found at Star Carr in England. Some experts think that antlers were worn by a kind of priest called a shaman, perhaps in a coming-of-age ceremony or to bring good luck in that season's hunt.

CLAY GODDESS
This female figure is made from clay and was found at Pazardzik in Bulgaria. Many prehistoric societies worshipped images of the earth goddess, or great mother. As the mother of the world, she gave life to plants, animals and humans, and so ensured the future of the human race.

STONE TEMPLE
This is Hgar Quim temple on the island of Malta. Many stone temples were built on Malta between 3600 B.C. and 2500 B.C. The oldest have walls at least 20 feet long and 111/2 feet tall. The most impressive temple is the Hypogeum, carved on three levels, deep underground.

STANDING STONES
Stonehenge was built over many centuries from about 2800 B.C. to 1400 B.C. The first Stonehenge was a circular earthwork made up of a bank and ditch. Later, large blocks of dressed (shaped) sarsen stones were put up. The stones are aligned with the midsummer sunrise and midwinter sunset, as well as the positions of the moon.

PASSAGE GRAVE
This stone lies at the entrance to a passage grave at Newgrange in Ireland. The grave is a circular mound with a single burial chamber at the center, reached by a long passage. Many of the stone slabs that line the passage are decorated with spirals and circles.

Wood henges, or circles, had up to five rings of timber posts, increasing in height toward the center.

4 Cover the base with uneven pieces of fake grass, glued into place. Be careful not to completely cover up the post holes.

5 Cut short sticks for the posts and lintels. Cut 7 more longer sticks. Paint the sticks with wood stain and leave to dry.

6 Glue the sticks in place using the post holes as guides. When dry, glue the lintels on top to complete your wood circle.

Journey Through Life

STONE AGE PEOPLE held ceremonies to mark the significant stages in their lives, such as birth, coming of age, marriage and death. Coming-of-age ceremonies marked the point when boys and girls were thought of as adults, playing a full part in the life of the clan. Life spans in Stone Age times were much shorter than they are today. Old people were valued members of the clan, as they were able to pass on their skills and knowledge. Most people lived into their thirties, but few survived into their sixties. There was little people could do fight illness and infection, and many infants died at birth. When game and food were plentiful, however, it seems that hunter-gatherers probably had an easier way of life than later farmers, whose work was hard and unending.

BURIAL SCENE
This burial from northeastern France was made in about 4500 B.C. at the time when farming was starting in that area. These farmers were buried in small cemetries, often with shell ornaments, adzes, and stones for grinding grain.

DOGGU FIGURE
This Jomon human figurine from Japan was made of clay between 2500 B.C. and 1000 B.C. These figurines were often used during funerary rituals and, in some cases, were also buried in graves.

A PASSAGE GRAVE

You will need: cardboard, compass and pencil, ruler, scissors, rolling pin and board, terra-cotta self-drying clay, modeling tool, white self-drying clay, white glue and glue brush, rich soil, spoon, green fabric.

1 Cut out 2 cardboard circles, with diameters of 8 inches and 10 inches. Roll out the clay and cut around the larger circle.

2 Put the smaller circle on top of the larger circle and cover it with clay. With a modeling tool, mark out the passage and chamber.

3 Roll out the white clay and cut it into squares. Form rocks from some squares and model the rest into stone slabs.

FAMILY GRAVE

This tomb at West Kennet in southern England was built around 3700 B.C. It was used for ceremonies involving the dead. The stone chambers inside the barrow (mound of earth) contain the bones of at least 46 people. The corpses were not placed inside the barrow right away, but were first left outside until most of the flesh had rotted away. Then the skeletons were disarticulated (divided up) and the bones placed in the tomb. Some of the skulls and long bones were removed, perhaps for a ceremony somewhere else. The barrow was blocked up and reopened many times over the thousand years it was in use.

burial chamber

barrow

entrance

Ditches dug around the outside of a barrow provided the soil to build the mound. Many people could be buried together in a burial site like this one.

4 When the clay is dry, build the walls and roof of the passage and chamber. Glue the slabs carefully in place.

5 Spoon soil gently over the chamber, heaping it up to make a large, even mound. Do not press on the clay chamber.

6 Cut out a piece of green fabric large enough to cover the mound of soil. Dip the fabric in glue and position it gently.

7 Place clay boulders all around the edge of the earthwork. When you are happy with their positions, glue them in place.

63

The End of an Era

THE END OF the Stone Age was marked by the growth of towns and cities. The very first town was probably Jericho in the Near East. In about 8000 B.C., a farming village was built there on the site of an earlier settlement. By about 7800 B.C., nearly 2700 people lived in Jericho. Çatal Hüyük in Turkey was the site of another, much larger town, dating from about 6500 B.C. and with a population of about 5000. The people who lived in these towns were not just farmers—they were also craftspeople, priests and traders. When metalworking became widespread, better tools allowed people to produce more food. Improved farming led to the first civilizations, with well-organized workforces, armies and governments ruled by kings and priests. These civilizations grew up in the fertile areas of Mesopotamia, Egypt, India and China, heralding the end of the Stone Age.

JERICHO
In about 8000 B.C., farmers built a settlement at Jericho in the Near East. It was surrounded by a ditch and massive stone walls. The walls were broken by a great round tower, the remains of which are shown here. The people of Jericho traded with bands of nomadic hunter-gatherers.

A SLIM FIGURINE
This female figurine was made around 2000 B.C. on the Cycladic Islands of Greece. Her slender shape contrasts greatly with the fuller figures of earlier female statuettes. She may have been created as a continuation of the tradition of fertility figurines, or mother goddesses, in new, town-based societies.

MAKE A FIGURINE
You will need: board, terra-cotta self-drying clay, modeling tool, glass tumbler, white glue (mixed with water for varnish) and brush.

1 First, mold a flattish, triangular shape from craft clay to form the body. Then roll out a fat sausage for the arms and legs.

2 Trim two lengths from the sausage to form the arms. Then cut the rest of the sausage to form two leg pieces.

3 Attach the arms to the body, smoothing down the seam and marking the shoulder area lightly with a modeling tool.

SARGON OF AKKAD

This Sumerian carving dates from about 2300 B.C. and depicts Sargon, king of Akkad. Sumer was the first civilization in the world. It arose in southern Mesopotamia (modern Iraq) in about 3200 B.C. The Sumerians were great traders.

REFINED POTTERY

This beautiful pottery jar is from the Jomon period in Japan and was made around 3000 B.C. The Japanese were making pottery as early as 10,500 B.C., and their Jomon culture thrived until as late as 300 B.C. Clay continued to be, and still is, an important material for the manufacture of ceramics.

WEIGHTS AND MEASURES

As trade grew, people needed a fair system of weights and measures. These weights and scales come from the city of Mohenjo-Daro, a center of the Harrapan civilization in Pakistan.

A prehistoric clay figure similar to this one has been nicknamed "The Thinker." It was made in Romania around 5200 B.C.

4 Roll out a piece of clay for the neck and a ball for the head. Sculpt features onto the face. Attach the head and neck to the body.

5 Lean the figure against a glass to support it. Attach the legs, molding the feet by pinching the ends of the rolls, as shown.

6 Bend each arm in turn and position so that the hands support the figurine's head and the elbows rest on its knees.

7 Leave the clay to dry, then gently remove the glass. Varnish the figurine lightly and leave it to dry again before moving it.

The Stone Age Today

THE SPREAD OF METALWORKING and farming changed the way people lived, but only very slowly. Huge areas of the world continued to live in the Stone Age. In many areas, people continued to live a hunter-gatherer way of life even when they knew about farming methods. In addition, large parts of the world remained isolated from each other until quite recently. Without the use of metal, Stone Age people evolved into complicated and advanced societies of their own. Incredibly, by 1000 B.C., people from southeastern Asia had colonized many of the Pacific islands, crossing up to 400 miles of open ocean. This was a great deal farther than people elsewhere had dared to travel without being in sight of land. Stone Age societies have survived right up to the twentieth century. The Inuit of the Arctic, the Aborigines of Australia and the San hunter-gatherers of southern Africa continue to preserve a way of life that is thousands of years old.

ARCTIC PEOPLES
This is a Nenet man from Siberia in Russia. The Nenet share a traditional way of life with the Inuit of North America. Today, most live in small settlements or towns, but they are very proud of their culture. They preserve their own language, art and songs, and regard hunting as an essential part of their way of life.

PAPUA NEW GUINEA
These men are taking part in one of the spectacular traditional dances of Papua New Guinea. The highland areas of Papua New Guinea have formed a natural barrier between different groups of people. This has helped to preserve a rich variety of cultures and languages. Many people in small villages continue to grow their own food and hunt for animals in the dense forests.

ABORIGINAL AUSTRALIANS

In Australia today, 200 years after the arrival of Europeans, some Aboriginal people are trying to maintain a traditional way of life. Thousands of years ago, their ancestors must have been well aware of how to grow plants such as yams, but they chose to continue as hunter-gatherers. In tune with their environment, they had a wide range of game and food plants available to them, making farming an unnecessary and more difficult way of life.

MARVELS IN STONE

Gigantic stone heads up to 40 feet high were carved out of volcanic rock and erected on Easter Island between A.D. 1100 and A.D. 1600. Easter Island is one of the most remote islands in the Pacific.

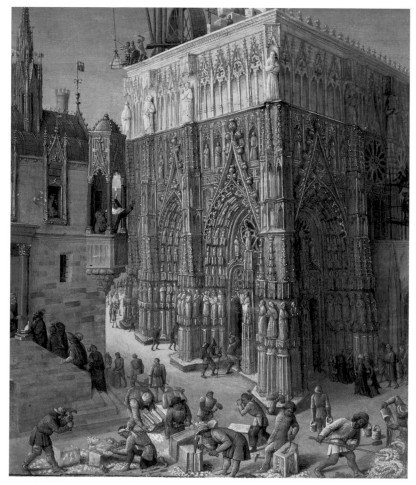

STONEMASONS

This is part of an illustration dating from the fifteenth century A.D., showing medieval stonemasons at work. Large workforces and metal tools gradually helped stone to take on a new role as a building material. Stone could be cut, shaped and transported on a much larger scale. Many impressive stone buildings were erected all over the world, some of which have stood for thousands of years.

ANCIENT EGYPT

PHILIP STEELE

CONSULTANT:
FELICITY COBBING

The Egyptian civilization that developed along the fertile banks of the river Nile 5,000 years ago was one of the most wealthy and creative in history. It was a glittering civilization shaped by thriving trade, the pride and power of pharaohs, and a religion peopled by animal gods. Extraordinary leaps were made in building techniques, and in the crafts of working precious metals and jewels, art, and writing. There were mighty tombs and pyramids, built at enormous cost, to house priceless treasures and elaborately preserved mummies. The glories of ancient Egypt lasted over 3,000 years.

The Kingdom on the Nile

EGYPT IS A COUNTRY at the crossroads of Africa, Europe and Asia. If you could step back in time 5,000 years, you would discover an amazing civilization—the kingdom of the ancient Egyptians.

Most of Egypt is made up of baking hot, sandy deserts. These are crossed by the river Nile as it snakes its way north to the Mediterranean Sea. Every year, floods cover the banks of the Nile with mud. Plants grow well in this rich soil, and 8,000 years ago farmers were planting crops here. Wealth from farming led to trade and to the building of towns. By 3100BC a great kingdom had grown up in Egypt, ruled by royal families.

Ancient Egypt existed for over 3,000 years, longer even than the Roman Empire. Pyramids, temples and artifacts survive from this period to show us what life was like in the land of the pharaohs.

HORUS' EYE
This symbol can be seen on many Egyptian artifacts. It is the eye of the god Horus.

AMAZING DISCOVERIES
In 1922, the English archaeologist Howard Carter made an amazing discovery. He found the tomb of the young pharaoh Tutankhamun. No single find in Egypt has ever provided as much evidence as the discovery of this well-preserved tomb.

LIFE BY THE NILE
Tomb paintings show us how people lived in ancient Egypt. Here people water and harvest their crops, using water from the river Nile.

TIMELINE 6000BC–2000BC

The kingdom of ancient Egypt existed for over 3,000 years. The most successful periods of Egyptian power are known as the Old Kingdom, the Middle Kingdom and the New Kingdom.

wheat

sheep

boat with sail

c6000BC
Early people settle in the fertile Nile valley. They grow wheat and barley.

c5020–4500BC
Craftsmen make clay figures and fine pottery vessels. They also carve objects from ivory.

c4800BC
Farmers keep sheep, cattle and other animals.

c4000BC
Sails are used on Egyptian ships for the first time.

6000BC   5500BC   5000BC   4500BC   4000BC

Alexandria
Rosetta (el-Rashid)
Nile delta
Giza
Saqqara
Memphis
LOWER EGYPT
Dahshur
Maidum
Sinai

Beni-Hasan
River Nile
Akhetaten (el-Amarna)
UPPER EGYPT

Abydos
Valley of the Kings
Karnak
Thebes (Luxor)

Kha'rga Oasis

Aswan
Philae

▲ Pyramid
⬟ Valley of the Kings
⚵ Ancient Site

Abu Simbel

THE KINGDOM OF EGYPT

This map of Egypt today shows where there were important cities and sites in ancient times. The ancient Egyptians lived mostly along the banks of the river Nile and in the green, fertile lands of the delta. Through the ages, the Egyptians built many imposing temples in honor of their gods and mysterious tombs to house their dead. Most of these temples and tombs were built close to the major cities of Memphis and Thebes.

SURVIVORS OF THE DESERT

The face of the great pharaoh Ramesses II stares out at us. Huge statues of Ramesses were part of a temple cut from the rock face at Abu Simbel in 1269BC. During the 1960s the statues had to be raised because a new dam at Aswan turned this part of the Nile into a lake. Temples, tombs and statues such as those at Abu Simbel have survived for thousands of years in the dry desert heat. More recently, many monuments have started to disintegrate because of the polluted air around modern cities such as Luxor.

c4000–3500BC
Reed shrines are built.

The first buildings are made from mud brick.

Craftsmen paint the first wall paintings and make stone statues.

one of over 750 hieroglyphic symbols in the Egyptian writing system

c3400BC Walled towns are built in Egypt.

3100BC The first of the great royal families govern Egypt. The Early Dynastic period begins.

King Narmer unites Egypt. He creates a capital at Memphis.

Egyptians use hieroglyphs.

2686BC Old Kingdom period.

2667BC Zoser becomes pharaoh.

2650BC Stepped pyramid built at Saqqara.

Stepped Pyramid

2600BC Pyramid built at Maidum.

2589BC Khufu becomes pharaoh. He later builds the Great Pyramid at Giza.

Great Sphinx

c2500BC Khafra, son of Khufu, dies. During his reign the Great Sphinx was built at Giza.

2181BC The Old Kingdom comes to an end.

The Intermediate Period begins. Minor kings in power.

4000BC   3500BC   3000BC   2500BC   2000BC

Famous Pharaohs

FOR THOUSANDS OF YEARS ancient Egypt was ruled by royal families. We know much about the pharaohs and queens from these great dynasties because of their magnificent tombs and the public monuments raised in their honor.

Egypt's first ruler was King Narmer, who united the country in about 3100BC. Later pharaohs such as Zoser and Khufu are remembered for the great pyramids they had built as their tombs.

Pharaohs usually succeeded to the throne through royal birth. However, in some cases military commanders such as Horemheb came to power. Although Egypt's rulers were traditionally men, a few powerful women were made pharaoh. The most famous of these is the Greek queen Cleopatra, who ruled Egypt in 51BC.

KHAFRA
(reigned 2558–2532BC)
Khafra is the son of the pharaoh Khufu. He is remembered for his splendid tomb, the Second Pyramid at Giza and the Great Sphinx that guards it.

AMENHOTEP I
(reigned 1525–1504BC)
The pharaoh Amenhotep led the Egyptian army to battle in Nubia. He also founded the workmen's village at Deir el-Medina.

HATSHEPSUT
(reigned 1498–1483BC)
Hatshepsut was the half-sister and wife of Thutmose II. When her husband died, she was appointed to rule Egypt until her young stepson Thutmose III was old enough. However Queen Hatshepsut was ambitious and had herself crowned pharaoh. Hatshepsut is famous for her trading expeditions to the land of Punt. The walls of her temple at Deir el-Bahri show these exotic trips.

TIMELINE 1200BC–AD1960

1198BC Mediterranean Sea peoples attack Egypt.

1182BC Ramesses III, the last great warrior pharaoh, comes to power. He defeats the Mediterranean Sea peoples in battles.

1151BC The last great pharaoh, Ramesses III, dies.

Ramesses III

c1070BC The New Kingdom ends. Start of Third Intermediate Period.

900–700BC Brief periods of calm between conquest by invading armies.

671BC Assyrians conquer Egypt as far as Memphis.

Darius I

525BC Beginning of the Late Dynastic Period.

525BC Egypt becomes part of the Persian Empire.

332BC Egypt is invaded by Alexander the Great and is ruled by Greek kings. Alexandria is built. *Alexander the Great*

305BC Ptolemy I, a commander in Alexander the Great's army, takes power after his death.

51BC Cleopatra VII, Ptolemy's XII's daughter, reigns in Egypt.

Cleopatra VII

30BC Egypt becomes part of the Roman Empire under the emperor Augustus.

1200BC   900BC   600BC   300BC   AD0

TUTANKHAMUN
(reigned 1334–1325BC)
This pharaoh came to the throne when he was only nine years old. He died at the age of 18. Tutankhamun is remembered for his tomb in the Valley of the Kings, which was packed with amazing treasure.

THUTMOSE III
(reigned 1479–1425BC)
Thutmose III is remembered as a brave warrior king. He launched many military campaigns against the Syrians in the Near East. Records from the time tell of Thutmose marching fearlessly into battle at the head of his army, unconcerned about his own safety. He won a famous victory at Megiddo and then later at Kadesh. Thutmose III was buried in the Valley of the Kings.

AKHENATEN
(reigned 1379–1334BC)
The Egyptians believed in many gods. However, when Akhenaten came to power, he introduced worship of one god, the Sun disc Aten. He moved the capital from Memphis to Akhetaten (now known as el-Amarna). His chief wife was the beautiful Queen Nefertiti.

RAMESSES II
(reigned 1279–1212BC)
One of the most famous pharaohs of all, Ramesses II, was the son of Seti I. He built many fine temples and defeated the Hittites at the Battle of Kadesh in 1274BC. The chief queen of Ramesses was Nefertari. Carvings of this graceful queen can be seen on Ramesses II's temple at Abu Simbel. Ramesses lived a long life and died at the age of 92. He was buried in the Valley of the Kings.

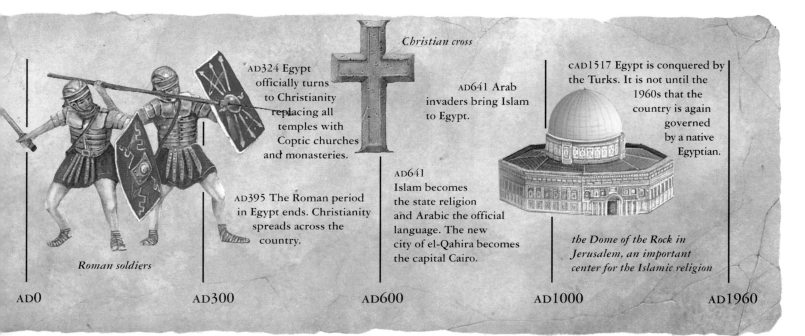

Christian cross

AD324 Egypt officially turns to Christianity replacing all temples with Coptic churches and monasteries.

AD641 Arab invaders bring Islam to Egypt.

cAD1517 Egypt is conquered by the Turks. It is not until the 1960s that the country is again governed by a native Egyptian.

AD395 The Roman period in Egypt ends. Christianity spreads across the country.

AD641 Islam becomes the state religion and Arabic the official language. The new city of el-Qahira becomes the capital Cairo.

Roman soldiers

the Dome of the Rock in Jerusalem, an important center for the Islamic religion

AD0   AD300   AD600   AD1000   AD1960

The Land of the Gods

HORUS
Horus the falcon god was the son of Isis. He was god of the sky and protector of the reigning pharaoh. The name Horus meant "He who is far above". Here he holds an *ankh*, the symbol of life. The holder of an *ankh* had the power to give life or take it away. Only pharaohs and gods were allowed to carry them.

THE ANCIENT EGYPTIANS believed that the ordered world in which they lived had been created out of nothingness. Chaos and darkness could return at any time if the proper religious rituals were not followed. The spirit of the gods lived inside the pharaohs, who were honored as god-kings. They looked after the everyday world for the gods. Over 2,000 gods were worshipped in ancient Egypt. Many gods were linked to a particular region. The mighty Amun was the god of Thebes. Some gods appeared as animals— Sebek the water god was a crocodile. Gods were also connected with jobs and interests. The hippopotamus goddess, Tawaret, looked after babies and childbirth.

Many ordinary Egyptians understood little about the religion of the court and nobles. They believed in magic, local spirits and superstitions.

LOTUS FLOWER
The lotus was a very important flower to the Egyptians. This sacred symbol was used to represent Upper Egypt.

THE GODDESS NUT
Nut, covered in stars, was goddess of the heavens. She is often shown with her body stretched across the sky. The Egyptians believed that Nut swallowed the Sun each evening and gave birth to it the next morning. She was married to the Earth god, Geb, and gave birth to the gods Isis and Osiris.

AMUN OF THEBES

Amun was originally the god of the city of Thebes. He later became popular throughout Egypt as the god of creation. By the time of the New Kingdom, Amun was combined with other powerful gods such as Ra, god of the Sun, and became known as Amun-Ra. He was believed to be the most powerful god of all. Amun is sometimes shown as a ram.

HOLY BEETLES

Scarabs are beetles that were sacred to the ancient Egyptians. Pottery or stone scarabs were used as lucky charms, seals, or as ring decorations. The base of these scarabs was often inscribed with stories telling of some great event.

OSIRIS, KING OF THE UNDERWORLD

The great god Osiris stands dressed as a king. He was one of the most important gods in ancient Egypt, the master of life and the spirit world. He was also the god of farming. Egyptian tales told how Osiris was murdered and cut into pieces by his brother Seth, the god of chaos. Anubis, the jackal-headed god of embalming, gathered the pieces together and his sister, Isis, brought Osiris back to life.

CAT MUMMIES

The Egyptians worshiped gods in the forms of animals from the Old Kingdom onwards. The cat goddess Bastet was said to be the daughter of the great Sun god, Ra. Cats were so holy to the Egyptians that at one time many of them were embalmed, wrapped in linen bandages and preserved as mummies. It is thought that bronze cat figures and these mummified cats were left as offerings to Bastet at her temple.

MIW THE CAT

Cats were holy animals in ancient Egypt. They even had their own god! The Egyptians' love of cats dated back to the early farmers who tamed cats to protect stores of grain from mice. Cats soon became popular pets. The Egyptian word for cat was *miw*, which was like a mew or meow!

Priest, Politician and God

THE CROOK AND FLAIL
These emblems of the god Osiris became badges of royal authority. The crook stood for kingship and the flail for the fertility of the land.

flail

crook

THE WORD PHARAOH comes from the Egyptian *per-aa*, which meant great house or palace. It later came to mean the man who lived in the palace, the ruler. Pictures and statues show pharaohs with special badges of royalty, such as crowns, headcloths, false beards, scepters and a crook and flail held in each hand.

The pharaoh was the most important person in Egypt. As a god-ruler, he was the link between the people and their gods. He therefore had to be protected and cared for. The pharaoh led a busy life. He was the high priest, the chief law-maker, the commander of the army and in charge of the country's wealth. He had to be a clever politician, too. The ancient Egyptians believed that on his death, the pharaoh became a god in his own right.

Pharaohs were generally men, but queens sometimes ruled Egypt if the pharaoh was too young. A pharaoh could take several wives. Within royal families it was common for fathers to marry daughters and for brothers to marry sisters. Sometimes pharaohs married foreign princesses in order to make an alliance with another country.

MOTHER GODDESS OF THE PHARAOHS
Hathor was worshipped as the mother goddess of each pharaoh. Here she is shown welcoming the pharaoh Horemheb to the afterlife. Horemheb was a nobleman who became a brilliant military commander. He was made pharaoh in 1323BC.

MAKE A CROWN

You will need: 2 sheets of cardboard (red and white), pencil, ruler, scissors, masking tape, small cardboard tube, muslin, white glue and brush, acrylic paint (white, gold), brush, beads, skewer and water bowl.

White crown of Upper Egypt

18 in

16 in

3 in

21 in

8 in

22 in

Snake

6 in

Red crown of Lower Egypt

Mark out these patterns onto your cardboard. Cut around them with scissors.

1 Bend the white cardboard into a cylinder-shape, as shown. Use lengths of masking tape to join the two edges firmly together.

RAMESSES MEETS THE GODS

This painting shows the dead pharaoh Ramesses I meeting the gods Horus (left) and Anubis (right). Pharaohs had to pass safely through the afterlife or the link between the gods and the world would be broken forever.

THE QUEEN'S TEMPLE

This great temple (*below*) was built in honor of Queen Hatshepsut. It lies at the foot of towering cliffs at Deir el-Bahri, on the west bank of the Nile near the Valley of the Kings. The queen had the temple built as a place for her body to be prepared for burial. Pyramids, tombs and temples were important symbols of power in Egypt. By building this temple, Hatshepsut wanted people to remember her as a pharaoh in her own right.

HATSHEPSUT

A female pharaoh was so unusual that pictures of Queen Hatshepsut show her with all the trappings of a male king, including a false beard! Here she wears the pharaoh's crown. The cobra on the front of the crown is the symbol of Lower Egypt.

The double crown worn by the pharaohs was called the pschent. *It symbolized the unification of the two kingdoms. The white section at the top (hedjet) stood for Upper Egypt, and the red section at the bottom (deshret) for Lower Egypt.*

2 Tape the cardboard tube into the hole at the top. Plug its end with a ball of muslin. Then tape the muslin in position and glue down the edges.

3 Wrap the white cardboard with strips of muslin. Paint over these with an equal mixture of white paint and glue. Allow the crown to dry.

4 Now take the shape made from the red cardboard. Wrap it tightly around the white cardboard, joining the edges with masking tape.

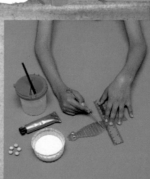

5 Now paint the snake gold, sticking on beads as eyes. When dry, score lines across its body with the skewer. Bend the snake and glue it to the crown.

83

Court and Nobles

EGYPTIAN PALACES were vast complexes. They included splendid public buildings where the pharaoh would meet foreign rulers and carry out important ceremonies. Members of the royal family lived in luxury in beautiful townhouses with painted walls and tiled floors near the palace.

The governors of Egypt's regions also lived like princes, and pharaohs had to be careful that they did not become too rich and powerful. The royal court included large numbers of officials and royal advisors. There were lawyers, architects, tax officials, priests and army officers. The most important court official of all was the vizier, who carried out many of the pharaoh's duties for him.

The officials and nobles were at the top of Egyptian society. But most of the hard work that kept the country running smoothly was carried out by merchants and craft workers, by farmers, laborers and slaves.

GREAT LADIES
Ahmose-Nefertari was the wife of Ahmose I. She carries a lotus flower and a flail. Kings could take many wives and it was also common for them to have a harem of beautiful women.

A NOBLEMAN AND HIS WIFE
This limestone statue shows an unknown couple from Thebes. The man may have worked in a well-respected profession, as a doctor, government official, or engineer. Noblewomen did not work but were quite independent. Any property that a wife brought into her marriage remained hers.

THE SPLENDORS OF THE COURT
This is the throne room of Ramesses III's palace at Medinet Habu, on the west bank of the Nile near Thebes. Pharaohs often had many palaces and Medinet Habu was one of Ramesses III's lesser ones. Surviving fragments of tiles and furniture give us an idea of just how splendid the royal court must have been. A chamber to one side of the throne room is even believed to be an early version of a shower stall!

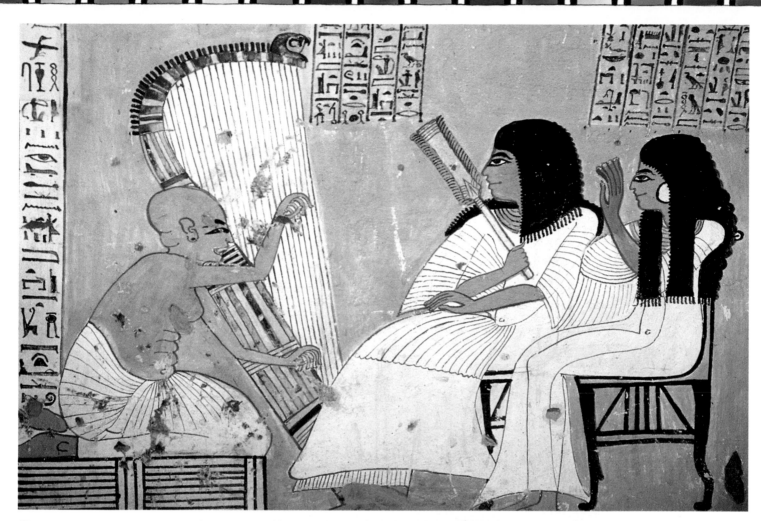

RELAXATION

Ankherhau (*above*), a wealthy overseer of workmen, relaxes at home with his wife. They are listening to a harpist. Life was pleasant for those who could afford it. Kings and nobles had dancers, musicians and acrobats to entertain them. Cooks worked in their kitchens preparing sumptuous meals. By comparison, ordinary people ate simple food, rarely eating meat except for the small animals they caught themselves.

HAIR CARE

The royal family was waited on by domestic servants who attended to their every need. Here (*left*), the young Queen Kawit, wife of the pharaoh Mentuhotep II, has her hair dressed by her personal maid. Although many of the female servants employed in wealthy households were slaves, a large number of servants were free. This meant that they had the right to leave their employer at any time.

Towns, Homes and Gardens

THE GREAT CITIES of ancient Egypt, such as Memphis and Thebes, were built along the banks of the river Nile. Small towns grew up haphazardly around them. Special workmen's towns such as Deir el-Medina were also set up around major burial sites and temples to help with building work.

Egyptian towns were defended by thick walls and the streets were planned on a grid pattern. The straight dirt roads had a stone drainage channel, or gutter, running down the middle. Parts of the town housed important officials, while other parts were home to craft workers and poor laborers.

Only temples were built to last. They were made of stone. Mud brick was used to construct all other buildings from royal palaces to workers' dwellings. Most Egyptian homes had roofs supported with palm logs and floors made of packed earth. In the homes of wealthier Egyptians, walls were sometimes plastered and painted. The rooms of their houses included bedrooms, living rooms, kitchens in thatched courtyards and workshops. Homes were furnished with beds, chairs, stools and benches. In the cool of the evenings people would sit on the flat roofs or walk and talk in cool, shady gardens.

THE GARDEN OF NAKHT
The royal scribe Nakht and his wife Tjiui take an evening stroll through their garden. Trees and shrubs surround a peaceful pool. Egyptian gardens included date palms, pomegranates, grape vines, scarlet poppies and blue and pink lotus flowers. Artists in ancient Egypt showed objects in the same picture from different angles, so the trees around Nakht's pool are flattened out.

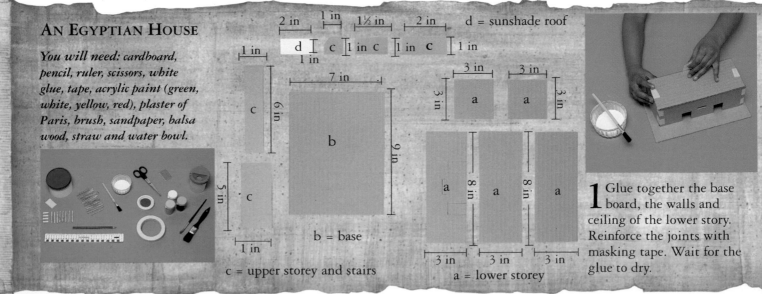

AN EGYPTIAN HOUSE

You will need: cardboard, pencil, ruler, scissors, white glue, tape, acrylic paint (green, white, yellow, red), plaster of Paris, brush, sandpaper, balsa wood, straw and water bowl.

d = sunshade roof

b = base

c = upper storey and stairs

a = lower storey

1 Glue together the base board, the walls and ceiling of the lower story. Reinforce the joints with masking tape. Wait for the glue to dry.

ABOVE THE FLOODS

The homes of wealthy people were often built on platforms to stop moisture through the mud brick walls. This also raised it above the level of any possible flood damage.

SOUL HOUSES

Pottery models give us a good idea of how the homes of poorer Egyptians looked. During the Middle Kingdom, these soul houses were left as tomb offerings. The Egyptians placed food in the courtyard of the house to feed the person's soul after death.

MUD BRICK

The Egyptians made mud bricks from the thick clay soil left behind by the Nile floods. The clay was taken to the brickyard and mixed with water, pebbles and chopped straw. Mud brick is still used as a building material for houses in Egypt today and is made in the same way.

straw

mud

BRICK MAKING

A group of laborers make bricks. First mud was collected in leather buckets and taken to the building site. There, it was mixed with straw and pebbles. Finally the mixture was put into a mold. At this stage, bricks were sometimes stamped with the name of the pharaoh or the building for which they were made. They were then left to dry in the hot sunshine for several days, before being carried away in a sling.

Egyptian houses had a large main room that opened directly onto the street. In many homes, stairs led up to the roof. People would often sleep there during hot weather.

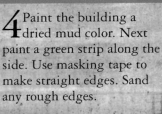

2 Now glue together the top story and stairs. Again, use masking tape to reinforce the joints. When the top story is dry, glue it to the lower story.

3 Glue the balsa pillars into the front of the top story. When the house is dry, cover it in wet paste of plaster of Paris. Paint the pillars red or a colour of your choice.

4 Paint the building a dried mud color. Next paint a green strip along the side. Use masking tape to make straight edges. Sand any rough edges.

5 Now make a shelter for the rooftop. Use four balsa struts as supports. Make the roof from cardboard glued with straw. Glue the shelter into place.

Skilled Workers

IN ANCIENT EGYPT, skilled workers formed a middle class between the poor laborers and the rich officials and nobles. Wall paintings and models show us craft workers carving stone or wood, making pottery, or working precious metals. There were boat builders and chariot makers, too.

Artists and craft workers could be well rewarded for their skills, and some became famous for their work. The house and workshops of a sculptor called Thutmose was excavated in el-Amarna in 1912. He was very successful in his career and was a favorite of the royal family.

Craft workers often lived in their own part of town. A special village was built at Deir el-Medina, near Thebes, for the builders of the magnificent, but secret, royal tombs. Among the 100 or so houses there, archaeologists found delivery notes for goods, sketches and plans drawn on broken pottery. Working conditions cannot always have been very good, for records show that the workers once went on strike. They may well have helped to rob the tombs that they themselves had built.

GLASS IN GOLD
This pendant shows the skill of Egyptian craft workers. It is in the form of Nekhbet the vulture, goddess of Upper Egypt. Glass of many colors has been set in solid gold using a technique called cloisonné. Like many other such beautiful objects, it was found in the tomb of Tutankhamun.

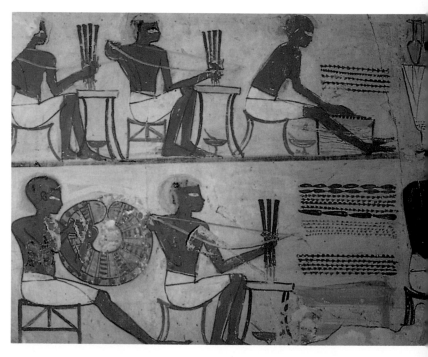

JEWELERS AT WORK
Jewelers are shown at their work benches in this wall painting from 1395BC. One is making an ornamental collar while the others are working with precious stones or beads. The bow strings are being used to power metal drill bits.

A HIVE OF INDUSTRY

Skilled craftsmen are hard at work in this bustling workshop. Carpenters are sawing and drilling wood, potters are painting pottery jars, and masons are chiseling stone. A foreman would inspect the quality of each finished item.

DEIR EL-MEDINA

The stone foundations of the village of Deir el-Medina may still be seen on the west bank of the Nile. They are about 3,500 years old. In its day, Deir el-Medina housed the skilled workers who built and decorated the royal tombs in the Valley of the Kings. The men worked for eight days out of ten. The village existed for four centuries and was large and prosperous. Nevertheless, the workmen's village did not have its own water supply, so water had to be carried to the site and stored in a guarded tank.

SURVEYING THE LAND

Officials stretch a cord across a field to calculate its area. These men were employed to survey an estate for government records.

bow drill

awl

smoothing stone

chisel

drill

oil flask

adze

saw

axe

pull saw

TOOLS OF THE TRADE

A carpenter's tool kit included chisels, saws, mallets, axes and knives. Bradawls were also used for making starter holes before drilling. The tools were generally made of wood and copper. Carpenters made fine chairs, beds, chests, boxes and beautiful coffins with these sophisticated tools.

Arts and Crafts

THE ANCIENT EGYPTIANS loved beautiful objects, and the craft items that have survived still amaze us today. There are shining gold rings and pendants, necklaces inlaid with glass and a dazzling blue pottery called faience. Jars made of a smooth white stone called alabaster have been preserved in almost perfect condition, along with chairs and chests made of cedar wood imported from the Near East.

Egyptians made beautiful baskets and storage pots. Some pottery was made from river clay, but the finest pots were made from a chalky clay found at Quena. Pots were shaped by hand or, later, on a potter's wheel. Some were polished with a smooth pebble until their surface shone. We know so much about Egyptian craft work because many beautiful items were placed in tombs, so that the dead person could use them in the next world.

ALABASTER ART
This elaborate jar was among the treasures in the tomb of Tutankhamun. Jars such as this would have held precious oils and perfumes.

GLASS FISH
This beautiful striped fish looks as if it should be swimming in the reefs of the Red Sea. In fact it is a glass jar used to store oils. Glass making became popular in Egypt after 1500BC. The glass was made from sand and salty crystals. It would then have been colored with metals and shaped while still hot.

MAKE A LOTUS TILE

You will need: cardboard, pencil, ruler, scissors, self-drying clay, modeling tool, sandpaper, acrylic paint (blue, gold, green, yellow), water bowl. Optional: rolling pin & board.

1 Using the final picture as reference, draw both tile shapes onto cardboard. Cut them out. Draw the pattern onto the sheet of cardboard and cut around the border.

2 Roll out the clay on a board. Place the overall outline over the clay and carefully trim off the edges. Discard the extra clay.

3 Mark the individual tile patterns into the clay, following the outlines carefully. Cut through the lines, but do not separate them out yet.

DESERT RICHES

The dwellers of the green Nile valley feared and disliked the desert. They called it the Red Land. However, the deserts did provide them with great mineral wealth, including blue-green turquoise, purple amethyst and blue agate.

blue agate　　*turquoise*　　*amethyst*

ROYAL TILES

Many beautiful tiles have been discovered by archaeologists. It is thought that they were used to decorate furniture and floors in the palaces of the Egyptian pharaohs.

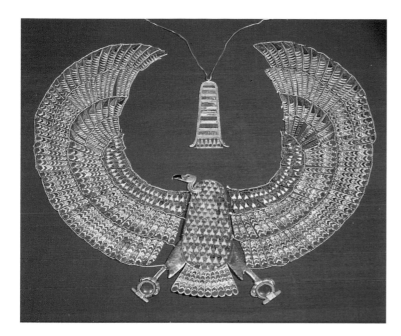

NEKHBET COLLAR

This splendid collar was one of 17 found in Tutankhamun's tomb. The spectacular wings of the vulture goddess Nekhbet include 250 feather sections made of colored glass set in gold. The vulture's beak and eye are made from a black, volcanic glass called obsidian. This and other amazing objects found in the young king's tomb show us the incredible skill of Egyptian craftsmen.

TUTANKHAMUN'S WAR CHEST

This painted chest shows Tutankhamun in battle against the Syrians and the Nubians. On the lid, the young king is also seen hunting in the desert. The incredible detail of the painting shows that this was the work of a very skilled artist. When Tutankhamun's tomb was opened, the chest was found to contain children's clothes. The desert air was so dry that neither the wood, leather nor fabric had rotted.

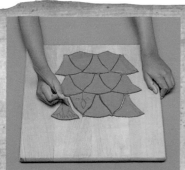

4 Now use the tool to score patterns of leaves and flowers into the surface of the soft clay, as shown. Separate the pieces and allow them to dry.

5 When one side of each tile has dried, turn it over. Leave the other side to dry. Then sand down the edges of the tiles until they are smooth.

6 The tiles are now ready for painting. Carefully paint the patterns in green, yellow, gold and blue. Leave them in a warm place to dry.

These tiles are similar to those found at a royal palace in Thebes. The design looks rather like a lotus, the sacred waterlily of ancient Egypt.

Wonder of the World

EARLY TOURISM

In the 1800s, many tourists climbed to the top of the Great Pyramid. From here, the best view of the Giza complex could be had. However, it was a dangerous climb and some visitors fell to their death.

FOR MANY YEARS the Great Pyramid at Giza was the largest building in the world. Its base is about 750 feet square, and its original point was 484 feet high. It is made up of about 2,300,000 massive blocks of stone, each one weighing about 2½ tons. It was the oldest of the seven ancient wonders of the world and is the only one left standing today. Even in ancient times, tourists came to marvel at the size of the Great Pyramid, and vast numbers of people still come to Giza today. The Great Pyramid is incredible in terms of both scale and age. It was built for the pharaoh Khufu, who died in 2566BC. Nearby was a great temple built in his honor. The purpose of the pyramid was to protect Khufu's body while he journeyed to meet the gods after his death. A 154-foot-long passage leads to one of the three burial chambers inside the pyramid, but the pharaoh's body was never found in the tomb. It had been robbed long ago.

GRAND GALLERY

This steep passage is known as the Grand Gallery. It leads up to the burial chamber in the Great Pyramid. After King Khufu's funeral, granite blocks were slid down the gallery to seal off the chamber. However, ancient Egyptian tomb robbers still managed to break into the chamber and steal its contents.

MAKE A PYRAMID

You will need: cardboard, pencil, ruler, scissors, white glue and brush, masking tape, acrylic paint (yellow, white, gold), plaster paste, sandpaper, water bowl and brush.

a   b

6 in | a   6 in | b

13 in   12 in

8 in | c

c   c

c   c

8½ in

Make the pyramid in two halves. Cut out one triangle (a) for the base, one triangle (b) for the inside and two of triangle (c) for the sides of each half.

1 Glue the half section of the pyramid together, binding the joints with pieces of masking tape. Now make the second half section in the same way.

INSIDE A PYRAMID

This cross-section shows the inside of the Great Pyramid. The design of the interior changed several times during its construction. An underground chamber may originally have been intended as Khufu's burial place. This chamber was never finished. A second chamber, known as the Queen's Chamber, was also found empty. The pharaoh was actually buried in the King's Chamber. Once the funeral was over, the tomb had to be sealed from the inside. Blocks of stone were slid down the Grand Gallery. The workmen left through a shaft and along a corridor before the stones thudded into place.

THE KING'S CHAMBER

The burial chamber in the Great Pyramid is known as the King's Chamber. It was the final resting place of the sarcophagus containing King Khufu's body. The chamber is made of granite. Each of the nine slabs which make up its roof weighs 50 tons. Strangely, the only place in the pyramid where Khufu's name can be seen is above the roof. Here graffiti was left by the workmen who built the pyramid.

ventilation shafts

King's Chamber

Grand Gallery

Queen's Chamber

escape shaft for workers

corridor

unfinished chamber

2 Mix up yellow and white paint with a little plaster paste to achieve a sandy texture. Add glue so that it sticks to the cardboard. Paint the pyramid sections.

3 Now leave the painted pyramid sections in a warm place to dry. Next sand down the tips until they are smooth and mask them off with tape.

4 Now paint the tips of each half of the pyramid gold and leave to dry. Finally, glue the two halves together and place your pyramid on a bed of sand.

The building of the Great Pyramid probably took about 23 years. Originally the pyramids were cased in pale limestone, so they would have looked a brilliant white. The capstone at the top of the pyramid was probably covered in gold.

The Valley of the Kings

IN 1550BC, the capital of Egypt moved south to Thebes. This marked the beginning of the New Kingdom. The ancient Egyptians no longer built pyramids as they were obvious targets for tomb robbers. The people still raised great temples to honor their dead rulers, but now the pharaohs were buried in secret underground tombs. These were hidden away in the cliffs bordering the desert on the west bank of the Nile, where the Sun set each night. It was from here that the pharaoh would journey to meet the Sun god on his death.

The burial sites near Thebes included the Valley of the Kings, the Valley of the Queens and the Valley of the Nobles. The tombs were packed with glittering treasure. Practical

items that the pharaoh would need in the next life were buried there too, such as food, royal clothing, gilded furniture, jewelery, weapons and chariots.

The tombs were guarded by a secret police force and were designed with traps to foil any intruders. Even so, many sites were robbed in ancient times. Luckily, some remained unspoiled and have given archaeologists an amazing look into the world of ancient Egypt.

THE KINGDOM OF THE DEAD
The Valley of the Kings lies across the Nile from the modern town of Luxor, on the edge of the Western desert. Sixty-two New Kingdom tombs have been discovered here so far.

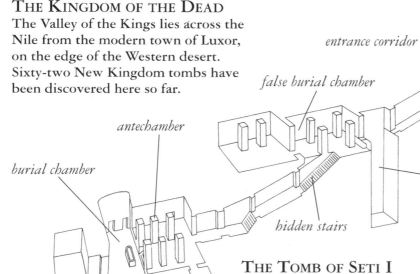

entrance corridor

false burial chamber

antechamber

burial chamber

shaft

hidden stairs

THE TOMB OF SETI I
One of the finest tombs in the Valley of the Kings belonged to the pharaoh Seti I, who died in 1279BC. Its splendid hall and burial chamber were protected by hidden shafts and stairs.

THE MASK
This beautiful mask was placed over the face of Tutankhamun's mummy. It presents the pharaoh in the image of the Sun god, Ra. This mask is made of solid gold and a blue stone called lapis lazuli. Tutankhamun's tomb was the most spectacular find in the Valley of the Kings. The inner chambers had not been disturbed for over 3,260 years.

GRAVE ROBBERS

When Howard Carter entered the tomb of Tutankhamun, he discovered that robbers had reached its outer chambers in ancient times. The Valley guards had resealed the tomb, but many items were left in heaps and piles. This picture shows two chariots, two beds, a chest, stools and food boxes.

UNTOLD TREASURES

This gold perfume box was found in Tutankhamun's burial chamber. The oval-shaped designs are called cartouches. They contain pictures of the pharaoh as a boy.

WORKERS ON SITE

The excavations of the 1800s and 1900s brought teams of Egyptian workers back into the Valley of the Kings for the first time in thousands of years. They dug down into tombs, carried out soil in baskets and shifted rocks. This photograph was taken in 1922 during Howard Carter's excavations that uncovered the tomb of Tutankhamun.

Mummies and Coffins

THE EARLY EGYPTIANS found out that people buried in the desert were often preserved in the dry sand. Their bodies dried out and became mummified. Over the ages, the Egyptians became experts at preserving bodies by embalming them. They believed that the dead would need to use their bodies in the next life.

The methods of mummification varied over the years. The process usually took about 70 days. The brains were hooked out through the nose and the other organs were removed and placed in special jars. Only the heart was left so that it could be weighed in the next life. Embalming involved drying the body out with salty crystals of natron. Afterwards it was stuffed and covered with oils and ointments and then wrapped in bandages. The mummy was then placed inside a series of coffins in the shape of the body.

MUMMY CASE
This beautiful gold case contains the mummy of a priestess. Once the embalmed body had been wrapped in bandages it was placed in a richly decorated coffin. Both the inside and outside would be covered in spells to help the dead person in the underworld. Sometimes more than one coffin was used. The inner coffins would be of brightly painted or gilded wood (*as left*) and the outer coffin would be a stone sarcophagus.

CANOPIC JARS
Special jars were used to store the body's organs. The human-headed jar held the liver. The baboon-headed jar contained the lungs. The stomach was put in the jackal-headed jar and finally the intestines were placed in the falcon-headed jar.

CANOPIC JARS

You will need: self-drying clay, rolling pin and board, ruler, modeling tool, sandpaper, masking tape, acrylic paint (white, blue, green, yellow, black), water bowl and brush.

1 Roll out ³/₄ of the clay and cut out a circle 3 in in diameter. This is the base of the jar. Roll out thin strips of clay and coil them from the base to make the sides.

2 Carefully press out the bumps between the coils until the sides of the jar are smooth and round. Finally trim the top of the jar with a modeling tool.

3 Now make a lid for the jar. Measure the size needed and cut out a circle of the remaining clay. Mold it into a dome. Model the head of a baboon on to the lid.

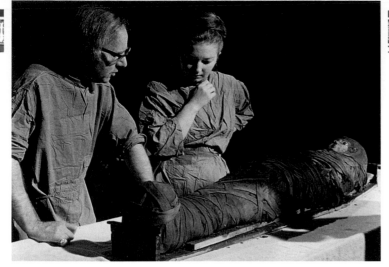

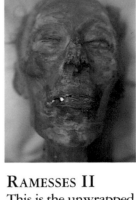

BENEATH THE BANDAGES

Unwrapping a mummy is a delicate operation. Today, archaeologists can use scanning or X-ray equipment to examine the mummies' bodies. It is possible to tell what food they once ate, the work they did and the illnesses they suffered from. X-rays also show the stuffing used to replace the internal organs.

RAMESSES II

This is the unwrapped head of the mummy of Ramesses II. Wadding was placed in his eye sockets to stop the natron (preserving salts) from destroying his features.

THE OPENING OF THE MOUTH CEREMONY

The last ritual before burial was led by a priest wearing the mask of the god Anubis. The human-shaped coffin was held upright and its face was touched with magical instruments. This ceremony enabled the mummy to speak, see and hear in the next world.

It was believed that any part of a person's body could be used against them. For this reason the organs were removed during mummification and stored in canopic jars. Spells written on the jars helped to protect them.

4 Hapy the baboon guarded the mummy's lungs, Use the modeling tool to make the baboon's eyes and nose. Leave the lid in a warm place to dry.

5 When both the jar and the lid are completely dry, rub them down with sandpaper until they are smooth. The lid should fit snugly onto the jar.

6 It is now time to paint your jar. Use masking tape to protect the baboon's face and to help you get the stripes straight. Follow the colors in the picture above.

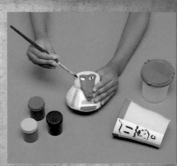

7 Paint hieroglyphs down the front of the jar as shown. Use the letters on page 46 to help you. The canopic jar is now ready for the funeral.

Egyptian Funerals

WHEN A PHARAOH died, everything possible was done to make sure he completed his journey to the gods in safety. During the New Kingdom, the ruler's coffin, containing his mummy, would be placed on a boat and ferried from Thebes to the west bank of the Nile. There it was placed in a shrine and hauled on a sled drawn by oxen to the Valley of the Kings. The funeral procession was spectacular.

Priests scattered offerings of milk and burned incense. Women played the part of official mourners, screaming and weeping. In front of the tomb there was dancing and a priest read out spells. After a ceremony and a banquet, the coffin was placed in the tomb with food, drink and treasure. The tomb was then sealed.

LIFE AFTER DEATH

The *ba*, or personality, of a dead person hovers over the mummy. It appears as a bird. Its job is to help the dead body rejoin its spirit, or *ka*, so it can live in the next world. This picture is taken from a papyrus called the Book of the Dead. This book acted as a guide to the afterlife for the dead. It contained spells to guarantee safe passage through the underworld. Priests read from it at the funeral and then it was buried with the mummy.

SHABTI FIGURES

Shabti were model figures placed in a tomb. Their purpose was to work for the dead person in the next life, acting as servants or laborers. They would be brought to life by a spell.

MAKE AN UDJAT EYE

You will need: self-drying clay, modeling tool, sandpaper, acrylic paint (red, blue, black, white), water bowl and brush. Optional: rolling pin and board.

1 Begin by rolling out the clay on the board. Use the modeling tool to cut in the pattern of the eye pieces. Refer to step 2 for the shape of each piece.

2 Remove all extra clay and arrange the eye pieces on the board. The eye is meant to represent the eye of the falcon-headed god Horus.

3 Next, press the pieces together until you have the full shape of the eye. Use the modeling tool if necessary. Now leave the eye to dry.

THE FUNERAL PROCESSION

The coffin lies inside a boat-shaped shrine on a sled. The priests chant and pray as they begin to haul the sled up towards the burial place. A burial site such as the Valley of the Kings is called a necropolis, which means "the city of the dead". The coffin would be taken into the tomb through a deep corridor to its final resting place. In the burial chamber, it would be surrounded by fine objects and riches.

FUNERARY BOAT

This beautiful model boat was placed in the tomb of Tutankhamun. It is made of alabaster and shows two female mourners who represent the goddess Isis and her sister Nephthys. They are mourning the death of the murdered god Osiris. Between them is an empty sarcophagus (stone coffin casing), which may once have been used to hold oils. Many other boats were found in the tomb. They were meant to carry the pharaoh after he had died, just as a boat had carried Ra, the Sun god, through *Dwat*, the underworld.

4 Smooth the surface with sandpaper to prepare it for painting. Horus was said to have lost his eye in a battle with Seth, the god of Chaos.

5 Paint in the white of the eye and add the black eyebrow and pupil. Next, paint in the red liner. Finally, paint the rest of the eye blue and let dry.

When Horus lost his eye, it was made better by the goddess Hathor. Udjat meant making better. Udjat eye and other charms, or amulets, were wrapped up with mummies to protect them in the next life.

101

Priests, Temples and Festivals

MASSIVE TEMPLES were built in honor of the Egyptian gods. Many can still be seen today. They have great pillars and massive gates, courtyards and avenues of statues. Once, these would have led to a shrine that was believed to be the home of a god.

Ordinary people did not gather to worship in an Egyptian temple as they might today in a church. Only priests were allowed in the temples. They carried out rituals on behalf of the pharaoh, making offerings of food, burning incense, playing music and singing. They had complicated rules about washing and shaving their heads, and some had to wear special clothes such as leopard skins. Noblewomen served as priestesses during some ceremonies. Many priests had little knowledge of religion and just served in the temple for three months before returning to their normal work. Other priests studied the stars and spells.

There were many religious festivals during which the god's shrine would be carried to other temples in a great procession. This was when ordinary Egyptians joined in worship. Offerings of food made to the gods were given back to the people for public feasting.

SACRED RITUALS

A priest engaged in a religious ritual wears a leopard skin garment. He is carrying a vase containing sacred water from the temple's holy lake. During ceremonies, this water would have been poured over offering tables to ensure the purity of the gifts made to the gods. Incense would also have been burned to purify the atmosphere of the temple.

KARNAK

This painting by David Roberts shows the massive temple of Karnak as it appeared in 1850. It still stands just outside the modern town of Luxor. The temple's most important god was Amun-Ra. The site also includes courts and buildings sacred to other gods and goddesses, including Mut (a vulture goddess, wife of Amun) and Khons (the Moon god, son of Amun). The Great Temple was enlarged and rebuilt over about 2,000 years.

TEMPLE OF HORUS
A statue of Horus, the falcon god, guards the temple at Edfu. There was a temple on this site during the New Kingdom. However, the building that still stands today dates back to the period of Greek rule. This temple was dedicated to Horus and his wife, the cow goddess Hathor. Inside the temple there are stone carvings showing Horus fighting the enemies of Osiris, his father.

ANUBIS THE EMBALMER
A priest wears the mask of Anubis to embalm a body. This jackal-headed god was said to have prepared the body of the god Osiris for burial. He and his priests had strong links with mummies and the practice of embalming.

KALABSHA TEMPLE
The Kalabsha temple was one of the largest temples in Lower Nubia. In the 1960s, the Aswan Dam was built and Lower Nubia was flooded. Many monuments such as the temples at Abu Simbel and Philae had to be moved. The temple at Kalabsha was dismantled, and its 13,000 blocks of stone were moved to New Kalabsha, where it was rebuilt.

GATEWAY TO ISIS
The temple of Philae (*above*) was built in honor of Isis, the mother goddess. Isis was worshipped all over Egypt and in many other lands, too. Massive gateways called pylons guard the temple of Philae. Pylons guard the way to many Egyptian temples and were used for special ceremonies.

Workers and Slaves

The PHARAOHS may have believed that it was their links with the gods that kept Egypt going, but really it was the hard work of the ordinary people. It was they who dug the soil, worked in the mines and quarries, sailed the boats on the Nile river, marched with the army into Syria or Nubia, cooked food and raised children.

Slavery was not very important in ancient Egypt, but it did exist. Most of the slaves were prisoners who had been captured during the many wars that Egypt fought with its neighbors in the Near East. Slaves were usually treated well and were allowed to own property.

Many Egyptian workers were serfs. This meant that their freedom was limited. They could be bought and sold along with the estates where they worked. Farmers had to be registered with the government. They had to sell crops at a fixed price and pay taxes in the form of produce. During the season of the Nile floods, when the fields lay under water, many workers were recruited into public building projects. Punishment for those who ran away was harsh.

PLOWING WITH OXEN
This model figure from a tomb is plowing the soil with oxen. The Egyptian farm workers' daily toil was hard. Unskilled peasant laborers did not own land and were paid little.

TRANSPORTING A STATUE
These workers are moving a huge stone statue on a wooden sled hauled by ropes. Many farm workers had to labor on large public building works, building dams or pyramids, each summer and autumn. Their food and lodging were provided, but they were not paid wages. Only the official classes were exempt from this service, but anyone rich enough could pay someone else to do the work for them. Slaves were used for really hard labor, such as mining and quarrying.

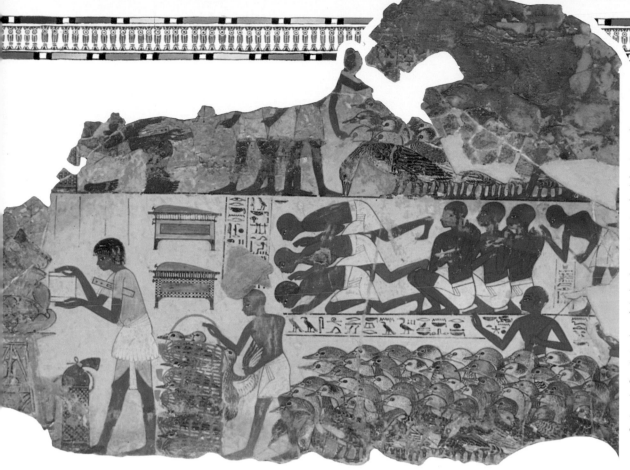

COUNTING GEESE
A farmer's flock of geese is counted out in this wall painting. Every other year, government officials visited each farm. They would count the animals to see how much tax had to be paid to the pharaoh. Taxes were paid in produce rather than money. The scribe on the left is recording this information. Scribes were members of the official classes and therefore had a higher position than other workers.

CARRYING BREAD
A woman carries a tray of loaves on her head. Most of the cooking in large houses and palaces was done by male servants, but baking bread was the job of the women. Baking was one of the few public jobs open to women.

GRINDING CORN
This model from 2325BC shows a female servant grinding wheat or barley grains into flour. She is using a stone hand-mill called a quern.

GIVE THAT MAN A BEATING
This tomb painting shows an official overseeing work in the fields. Unskilled peasant farmers were attached to an estate belonging to the pharaoh, a temple, or a rich landowner. Farmers who could not or would not give a large percentage of their harvest in rent and taxes to the pharaoh were punished harshly. They might be beaten, and their tools or their house could be seized as payment. There were law courts, judges and local magistrates in place to punish tax collectors who took bribes.

Farmers and Crops

HARVEST FESTIVAL
A priestess makes an offering of harvest produce in the tomb of Nakht. The picture shows some of the delicious fruits grown in Egypt. These included figs, grapes and pomegranates.

FARMING TOOLS
Hoes were used to break up soil that had been too heavy for the plows. They were also used for digging soil. The sharp sickle was used to cut grain.

sickle   *hoes*

THE ANCIENT EGYPTIANS called the banks of the Nile the Black Land because of the mud that was washed downstream each year from Central Africa. The Nile flooded in June, depositing this rich, fertile mud in Egypt. The land remained underwater until autumn.

By November the ground was ready for plowing and then sowing. Seeds were scattered over the soil and trampled in by the hooves of sheep or goats. During the drier periods of the year, farmers dug channels and canals to bring water to irrigate their land. In the New Kingdom, a lifting sytem called the *shaduf* was introduced to raise water from the river. The success of this farming cycle was vital. Years of low flood or drought could spell disaster. If the crops failed, people went hungry.

Farm animals included ducks, geese, pigs, sheep and goats. Cows grazed the fringes of the desert or the greener lands of the delta region. Oxen were used for hauling plows and donkeys were widely used to carry goods.

TOILING IN THE FIELDS
Grain crops were usually harvested in March or April, before the great heat began. The ears of wheat or barley were cut off with a sickle made of wood and sharpened flint. In some well-irrigated areas there was a second harvest later in the summer.

MAKE A SHADUF

You will need: cardboard, pencil, ruler, scissors, white glue and brush, masking tape, acrylic paint (blue, green, brown), balsa wood, stones, twig, clay, muslin, string, water bowl and brush.
Note: mix green paint with dried herbs for the grass mixture.

c = water tank

6 in   1 in   1½ in
2 in   2 in   3½ in   c   3½ in   3½ in
9 in   9 in   a   9 in   1½ in   1 in
1½ in   2½ in
6½ in   1½ in   1½
2 in   2 in   9 in   9 in   9 in
6 in   b   3 in
a = irrigation channel & river bank   1¼ in   1½ in
Cut out the cardboard shapes (a), (b) and (c) as shown.   2½ in
b = river

1 Glue the edges of boxes (a), (b) and (c), as shown. Bind them with masking tape until they are dry. Paint the river (b) and the water tank (c) blue and let dry.

HERDING THE OXEN

This New Kingdom wall painting shows oxen being herded in front of a government inspector. Cattle were already being bred along the banks of the Nile in the days before the pharaohs. They provided milk, meat and leather. They hauled wooden plows and were killed as sacrifices to the gods in the temples.

NILE CROPS

The chief crops were barley and wheat, used for making beer and bread. Beans and lentils were grown alongside leeks, onions, cabbages, radishes, lettuces and cucumbers. Juicy melons, dates and figs could be grown in desert oases. Grapes were grown in vineyards.

leek   *onions*

WATERING MACHINE

The *shaduf* has a bucket on one end of a pole and a heavy weight at the other. First the weight is pushed up, lowering the bucket into the river. As the weight is lowered, it raises up the full bucket.

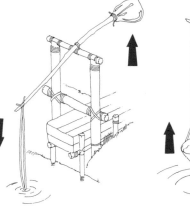

The mechanical lifting system called the shaduf was invented in the Middle East. It was brought to Egypt 3,500 years ago.

2 Paint the river bank with the green grass mixture on top, brown on the sides and the irrigation channel blue. Now find the balsa strips for the frame.

3 Glue the strips together, supporting them with masking tape and cardboard. When dry, paint the frame brown. Glue stones onto the tank.

4 Use a twig for the shaduf pole. Make a weight from clay wrapped in muslin. Tie it to one end of the pole. Make a bucket from clay, leaving holes for the string.

5 Thread the string through the bucket and tie to the pole. Tie the pole, with its weight and bucket, to the shaduf frame. Glue the frame to the bank.

Food and Banquets

WORKING PEOPLE in Egypt were often paid in food. They ate bread, onions and salted fish, washed down with a sweet, grainy beer. Flour was often gritty and the teeth of many mummies show signs of severe wear and tear. Dough was kneaded with the feet or by hand, and pastry cooks produced all kinds of cakes and loaves.

BEAUTIFUL BOWLS
Dishes and bowls were often made of faience, a glassy pottery. The usual color for this attractive tableware was blue-green or turquoise.

A big banquet for a pharaoh was a fancy affair, with guests dressed in their finest clothes. A royal menu might include roast goose or stewed beef, kidneys, wild duck or tender gazelle. Lamb was not eaten for religious reasons, and in some regions certain types of fish were also forbidden. Vegetables such as leeks were stewed with milk and cheese. Egyptian cooks were experts at stewing, roasting and baking.

Red and white wines were served at banquets. They were stored in pottery jars marked with their year and their vineyard, just like the labels on modern wine bottles.

A FEAST FIT FOR A KING
New Kingdom noblewomen exchange gossip at a dinner party. They show off their jewelry and best clothes. The Egyptians loved wining and dining. They would be entertained by musicians, dancers and acrobats during the feast.

MAKE A CAKE

You will need: 1 1/2 cups stone-ground flour, 1/2 tsp salt, 1 tsp baking powder, 4 tbsp butter, 1 cup honey, 3 tbsp milk, caraway seeds, bowl, wooden spoon, floured surface, baking tray.

1 Begin by mixing together the flour, salt and baking powder in the bowl. Next, chop up the butter and add it to the mixture.

2 Using your fingers, rub the butter into the mixture, as shown. Your mixture should look like fine breadcrumbs when you have finished.

3 Now it is time to add half a cup of honey. Combine it with your mixture. This will sweeten your cakes. The Egyptians did not have sugar.

WOMAN MAKING BEER

This wooden tomb model of a woman making beer dates back to 2400BC. Beer was made by mashing barley bread in water. When the mixture fermented, becoming alcoholic, the liquid was strained off into a wooden tub. There were various types of beer, but all were very popular. It was said that the god Osiris had brought beer to the land of Egypt.

DRINKING VESSEL

This beautiful faience cup could have been used to drink wine, water or beer. It is decorated with a pattern of lotus flowers.

DESERT DESSERTS

An Egyptian meal could be finished off with nuts such as almonds or sweet fruits—juicy figs, dates, grapes, pomegranates or melons. Sugar was still unknown so honey was used to sweeten cakes and pastries.

pomegranates

dates

PALACE BAKERY

Whole teams of model cooks and bakers were left in some tombs. This was so that a pharaoh could order them to put on a good banquet to entertain his guests in the other world. Models are shown sifting, mixing and kneading flour, and making pastries. Most of our knowledge about Egyptian food and cooking comes from the food boxes and offerings left in tombs.

Egyptian pastries were often shaped in spirals like these. Other popular shapes were rings like donuts, pyramids and discs like cookies.

4 Add the milk and stir the mixture until it forms a dough. Place your ball of dough on a floured board or surface. Divide it into three.

5 Roll the dough into long strips, as shown. Take the strips and coil them into a spiral to make one cake. Make the other cakes in the same way.

6 Now sprinkle each cake with caraway seeds and place them on a greased baking tray. Finish by glazing the cakes carefully with honey.

7 Ask an adult to bake them in an oven at 355°F for 20 minutes. When they are ready, take them out and leave on a baking rack to cool.

Egyptian Dress

THE MOST COMMON TEXTILE in Egypt was linen. It was mostly a spotless white. Dyes such as iron (red), indigo (blue) and saffron (yellow) were sometimes used, but colored and patterned clothes were usually the mark of a foreigner. However, the Egyptians did decorate their clothes with beads and beautiful feathers. Wool was not used for weaving in ancient Egypt. Silk and cotton did not appear until foreign rulers came to power in Egypt, after about 1000BC.

The basic items of dress for men were a simple kilt, loin-cloth or tunic. Women wore a long, closely fitting dress of fine fabric. Fashions for both men and women varied over the ages, with changes in the straps, pleating and folds.

Although more elaborate styles of clothing did appear in the New Kingdom, clothing was relatively simple, with elaborate wigs, jewelry and eye makeup creating a more dramatic effect.

LUCKY BRACELET
The bracelet above features an *udjat* eye—this eye charm was thought to protect those who carried it. Many items of jewelry featured such charms for decoration as well as for superstitious reasons. Some necklaces and earrings featured magic charms to prevent snake bites or other disasters.

GOLDEN SANDALS
These gold sandals were found in the tomb of Sheshonq II. Sandals for the rich were usually made of fine leather, while the poor used sandals made of papyrus or woven grass.

110

Linen was made from the plant flax. Its stalks were soaked, pounded and then rolled into lengths. The fiber was spun into thread by hand on a turning spindle, and the thread kept moist in the mouths of the spinners. It was then ready for weaving. The first Egyptian looms were flat, but upright looms were brought in during the Hyksos period.

linen

FIT FOR A KING AND QUEEN

This panel from a golden throne shows Tutankhamun and his wife, Ankhesenamun, in their palace. The pictures are made from glass, silver, precious stones and faience (glazed pottery). The queen is wearing a long, pleated dress, while the pharaoh wears a pleated kilt. Garments were draped around the wearer rather than sewn, and pleating was very popular from the Middle Kingdom onwards. Both Tutankhamun and his wife wear sandals, bracelets, wide collars and beautiful headdresses or crowns. The queen is offering her husband perfume or ointment from a bowl.

FIRST FASHIONS

This shirt was found in the tomb of Tarkhan. It was made nearly 5,000 years ago during the reign of the pharaoh Djet. The fabric is linen and there are pleats across the shoulders.

COLORFUL COLLARS

Wide, brilliantly colored collars were made of glass beads, flowers, berries and leaves. They were worn for banquets and other special occasions. Collars found in Tutankhamun's tomb included those made of olive leaves and cornflowers. By examining such plants, archaeologists can find out important information about gardening, farming, the climate and insect life in ancient Egypt.

Science and Technology

THE ANCIENT EGYPTIANS had advanced systems of numbering and measuring. They put their knowledge to good use in building, engineering and in surveying land. However, their knowledge of science was often mixed up with superstitions and belief in magic. For example, doctors understood a lot about broken bones and surgery, but at the same time they used all kinds of spells, amulets and magic potions to ward off disease. Much of their knowledge about the human body came from their experience of preparing the dead for burial.

The priests studied the stars carefully. They thought that the planets must be gods. The Egyptians also worked out a calendar, and this was very important for deciding when the Nile floods would arrive and when to plant crops.

MATHEMATICAL PAPYRUS
This papyrus shows methods for working out the areas of squares, circles and triangles. It dates from around 850BC. These methods would have been used in calculations for land areas and pyramid heights on Egyptian building projects. Other surviving Egyptian writings show mathematical calculations to work out how much grain would fit into a store. The Egyptians used a decimal system of numbering, with separate symbols for one, ten, 100 and 1,000. Eight was shown by eight one symbols—11111111.

CUBIT MEASURE
Units of measurement included the royal cubit of 20 inches and the short cubit of 18 inches. A cubit was the length of a man's forearm and was subdivided into palms and fingers.

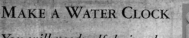

MAKE A WATER CLOCK
You will need: self-drying clay, plastic flowerpot, modeling tool, skewer, pencil, ruler, masking tape, scissors, acrylic paint (yellow), varnish, water bowl. Optional: rolling pin and board.

1 Begin by rolling out the clay. Take the plastic flowerpot and press its base firmly into the clay. This will be the bottom of your water clock.

2 Cut out an oblong of clay large enough to mold around the flower pot. Add the base and use your modeling tool to make the joints smooth.

3 Make a small hole near the bottom of the pot with a skewer. Leave the pot in a warm place to dry. When the clay has dried, remove the flowerpot.

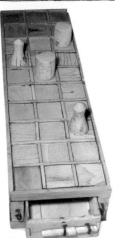

THE LAST GAME

This gameboard comes from Tutankhamun's tomb. Board games were so popular that they were placed in tombs to offer the dead person some fun in the next life.

HOLDS AND THROWS

Wrestling was one sport that any Egyptian could do. It did not need expensive chariots or any other special equipment. It was popular with rich and poor alike.

HUNTING BIRDS IN THE MARSHES

Nebamun, a nobleman, is enjoying a day's bird-hunt in the marshes of the Nile Delta. He stands in his reed boat and hurls a throwing stick, a kind of boomerang, at the birds flying out of the reeds. His cat already seems to have caught several birds.

Mehen, the snake game, was popular in Egypt before 3000 BC.

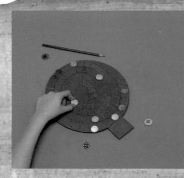

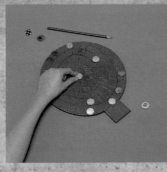

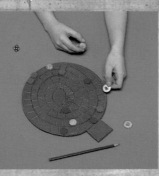

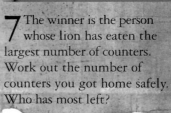

4 Start all of your counters on the board before advancing any of the others. A throw of one ends a go and allows your opponent to take their turn.

5 Exact numbers are needed to reach the center. Once there, turn your counter over for its return journey. When it gets back to the start, your lion can begin.

6 The lion moves to the center in the same way as the other counters. On its return journey, it can eat any of your opponent's counters in its way.

7 The winner is the person whose lion has eaten the largest number of counters. Work out the number of counters you got home safely. Who has most left?

A Child's World

ALTHOUGH EGYPTIAN CHILDREN had only a brief period of childhood before education and work, they did enjoy playing with rattles, balls, spinning tops, toy horses and toy crocodiles. They wrestled in the dust, ran races and swam in the river.

Girls from ordinary Egyptian families received little schooling. They were taught how to look after the household, how to spin, weave and cook. When girls grew up there were few jobs open to them, although they did have legal rights and some noblewomen became very powerful. Boys were mostly trained to do the same jobs as their fathers. Some went to scribe school, where they learned how to read and write. Slow learners were beaten without mercy. Boys and some girls from noble families received a broader education, learning how to read, write and do math.

TOY HORSE
This wooden horse dates from the period when the Greeks or Romans ruled Egypt. It would have been pulled along on its wheels by a piece of string.

FUN FOR ALL
Spinning tops were popular toys with children in Egypt. They were made of glazed stone and would have been cheap enough for poorer families to buy.

ISIS AND HORUS
Many statues show the goddess Isis with Horus as a child sitting on his mother's lap. The young Horus was believed to protect families from danger and accidents. The Egyptians had large families and family life was important to them.

A LION THAT ROARS
You will need: self-drying clay, rolling pin and board, modeling tool, cardboard, skewer, balsa wood, sandpaper, acrylic paint (white, green, red, blue, black, yellow), masking tape, string, water bowl.

1 Begin by rolling out the clay. Cut the pieces to the shapes shown. Mold the legs onto the body and the base. Put the jaw piece to one side.

2 Use your modeling tool to make a hole between the lion's upper body and the base, as shown. This hole is for the lower jaw to fit into.

3 Insert the lower jaw into the hole you have made and prop it up with cardboard. Make a hole through the upper and lower jaws with a skewer.

THE LOCK OF YOUTH

When they were young, boys and girls wore a special haircut, a shaved head with a lock of plaited hair. This plait, or lock of youth, was allowed to grow over one side of children's faces. When they reached adulthood, many Egyptians would have their heads shaved and wear an elaborate wig.

Originally this toy would have been made of wood, with a bronze tooth.

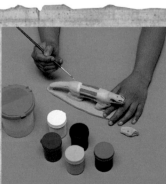

BOUNCING BACK

Egyptian children enjoyed playing games with balls made from rags, linen and reeds. However, archaeologists are not certain whether the balls above were used for the playing of games or as a type of rattle for younger children.

A TOY LION

Pull the string, and the lion roars! Or is it a cat meowing? Children once played with this animal on the banks of the Nile. At the time, this toy would have been brightly painted.

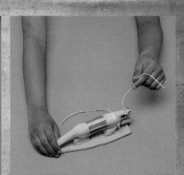

4 Now use the skewer to make a hole from right to left through the lion's upper body. String will go through these holes later to be connected to the jaw.

5 Push a small piece of balsa wood into the mouth. This will form the lion's tooth. Leave the clay lion to dry and then sand down the surface.

6 Paint the lion in white, yellow, blue, black and red. Use masking tape to make your lines straight. Leave the lion in a warm place to dry.

7 Thread the string through the holes in the upper body and tie it to secure. A second string goes through the lower and upper jaws of the lion.

Weapons and Warriors

GYPT WAS SURROUNDED by harsh deserts on three sides. In the north were the marshes of the delta and to the south the Nile ran over a series of rapids and waterfalls, the cataracts. All these formed barriers to invading armies. Even so, Egyptian towns were defended with forts and walls, and many pharaohs went into battle against their neighbors. Wars were fought against the Libyans, the Nubians, the Hittites and the Syrians.

There were professional soldiers in Egypt, but most were conscripted against their will. For slaves, fighting in the army was a chance to gain their freedom. At times, foreign troops were also hired to fight. Young men in the villages learned to drill in preparation for war. Soldiers carried shields of leather and wood. They were armed with spears, axes, bows and arrows, daggers and swords. Later, war chariots drawn by horses were used. Special awards, such as the golden fly, were handed out for bravery in battle.

KING DEN
This ivory label from 3000BC shows King Den striding into battle against an eastern enemy. He stands beneath the flag, or standard, of the jackal-headed god Anubis. He is armed with a club, or mace.

RIDING TO VICTORY
Egyptian art often shows scenes of a pharaoh riding into battle or returning home in triumph. The king is shown in a fine chariot, driving prisoners before him. Artists often showed the enemy as very small, to show the importance and power of the pharaoh. This plaque of red gold shows Tutankhamun as the all-conquering hero.

MAKE A GOLDEN FLY

You will need: cardboard, pencil, ruler, scissors, self-drying clay, white glue and brush, acrylic paint (gold), gold or white ribbon (16 in long x 1/2 in wide), water bowl.

1 Begin by making the body and wings of the fly. Use a ruler and pencil to draw the fly shape onto the cardboard. Then cut it out with scissors.

2 Next, mold the face of the fly in clay. Roll two small balls for the eyes and outline them with coils of clay. This will make the eyes look larger.

3 Take the cardboard, bend over the tab and glue it down, as shown. This will make a loop. Ribbon will be threaded through this loop later.

124

BATTLE AXE

This axe has a silver handle and a long blade designed to give a slicing movement. The battle axe was the Egyptian foot soldiers' favorite weapon. Its head of copper or bronze was fitted into a socket or lashed to the wooden handle with leather thongs. Soldiers did not wear armor in battle. Their only protection against weapons such as the heavy axes and spears was large shields made of wood or leather. The mummy of the pharaoh Seqenenre Tao shows terrible wounds to the skull caused by an axe, a dagger and a spear on the battlefield.

DAGGERS

These ceremonial daggers were found in Tutankhamun's tomb. They are similar to those that would have been used in battle. Egyptian daggers were short and fairly broad. The blades were made of copper or bronze. An iron dagger was also found in Tutankhamun's tomb, but this was very rare. It may have been a gift from the Hittite people, who were mastering the new skill of ironworking.

The Golden Fly was a reward for brave soldiers. This is a model of the golden fly given to Queen Aahotep for her part in the war against the Hyksos.

4 Glue four small strips of white cardboard onto the face, as shown. Push them into the modeling clay. Leave the fly's face in a warm place to dry.

5 Now glue the completed clay fly in place on the cardboard wings. Leave the finished fly to dry for 20 minutes or so before painting it.

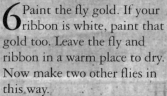

6 Paint the fly gold. If your ribbon is white, paint that gold too. Leave the fly and ribbon in a warm place to dry. Now make two other flies in this way.

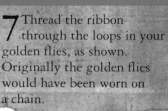

7 Thread the ribbon through the loops in your golden flies, as shown. Originally the golden flies would have been worn on a chain.

Boats and Ships

THE EGYPTIANS were not great seafarers. Their ocean-going ships did sail the Red Sea and the Mediterranean, and may even have reached India, but they mostly kept to coastal waters. However, the Egyptians were experts at river travel, as they are today. They built simple boats from papyrus reed, and these were used for fishing and hunting.

Egypt had little timber, so wooden ships were often built from cedar imported from Lebanon. Boats and model ships were often placed in tombs, and archaeologists have found many well-preserved examples.

The Nile was Egypt's main road, and all kinds of boats traveled up and down. There were barges transporting stones to building sites, ferries taking people across the river, and royal pleasure boats.

THE FINAL VOYAGE
Ships often appear in Egyptian pictures. They were important symbols of the voyage to the next world after death.

ALL ALONG THE NILE
Wooden sailing ships with graceful, triangular sails can still be seen on the Nile river today. They carry goods and people up and down the river. The design of these boats, or *feluccas*, has changed since the time of the ancient Egyptians. The sails on their early boats were tall, upright and narrow. Later designs were broader, like the ones shown. In Egypt, big towns and cities have always been built along the river, so the Nile has served as an important highway.

MAKE A BOAT

You will need: a large bundle of straw 12 inches long, scissors, string, balsa sticks, red and yellow cardboard, white glue and brush.

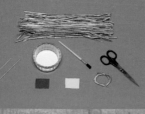

1 Divide the straw into five equal bundles and then cut three of them down to 6 inches in length. Tie the bundles securely at both ends and in the middle, as shown.

2 Take the two long bundles and tie them together at one end as shown. These bundles will form the outer frame of the boat.

3 Next take the three short bundles of straw and bind them together at both ends. These will form the inner surface of the straw boat.

STEERING AROUND SAND BANKS

This wooden tomb model shows a boat from 1800BC with high curved ends. Long steering oars kept the boat on course through the powerful currents of the flooding river. Although timber was the main material for building larger boats, their designs were similar to those of the simple reed vessels.

SAILING TO ABYDOS

These boats are making a pilgrimage to Abydos. This was the city of Osiris, the god of death and rebirth. Mummies were taken here by boat. Ships and boats played a major part in the religious beliefs of the Egyptians. Ra the Sun god traveled on a boat across the sky. In October 1991, a fleet of 12 boats dating from about 3000BC was found at Abydos near Memphis. The boats were up to 98 feet in length and had been buried beneath the desert sands. The vessels found in these pits are the oldest surviving large ships in the world.

SIGN OF THE NORTH

This hieroglyphic symbol means boat. It looks a bit like the papyrus reed vessels with their curved ends. This sign later came to mean north. A ship without a mast would always travel north with the current of the Nile.

Early boats were made from papyrus reeds. These were bound with string made from reed fibers.

4 Next push the short bundles into the center of the long pair firmly. Tie the bundles together with string at one end, as shown.

5 Bring the rear of the long pair of bundles together and tie them securely, as shown. Bind the whole boat together with string.

6 Thread a string lengthwise from one end to the other. The tension on the string should create the boat's curved prow and stern.

7 Finally, cut the card and glue it to the balsa sticks to make the boat's paddle and harpoon. Boats like these were used for fishing and hunting hippos.

Trade and Conquest

AT ITS HEIGHT, the Egyptian empire stretched all the way from Nubia to Syria. The peoples of the Near East who were defeated by the pharaohs had to pay tribute in the form of valuable goods such as gold or ostrich feathers. However, the Egyptians were more interested in protecting their own land from invasion than in establishing a huge empire. They preferred to conquer by influence rather than by war.

Egyptian trading influence spread far and wide as official missions set out to find luxury goods for the pharaoh and his court—timber, precious stones or spices. Beautiful pottery was imported from the Minoan kingdom of Crete. Traders employed by the government were called *shwty*. The ancient Egyptians did not have coins, and so goods were exchanged in a system of bartering.

Expeditions also set out to the land of Punt, a part of east Africa. The traders brought back pet apes, greyhounds, gold, ivory, ebony and myrrh. Queen Hatshepsut particularly encouraged these trading expeditions. The walls of her mortuary temple record details of them and also show a picture of Eti, the Queen of Punt.

WOODS FROM FARAWAY FORESTS
Few trees grew in Egypt, so timber for making fine furniture had to be imported. Cedarwood came from Lebanon and hardwoods such as ebony from Africa.

ALL THE RICHES OF PUNT
Sailors load a wooden sailing boat with storage jars, plants, spices and apes from the land of Punt. Goods would have been exchanged in Punt for these items. Egyptian trading expeditions traveled to many distant lands and brought back precious goods to the pharaoh. This drawing is copied from the walls of Hatshepsut's temple at Deir el-Bahri.

SYRIAN ENVOYS

Foreign rulers from Asia and the Mediterranean lands would send splendid gifts to the pharaoh, and he would send them gifts in return. These Syrians have been sent as representatives of their ruler, or envoys. They have brought perfume containers made of gold, ivory and a beautiful stone called lapis lazuli. The vases are decorated with gold and lotus flower designs. The pharaoh would pass on some of the luxurious foreign gifts to his favorite courtiers.

NUBIANS BRINGING TRIBUTE

Nubians bring goods to the pharaoh Thutmose IV—gold rings, apes and leopard skins. Nubia was the land above the Nile cataracts (rapids), now known as northern Sudan. The Egyptians acquired much of their wealth from Nubia through military campaigns. During times of peace, however, they also traded with the princes of Nubia for minerals and exotic animals.

EXOTIC GOODS

Egyptian craftsmen had to import many of their most valuable materials from abroad. These included gold, elephant tusks (for ivory), hardwoods, such as ebony, and softwoods, such as cedar of Lebanon. Copper was mined in Nubia and bronze (a mixture of copper and tin) was imported from Syria.

ivory

ebony

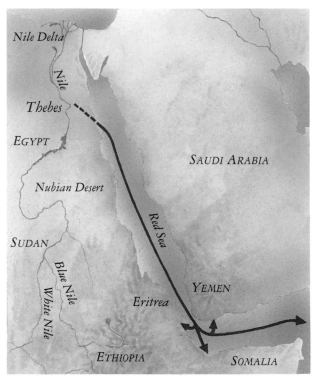

A WORLD OF TRADE

The Egyptians traveled over the Red Sea to the mysterious land of Punt. The map shows the voyage the traders would have made. No one is sure of the exact location of Punt, but it was probably modern day Somalia, Eritrea, Yemen or southern Sudan.

Glossary

A

alabaster A gleaming white stone, a type of gypsum.

amethyst A purple crystal, a type of quartz.

amulet A lucky charm.

artifact An object that has been preserved from the past.

amulet

C

canopic jar A pottery jar used to hold the lungs, liver, intestines and stomach of a dead person.

cataract Waterfalls or white-water rapids.

chariot A horse-drawn cart, used for warfare or racing.

civilization A society that makes advances in arts, sciences, technology, law or government.

chariot

conscript Someone who is called up by the government to serve in the army.

cosmetics Makeup.

crook and flail A hooked stick and a jointed stick, sacred to the god Osiris. The pharaohs carried the crook and flail as symbols of royal authority.

cubit A unit of measurement, the length of a forearm.

D

delta A coastal region where a river splits into separate waterways before flowing into the sea.

demotic A simplified script used in the later periods of ancient Egypt.

drought A long, dry period without rainfall.

dynasty A royal family, or the period it remains in power.

E

embalm To preserve a dead body.

empire A number of different lands coming under the rule of a single government.

F

faience A type of opaque glass that is often blue or green. It is made from quartz or sand, lime, ash and natron.

flax A blue-flowered plant grown for its fiber, which is used to make linen. It also has seeds that produce linseed oil.

furl To roll up the sail of a ship.

faience china

G

gazelle A small, graceful antelope.

golden fly A badge given as a reward to soldiers for bravery in battle.

grid pattern A plan dividing towns into blocks and straight streets at right angles.

H

henna A reddish dye for the hair or skin, made from the leaves of a shrub.

hieratic A shorthand version of hieroglyphic script, used by priests.

hieroglyph A picture symbol used in ancient Egyptian writing.

Hyksos A people from the region of Palestine, who settled in Egypt after 1800BC and ruled the country.

Hyksos

I

incense Sweet-smelling gum or bark burnt as part of religious ceremonies.

indigo A dark blue dye taken from plants.

irrigate To bring water to dry land.

J

jackal A wild dog that lives in Asia and Africa.

L

loom A frame on which cloth is woven.

Lower Egypt The northern part of Egypt, especially the Nile delta.

lute A string musical instrument.

lyre A harp-like musical instrument.

M

Middle Kingdom The period of Egyptian history between 2050 and 1786BC.

mummy A human, or sometimes animal, body preserved by drying.

N

natron Salty crystals used in preparing mummies.

Nekhbet The name of the vulture goddess.

New Kingdom The period of Egyptian history between 1550–1070BC.

Nilometer A series of measured steps or a column used to measure the depth of the Nile floods.

O

oasis A place where there is water in a desert area.

obelisk A pointed pillar, erected as a monument.

ocher A red or yellow iron ore.

Old Kingdom The period of Egyptian history between 2686 and 2181BC.

obelisk

P

papyrus A tall reedy plant that grows in the river Nile. It is used for making paper.

pendant A piece of jewelry hung in a chain around the neck.

pharaoh The ruler of ancient Egypt.

pigment Any coloring used to make paint.

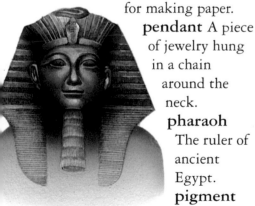

the pharaoh Thutmose III

potter's wheel A round slab, spun round to help shape the wet clay when making pots by hand.

prow The front end of a ship.

pyramid A large pointed monument with a broad, square base and triangular sides.

R

ritual A ceremony that is often religious.

S

saffron An orange spice and dye, taken from crocuses.

sarcophagus The stone casing for a coffin.

sceptre A rod carried by a king, queen or emperor as an emblem of rule.

scribe A professional writer, a clerk or civil servant.

script A method of writing.

serfs People who are not free to move from the land they farm without the permission of their lord.

shaduf A bucket on a weighted pole, used to move water from the river Nile into the fields on the banks.

shrine A container of holy relics, a place for worship.

side lock A braid of hair worn by children in ancient Egypt.

sistrum A metal rattle, used as a musical instrument in ancient Egypt.

a sistrum

sphinx The statue of a mythical creature, half lion, half human.

spindle A rod used to twist fibers into yarn while spinning.

stern

stern The rear end of a ship.

strike A work stoppage, part of a demand for better conditions.

superstition An illogical belief in good luck or bad luck.

survey To measure land or buildings.

T

tax Goods, money or services paid to the government.

textile Any cloth produced by the process of weaving.

tribute Goods given by a country to its conquerors, as a mark of submission.

turquoise A blue-green stone.

U

Upper Egypt The southern part of Egypt.

V

Vizier The treasurer or highest-ranking official in the Egyptian court.

wildfowling

W

wildfowling Hunting wild ducks, geese and other water birds using throw sticks.

ANCIENT
GREECE

RICHARD TAMES

CONSULTANT: LOUISE SCHOFIELD

ΑΧΙΛΛΕΥΣ

Over a period of 2,000 years, the ancient Greeks laid many of the foundations of the modern world. Many of their ideas about medicine, mathematics and how towns and countries are governed are still in use, even though the people who developed them lived 3-4,000 years ago. Greeks introduced the theater for entertainment, and new styles of art and architecture that are still being used today. Theirs was a civilization of spectacular achievements and adventure as they traded, traveled, and fought their way through the known world. Their heroes, poets, politicians, and colorful, imperfect gods made ordinary daily life rich and more exciting.

The Mycenaeans

THE FIRST IMPORTANT CIVILIZATION on mainland Greece developed in the northeastern part of the Peloponnese between 1600 and 1200 B.C. A series of small kingdoms and great fortresses were built during this period. The most powerful of these kingdoms was Mycenae. The Mycenaeans did not keep historical records, and therefore our knowledge of them comes largely from archaeological evidence. We know that they were an advanced culture, as they communicated in a written language and developed technology.

FRUIT OF LABOR
This gold pomegranate pendant was found in a tomb on the island of Cyprus. The surface is decorated with fine grains of gold using a process known as the granulation technique. It took a skilled artist to make such a detailed piece of jewelry.

The Mycenaeans had the ability to quarry and build. Excavations have revealed high walls made from huge stone slabs. They learned how to sail ships and developed extensive trade routes to Egypt, the Near East and the Baltic Sea. From these distant shores they imported gold, tin to make bronze, and amber for jewelry. Local resources such as olive trees were exploited for large financial gain.

Oil was extracted from the olives, then perfumed and bottled for export.

Around 1200 B.C. the Mycenaean culture suffered an economic recession that led to its downfall. Historians believe that earthquakes, wars and fires may have triggered the recession.

BOAR HELMET
The Mycenaeans favored elaborate armor, such as this 13th-century B.C. helmet plated with boar's tusks. Other materials used to make armor included linen, leather and bronze. A great deal of weaponry has been excavated from the royal shaft graves at Mycenae.

COPYCAT CUTTLEFISH
The Mycenaeans developed many of their ideas from those of the Minoans who lived on the island of Crete. Cuttlefish designs similar to the one shown here are also found on Minoan pottery. Mycenaean pottery was widely traded and has been found as far away as northern Italy and eastern Spain. Small jars for holding perfumed olive oil were among the most popular wares.

DECORATED DAGGER

This inlaid bronze dagger came from the tomb of a wealthy Mycenaean who was buried between 1550 and 1500 B.C. The large number of weapons placed in the tombs of high-ranking individuals suggests that the Mycenaeans were a warlike people. Several such daggers have been discovered during excavations. This one is the most well preserved of them. The scene on the blade of the dagger shows leopards hunting in the forest. The illustration was built-up with inlays of different metals, including gold, silver and copper.

This dagger is the only one discovered with its golden hilt still attached.

MASKED MONARCH

Gold death masks like this are unique to Mycenae. They were made by beating a sheet of gold over a wooden mold, which had been carved in the image of the deceased. The mask was then laid over the face of the dead man when he was buried. This one was discovered by the archaeologist Heinrich Schliemann in the 1870s, after his excavation of Troy. In the past, people have incorrectly thought that the mask belonged to the heroic King Agamemnon. In fact, the mask is approximately three centuries older than first thought and dates from around 1500 B.C. It is now believed to be the death mask of one the earliest kings of Mycenae.

RICHES FROM GRAVES

Heinrich Schliemann's excavations at Mycenae in 1876 led to the uncovering of five royal shaft graves. They contained 16 bodies and rich treasures made of gold, silver, ivory and bronze. The contents of the graves prove that the Mycenaeans were a wealthy civilization. Important tombs were hollowed out of soft rock or built of stone. Ordinary people were buried in stone-slab coffins or simple pits.

Politics and Government

THE GREEK WORLD WAS MADE UP of about 300 separate city-states. Some were no bigger than villages, while others centered around cities such as Sparta or Athens. Each city-state was known as a *polis* (from which we take our word politics is derived) and had its own laws and government. In the 4th century B.C., the Greek philosopher, Aristotle, wrote that there were three types of government. The first was power held by one person. He could either be a king (who ruled on account of his royal birth) or a tyrant (who ruled by force). The second type was government by the few which meant rule by an aristocracy (governing by right of noble birth) or an oligarchy (a ruling group of rich and powerful men). The third type was a democratic government (rule by the many) which gave every male citizen the right to vote, hold public office or serve on a jury. Democracy was only practiced in Athens. Even there women, slaves and foreigners were not counted as full citizens.

BEHIND THE SCENES
Women were not allowed to take an active part in politics in ancient Greece. However, some played an important role behind the scenes. One such woman was Aspasia. As a professional entertainer, she met and became mistress to Pericles (one of the most influential Athenian statesmen of the 5th century B.C.). Pericles confided in his mistress about affairs of state, and he came to rely on her insight and wisdom in his judgment of people and situations.

SET IN STONE
The laws of the city of Ephesus were carved on stone tablets in both Greek and Latin. The Greeks believed that their laws had to be clearly fixed (set in stone) and seen by everyone if all citizens were expected to obey them.

VOTING TOKENS
You will need: compass, thin card stock, pencil, ruler, scissors, rolling pin, cutting board, self-hardening clay, modeling tool, balsa wood stick 2 in. long, piece of drinking straw 2 in. long, bronze-colored paint, paintbrush, water bowl.

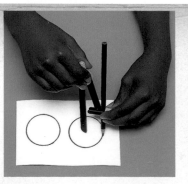

1 Make two templates. Use a compass to draw two circles, on a piece of thin card stock. Make each one 1½ in. in diameter. Cut them out.

2 Use a rolling pin roll out the clay to 1-in. thickness. Use a modeling tool to cut around the card stock circles into the clay. Press down hard as you do this.

3 Make a hole in the center of each clay circle. Use the balsa wood to make one hole (innocent token). Use the straw to make the other hole (guilty token).

PEOPLE POWER

Solon the Lawgiver was an Athenian statesman and poet who lived from 640 to 559 B.C. Around 594 B.C., when serving as chief magistrate, he gave Athens new laws that enabled more people to take part in politics. His actions prevented a potential civil war between the few nobles in power and the people who suffered under their rule.

VOTE HERE

This terra-cotta urn was used to collect voting tokens. They were used in Athens when votes needed to be taken in law courts or when the voters' intentions needed to be kept secret. Each voter put a bronze disk in the urn to register his decision. Normally, voting was done by a show of hands, which was difficult to count precisely.

FACE-TO-FACE

The ruins of this council chamber at Priene in present-day Turkey show how seating was arranged. The tiered, three-sided square enabled each councilor to see and hear clearly all of the speakers involved in a debate. Even in the democracies of ancient Greece, most everyday decisions were taken by committees or councils and not by the assembly of voters.

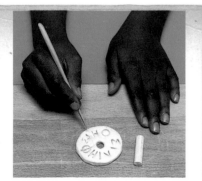

4 Write a name on the innocent token using the modeling tool. Carefully push the balsa stick through the hole. Let dry.

5 Write another name on the guilty token using the modeling tool. Carefully push the drinking straw through the hole. Let dry.

6 Wait until the clay tokens are dry before painting them. The original tokens were made from bronze, so use a bronze-colored paint.

Jurors were issued with two tokens to vote with. A hollow center meant that the juror thought the accused was guilty. A solid center meant that the juror thought the accused was innocent.

Equality and Inequality

GREEK SOCIETY WAS DIVIDED by a strict social structure, enforced by its governments. Most city-states were ruled by a small group of people (*oligarchy*). Two exceptions to this rule were the powerful cities of Sparta and Athens. Sparta held on to its monarchy, while Athens introduced the first democratic government in history. In the city of Athens, all citizens could vote and hold office. However to be a citizen, it was necessary to be an adult male, born in the city itself. Even so-called democratic Athens was ruled by a minority of the people who lived there. The treatment of women, foreign residents (called *metics*), slaves and children was just the same in Athens as in other city-states.

Women had no legal rights and rarely took part in public life. Metics were obliged to pay extra taxes and serve in the military. They could not own land or marry an Athenian. The Athenians felt uneasy about the large number of metics living in their city, but their skills helped to make it rich. Slaves made up half the population of Athens. Most had either been born slaves or become slaves as prisoners of war or captives of pirates. Even native Greeks could become slaves by falling into debt, but they were freed once the debt was paid off.

WARRIORS AND WEALTH
Only the most wealthy members of society could afford to equip themselves for war as fully armed infantrymen. In earlier centuries the poor were given supporting jobs, such as slinger or carrier of supplies. They could not afford expensive bronze weapons. However, as cities grew richer, weapons were manufactured at public expense by slaves, and most male citizens were expected to carry arms.

A WOMAN'S PLACE
Greek women spent their lives at home. On this vase, made about 450 B.C., a woman ties her sandal before going out. As she has attendants, she must be wealthy. Poor women would leave the house to fetch water, work in the fields or shop in the market. Women with slaves, like this one, might leave home to visit relatives or to pray at a shrine or temple.

LOVED ONES
A young girl and her pet dog are seen on this tombstone from the 4th century B.C. The likely expense of such a detailed carving suggests that she was dearly loved. Not all children were cherished. Girl babies, and sick babies of either sex, were often left outside to die. Some were underfed and fell victim to diseases. Greek law required children to support their parents in old age, so childless couples were always eager to adopt and were known to rescue abandoned children.

CRAFTSMAN

This smith could be a slave working in a factory owned by a wealthy man. Most craftsmen were slaves, ex-slaves, or foreign residents (*metics*). They were looked down upon by other citizens. If a master owned a talented slave, he might set the slave up to run his own business. In return, the master would receive a share of the profits. This smith might also have been a free, self-employed man, with his own workshop and a slave or two working as his assistants.

PATH TO POWER?

Being able to read and write in ancient Greece was not an automatic key to success. The Greek alphabet could be learned quite easily. Even slaves could become highly educated scribes. However, illiterate men were unlikely to hold high positions, except perhaps in Sparta, where written records were rarely kept. Although women were denied the right to a formal education, they were often able to read and write enough to keep a record of household needs.

ENSLAVED BY LANGUAGE

This Roman bottle is made in the shape of an African slave girl's head. The Greeks also owned slaves. The Greek philosopher Aristotle argued that some people were "naturally" meant to be slaves. His opinion was shared by many of his countrymen. He felt that this applied most obviously to people who did not speak Greek. Slaves were treated with varying degrees of kindness and hostility. Some were worked to death by their owners, but others had good jobs as clerks or bailiffs. A few hundred slaves were owned by the city of Athens and served as policemen, coin-inspectors and clerks of the court.

The Golden Age of Athens

ATHENS WAS THE CHIEF CITY of the fertile region of Attica, in southern Greece. It grew rich from trade, manufacturing and mining silver. The city of Athens reached the height of its wealth and power in the 5th century B.C. By this time, it had built up a large empire which encompassed cities on both the mainland and the islands. Its 250,000 citizens enjoyed a vibrant golden age of art and culture. During this period, the Athenians celebrated a victory against Persian invaders by building a series of magnificent temples on the Acropolis in Athens. The Acropolis was a sacred hill that overlooked the city. Its most important temple was the Parthenon, which was dedicated to the city's goddess, Athena. Below, at the heart of the city was the marketplace (*agora*). Surrounded by temples and public buildings and crowded with stalls, the agora was the commercial center of Athens.

Between 431 and 404 B.C., Athens fought a crippling war against Sparta and the Persians. It lost the war and most of its maritime empire. As a result, Athens gave up its role as commercial and cultural leader in Greece to Sparta.

GODDESS OF WAR
On this 4th-century B.C. coin, Athena is shown wearing a helmet. It is wreathed with the laurel leaves of victory. Athena represented the disciplined side of fighting and was thought to have invented ships and chariots. As the goddess of war, she was known as Athena Nike, which means "Victory." Her counterpart was the god Ares who represented the madness and waste of war.

CROWNING GLORY
This temple to Hephaestus is a supreme example of the elegant architecture at which the Athenians excelled. It was built between 449 and 444 B.C. at the eastern end of the agora. Hephaestus was the god of fire and armorer of the gods. A bronze statue inside the temple showed Hephaestus at work making armor, wearing a blacksmith's cap and holding a hammer above an anvil. Excavations have revealed that the bronze sculptors worked on one side of the temple, while sculptors in marble worked on the other side.

PANATHENAIC FESTIVAL

Every year, the people of Athens marched or rode in a great procession up to Athena's temple on the Acropolis. Even foreign residents joined in. This frieze from the Parthenon shows young men getting ready to join the procession. At the temple, oxen and other animals were sacrificed, and the meat was given to the people to eat. Every fourth year, there was an extra celebration, when a new robe, (*peplos*), was presented to the goddess Athena. This event was celebrated with days of sporting and musical competitions, with prizes of money or olive oil.

BIRTH OF A GODDESS

According to Greek legend, Zeus swallowed a pregnant lover after a prophecy warned that their child would depose him. Not long after swallowing her, Zeus complained of a painful headache. Hephaestus offered to split open Zeus's head with an ax to ease the pain. When he did, the goddess Athena jumped out. She was fully grown and wearing the armor of a warrior (as seen here in the center of the painting).

BANISHMENT

Once a year, Athenians were allowed to banish an unpopular member of the community from the city for 10 years. Voters scratched the names on a fragment of pottery called an ostrakon, which is why the procedure was called ostracism. If at least 6,000 votes were cast in favor of exiling a person, they would have to leave the city within 10 days. Ostraka were also used for messages and shopping lists.

GODDESS OF WISDOM

The owl, symbolizing wisdom, was the emblem of Athena. This silver coin was issued in Athens in 479 B.C., after the Greeks won decisive victories against the Persians. Athenian coins were accepted throughout Greece, Italy and Turkey. This proves just how influential the city of Athens. Coins from other city-states were not widely accepted.

The Spartan Order

A T THE HEIGHT OF ITS POWER, Sparta was the only city-state to rival the influence of Athens. It controlled most of the area of southern Greece, called the Peloponnese. Sparta was an insular and militaristic state. It became so after losing control of its slave population in a rebellion, which lasted for 17 years. The slaves (helots) were descendants of the people of Messenia whom Sparta overran in the 8th century B.C. The helots outnumbered their Spartan overlords by seven to one. Although the Spartans defeated the rebellion, they continued to live in fear of one another. As a result, all male citizens were required by law to serve as full-time warriors. In addition, harsh restrictions were placed on the helots, who were forbidden to ride horses or stay out after nightfall. While the citizens were fully occupied with military training, the heavy work and domestic chores were done by the helots.

The Spartans imposed strict living conditions on themselves. Spartan boys and girls were separated from their parents and brought up in barracks. Boys were trained for battle from the age of seven. They were kept cold, barefoot and hungry, and regularly flogged to make them tough. At the age of 20 they joined groups of 15 men who became their comrades. In Sparta, comradeship between men was more important than family life. The girls also took part in physical training so as to be able to bear healthy children. The power of Sparta declined after its defeat by the Theban army in 371 B.C.

HEROIC KING
This bust from the 5th century B.C. may be of King Leonidas. There were two royal families in Sparta. A king was chosen from each family to govern Sparta at the same time. Their powers were limited. Their main responsibility was to lead Spartan forces into battle.

WINE FOR THE WARRIORS
This massive bronze krater (wine vessel) stands 5½ ft tall, weighs 460 lbs and holds 320 gals of liquid. It was made around 530 B.C. by a Spartan craftsman. The neck of the krater is decorated with Spartan warriors and chariots marching to war. The handles are crafted with the heads of female monsters called gorgons. It is thought that the vase was presented as a gift to the king of Lydia who wanted to form an alliance with Sparta. The Spartans were admired for the high quality of their bronze work.

DEATH AND GLORY

This modern monument was erected to commemorate the heroic self-sacrifice of King Leonidas and 300 Spartans. They died in 480 B.C. defending the pass at Thermopylae against a Persian army 250,000 strong. The pass was just 43 ft wide and the Spartans held their ground for two days while waiting for reinforcements. On the third day, a traitor showed the invading Persians another way through the mountain. Leonidas ordered a retreat, then led the rearguard in a fight to the death.

SEA POWER

The ivory relief pictured here has a Spartan warship carved into it. The pointed ram at the front was used for sinking enemy ships. Sparta was first and foremost a land power. Its navy was no match for that of Athens. A navy was expensive to run because specialized warships could not be used in peace-time. The Athenians financed their navy from their silver mines, but the Spartans were not so wealthy. They sometimes had to borrow money to keep their navy afloat.

BACKBONE OF THE ARMY

Spartan soldiers were easily distinguished on the battlefield because of their long hair and bright red cloaks. This figurine of a Spartan warrior probably dates from the 6th century B.C. His crested helmet incorporates a nose guard and cheek guards. He is also wearing greaves (armor to guard his lower legs) and a cuirass (armor to protect his chest).

LAW-GIVER

This Roman mosaic probably shows the figure of Lycurgus, wielding an axe. Little is known of his life, because so few records were kept in Sparta. It is generally believed that Lycurgus lived around 650 B.C. His main achievement was to reorganize the government of Sparta for effective warfare after its disastrous defeat by the state of Argos.

At Home

GREEK HOMES WERE BUILT of mud bricks and roofed with pottery tiles. They had small high windows with wooden shutters to keep out thieves, and floors of beaten earth, plaster or mosaic. Most houses started as small structures, and more rooms were added as the owner could afford them. This gave homes a random appearance and meant that streets were rarely straight. In rural areas, houses were often surrounded by a stone wall to protect the inhabitants and their domestic animals. Men and women lived in separate rooms and in different areas of the house. The women's quarters were usually found at the rear of the house. Richer households might also have rooms for cooking and bathing in. Most homes contained only a few pieces of plain furniture, which might include couches that doubled as beds, chairs and tables. Only wealthier people could afford richly decorated furniture such as couches inlaid with gold and ivory.

The roof was made of pottery tiles.

The andron was the room in which men entertained.

The mosaic floor was made from brightly colored pebbles.

HOME HEATING
In mountainous areas of Greece, the winter can be very cold. This bronze brazier, dating from the 4th century B.C., would have been filled with charcoal and used to heat a chilly room.

HEARTH GODDESS
Hestia was the goddess of the hearth and home. A fire was kept burning in her honor all year round. This fire was used for cooking, for heating water and to make charcoal as fuel for the braziers. Traditionally, when the Greeks founded a colony overseas, they took with them fire from their old home to link the new with the old.

DOLPHIN FRESCO
You will need: pencil, sheet of white paper 8 x 7½ in., rolling pin, white self-hardening clay, ruler, cutting board, modeling tool, pin, sandpaper, paintbrush, acrylic paints, water.

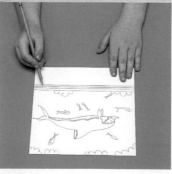

1 Draw a dolphin on the piece of white paper. Add some smaller fish and some seaweed. Refer to the final picture as a guide for your drawing.

2 Roll out a piece of clay until it measures 8 in. across and 7½ in. down. The clay should be about ¼ in. thick. Cut off any uneven edges.

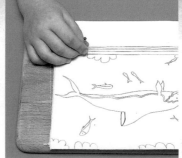

3 While the clay is still damp, place the dolphin picture over it. Following the outline of your picture, prick holes through the paper onto the clay.

Wooden shutters were used as windows.

HOT WORK
Food was usually cooked over an open fire. Cooking would take place either in an open courtyard, where smoke could escape upward or in a kitchen, where a chimney shaft might be installed.

OPEN HOUSE
At the heart of every Greek house was a courtyard. Many chores were carried out here. Most had an altar where offerings were made to the gods.

Frescoes are paintings applied to damp plaster. This one was inspired by a painting found on a wall of the Minoan palace at Knossos.

Clay walls were soft and could easily be burrowed through by enterprising thieves.

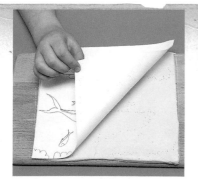

4 Lift the paper off the clay and let the base dry. Once the clay has dried completely, sand it down with fine sandpaper for a smooth finish.

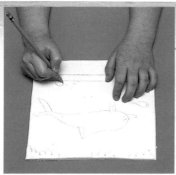

5 Using your pencil, join the dots of each outline together. When this is complete you will have a replica of your original drawing.

6 Paint the base of the fresco a light blue. Once this is dry, paint in the rest of the picture. Use colors that reflect those of the sea.

7 Finally, paint in the two stripes at the bottom of the picture. These indicate where the fresco would have ended on the wall. Let dry.

Country Living

MOST GREEKS LIVED IN the countryside and worked as farmers. The mountainous landscape, poor, stony soil and hot, dry climate restricted what crops they could produce and which animals they could keep. Olive trees and bees flourished in these conditions. Olives provided oil and bees supplied honey (the main sweetener in food) and wax. Grain, such as barley, was difficult to grow, and the land used for its production had to be left fallow every other year to recover its fertility. Country people kept oxen to pull plows and drag heavy loads, and they used donkeys to carry goods to market. Rural areas also produced important materials used by city craftworkers. These included timber, flax for linen, horn and bone for glue, and leather.

Country life was hazardous, as droughts, floods, wolves and warfare threatened their livelihoods. Over the centuries, another problem developed. As forests were cut down for timber and fuel, soil erosion increased, leaving even less fertile land. The search for new agricultural land prompted the growth of Greek colonies along the shores of the Mediterranean and the Black Sea.

OLIVE HARVEST
This vase shows men shaking and beating the branches of an olive tree to bring down its fruit. Olives were eaten and also crushed to extract their oil. The oil was used for cooking, cleaning, as a medicine and a fuel for lamps.

FOOD FOR THE POT
Meat was obtained through hunting and the rearing of domesticated animals. Hunting was considered a sport for the rich, but it was a serious business for the poor, who hoped to put extra food on their tables. Simple snares, nets and slings were used to trap lizards and hares and to bring down small birds.

GONE FISHING
Many Greeks lived near water. The sea, rivers and lakes provided fish and shellfish which were their main source of protein. Fish was smoked or salted for future use. Always at the mercy of storms and shipwreck, fishermen prayed to the sea god Poseidon to save them.

PLOWING WITH OXEN

This terra-cotta figure from Thebes shows a farmer plowing with two oxen. The plow was made of wood, but the part that broke up the earth was tipped with iron. Oxen were stronger and less expensive than horses, making them ideal for heavy work. When oxen died, they yielded hides for leather as well as horn, meat, sinew, which was used as twine, and fat that could be turned into candle tallow.

HARVEST GODDESS

Demeter was the goddess of grain and growth. She looked after plants, children and young people. The first part of her name *deme* is an ancient word for the earth, the second part, *meter*, means "mother." Farmers believed that their success depended on uncontrollable forces such as the rain, the sun, and diseases that attacked plants and livestock. Special prayers and sacrifices were made to Demeter to ask for her help in preventing such disasters. Festivals were held in honor of the goddess at crucial times during the harvest, before plowing, when the corn began to sprout, and after it had been harvested.

SNACKS

Drying food was a good way of preserving it in a warm country like Greece. The Greeks ate raisins and dried apricots as a dessert or used them to sweeten other foods. Olives were another popular snack or appetizer.

olives

apricots

raisins

Food and Drink

MEALS IN ANCIENT GREECE were based around home-baked bread, fish fresh from the sea and such vegetables as onions, beans, lentils, leeks and radishes. Chickens and pigeons were kept for their eggs and meat, and a cow or a few goats or sheep for milk and cheese. Occasionally a pig or goat was slaughtered for the table, or hunting provided boar, deer, hares and even thrushes. The Greeks cooked their meat in olive oil and flavored it with garlic and wild herbs. They ate fruits such as figs, apples, pears and pomegranates, which could be dried for the winter months. During hard times, people resorted to eating wild berries, hedgehogs and even locusts. Wine was the Greeks' favorite drink. It was usually very thick and had to be strained and then diluted with water for drinking. Sometimes it was mixed with resin, a preservative extracted from pine trees. It could then be kept for three to four years.

WASTE CONVERTER
This terra-cotta figure shows a butcher killing a pig. Pigs were a cheap source of meat because they could be kept on scrubby pasture and fed on acorns and kitchen scraps. Their skins were tanned to make leather and their hooves melted to make glue.

STORAGE ON A GRAND SCALE
Huge storage jars were used by the Greeks to store food and drink. These came from the palace, at Knossos in Crete. They probably contained olive oil, wine and cereals and were capable of holding hundreds of gallons. Handmade from clay, they kept food and drink cool in the hot Mediterranean climate.

PANCAKES WITH HONEY AND SESAME SEEDS
You will need: 3 ounces flour, sieve, mixing bowl, fork, ½ cup water, 8 tablespoons honey, frying pan, 1 tablespoon sesame seeds, spoon, 1 tablespoon oil, spatula.

1 First make the pancake batter. Sieve the flour into a mixing bowl. Then, using a fork stir the water into the flour. Measure the honey into a small bowl.

2 Spoon the honey into the mixture a bit at a time. Mix it with a fork, making sure that there are no lumps in the pancake batter.

3 Ask an adult to help you with the next two steps. Heat the frying pan. Sprinkle in the sesame seeds and cook until browned. Set aside.

STAFF OF LIFE

A team of bakers prepare bread for the oven in this terra-cotta model. In big cities, commercial bakeries produced many different kinds of bread. Ordinary loaves were made of barley or wheat flour, specialty breads were flavored with mountainside herbs, and delicious pastries came drenched in honey.

PLAY THE GAME

The Greeks drank from large, shallow cups such as this one. This picture shows a man playing a drinking game called *kottabos*. After much drinking, guests would compete to see who was most in control of their faculties by throwing the wine left in the bottom of their cup at a target. In another game, guests tried to make the loudest noise with their cup without spilling its contents.

GOD OF WINE

This Roman stone panel shows a procession of revelers following the Greek god Dionysus to a drinking party. Dionysus was the god of wine and was worshiped with special enthusiasm in vine-growing regions such as Athens, Boeotia and Naxos.

SERVICE

A carved relief shows servants carrying bowls of food. At formal banquets, the guests lay on their sides to eat, as this was thought to aid digestion. The Greeks adopted this custom from the peoples of Asia. They often ate and drank until they passed out on their couches, leaving the servants to clean up without waking them.

4 Heat a teaspoon of the oil in the frying pan. Pour a quarter of the batter into the pan. Cook on both sides for about 4 minutes, until light brown.

5 Serve the pancake on a plate. Sprinkle on a handful of sesame seeds and pour extra honey on top. Cook the rest of the batter the same way.

Pancakes were a popular snack in ancient Greece, especially with theater-goers. Food stalls were usually set up around theaters to catch the crowds who had come to view the latest play.

157

Women at Home

RESPECTABLE GREEK WOMEN were rarely seen out in the public domain. Their lives revolved around the household and family. From an early age, girls were trained in domestic skills, which would enable them to run a household once married. A girl might be married off by her father at the age of 13 or 14. Her husband was usually much older and would be given a dowry to offset the costs of providing for her. The purpose of marriage was to produce a son to continue the husband's name. A wife assumed a number of responsibilities in her new home. If she was fortunate enough to have the help of slaves, she would direct them in their daily tasks. If not, she carried out those chores herself. Chores would include cooking meals, cleaning the house and caring for the children. Some women even managed the family finances.

"SO SHE SAID..."
Wealthy women were largely confined to their houses. They often relied on friends or household slaves for news about events in the outside world. Women from poorer families, without slaves, had to leave the house to shop and fetch water. Public fountains were popular meeting places for gossiping.

A CONSTANT TASK
Weaving was considered a respectable occupation for women. This vase painting shows Penelope, wife of the absent hero Odysseus, spinning wool into yarn. Women were expected to produce all the fabric needed to clothe their family. The material they spun was also used for household furnishings such as wall hangings.

KNUCKLEBONES
You will need: self-drying modeling clay, modeling tool, work board, cream paint, paintbrush.

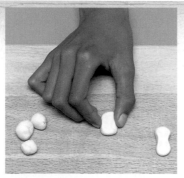

1 Divide the self-drying modeling clay into 5 equal pieces. Roll each piece into a ball. Press each ball into a figure eight shape, as above.

2 With the modeling tool, carve ridges around the middle of each shape. Make small dents in the end of each shape with your finger.

3 When the pieces have dried out, paint them. Use a cream colored paint. Once the paint has dried, the pieces are ready to play with.

HOPING FOR HEALTH

Married women from wealthy families rarely left the house. When they did, it was usually to take part in family celebrations or religious ceremonies. The family shown on this carved relief from the 5th century B.C. are sacrificing a bull to Asclepius, god of health, and Hygieia, his daughter.

Knucklebones were made from the ankle-joints of small animals. These small bones were used in different ways, depending on the type of game. The Greeks also used the knucklebones as dice.

YOUR TURN

Women were supposed to be fully occupied with household tasks. But many kept slaves, which allowed them some leisure time. These women are playing knucklebones. Another favorite pastime was checkers, played on a board with 36 squares.

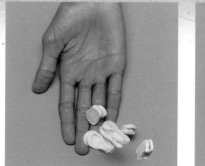

4 To play the game, gather the five pieces into the palm of one hand. Throw them into the air. Quickly flip your hand over.

5 Try to catch the pieces on the back of your hand. If you're lucky and you catch them all, you win the game. If not, then the game continues.

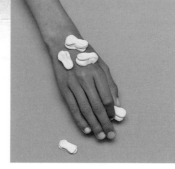

6 Try to pick up the fallen pieces with the others still on the back of your hand. Throw them up in the same way and try to catch them again.

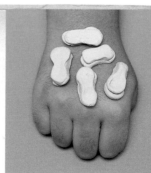

7 The winner is the first person to have all of the knucklebones on the back of their hand. It may take a few tries for you to get the hang of it.

159

Growing Up

BRINGING UP BABY
This baby is waving a rattle while sitting in a high chair. The chair also served as a potty. It might have wheels on it to help the baby learn how to walk.

CHILDREN FACED MANY OBSTACLES while growing up. When a baby was born, its father would decide whether to keep or abandon it. A sick or handicapped baby might be left outdoors at birth. Whoever rescued the child could raise it as their slave. Girls were more likely to be rejected because they could not provide for their parents in adulthood. Many children died in infancy through lack of health care.

Education was considered to be important for boys. Even so, it was usually only sons of rich families who received a complete schooling. They were taught a variety of subjects, including reading, music and gymnastics. Boys from poorer families often learned their father's trade. Education in domestic skills was essential for most girls. A notable exception was in Sparta, where girls joined boys in hard physical training.

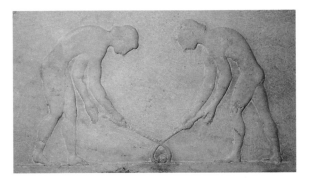

COMPETITION
These two boys are playing a game similar to hockey. On the whole, team sports were ignored in favor of sporting activities where an individual could excel. Wrestling is one such examples. Sports were encouraged as training for war.

YOU'RE IT
Two girls play a kind of tag game in which the loser has to carry the winner. Girls had less free time than boys did. They were supposed to stay close to home and help their mothers with housework, cooking and looking after the younger children.

MAKE A SCROLL
You will need: 2 12-in. rods of balsa wood, 2 in. in diameter, 4 doorknobs, double-sided tape, sheet of paper 12 x 12 in., 2½-in. rod of balsa wood, ¾ in. in diameter, craft knife, paintbrush, white glue, ink powder.

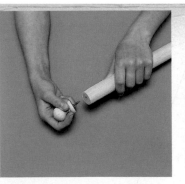

1 Carefully screw a door knob into either end of each 12-in. rod of balsa wood, or ask an adult to do it for you. These are the end pieces of the scroll.

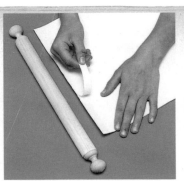

2 Cut two pieces of double-sided tape 12 in. long. Stick one piece of tape along the top of the paper and another along the bottom.

3 Wrap the top of the paper once around one of the pieces of balsa wood. Repeat this step again for the second piece at the bottom of the paper.

ACTION DOLL

The arms and legs on this terra-cotta figure are attached with cord so that the shoulders and knees can be moved. A doll such as this was a luxury item, which only a wealthy family could afford to buy for its children. Other popular toys were rattles and hoops.

THE ALPHABET

The first two of the Greek alphabet's 24 letters are called alpha and beta—these names give us the English word "alphabet."

ΑΒΓΔΕΖΗΘΙ
ΚΛΜΝΞΟΠΡΣ
ΤΥΦΧΨΩ

LIGHT OF LEARNING

This lamp takes the form of a teacher holding a scroll. Education involved learning poems and famous speeches from scrolls by heart. This was thought to help boys make effective speeches in court or public meetings. Good orators were always well thought of and could wield much influence.

Scrolls in ancient Greece were usually made from animal skin.

ΑΧΙΛΛΕΥΣ

A SECOND MOTHER

Greeks often hired wet nurses (on the left) to breastfeed their babies. Some nurses were forbidden to drink wine in case it affected their milk or made them so drunk that they might harm the baby.

4 Ask an adult to help you with this step. Take the 2½-in. piece of balsa wood, and use your craft knife to sharpen the end of it into a point.

5 Paint the nib of your pen with glue. This will stop the wood from soaking up the ink. Add water to the ink powder to make ink.

6 Write some letters or a word on your scroll with your pen. We've translated the Greek alphabet above in the fact box. Use this as a guide.

7 We have copied out some letters in ancient Greek. You could also write a word. Ask a friend to translate what you have written, using the alphabet.

Greek Fashion

PHYSICAL BEAUTY AND AN ATTRACTIVE appearance were admired in ancient Greece in both men and women. Clothes were styled simply. Both sexes wore long tunics, draped loosely for comfort in the warm climate, and held in place with decorative pins or brooches. A heavy cloak was added for traveling or in bad weather. The tunics of soldiers and laborers were cut short, so they would not get in the way. Clothes were made of wool and linen, which were spun at home. Fabrics were colored with dyes made from plants, insects and shellfish. The rich could afford more luxurious garments made from imported cotton or silk. Sandals were usually worn outdoors, though men sometimes wore boots. In such hot weather hats made of straw or wool kept off the sun. A suntan was not admired because it signified outdoor work as a laborer or a slave. Men wore their hair short, and women wore it long, coiled up in elaborate styles sometimes decorated with ribbons.

SEE FOR YOURSELF
Glass mirrors were not known to the Greeks. Instead, they used highly polished bronze to see their reflection in. This mirror has a handle in the shaped of a woman. Winged sphinxes sit on her shoulders.

GOLDEN LION
This heavy bracelet dates from around the 4th or 5th century B.C. It is made of solid gold and decorated with two lion heads. Gold was valuable because there was little of it to be found in Greece itself. Most of it was imported from Asia Minor or Egypt.

KEEP IT SIMPLE
The figurine above is wearing a peplos. This was a simple, sleeveless dress worn by Greek women. The only adornment was a belt tied underneath the bust. This statue comes from a Greek colony in southern Italy.

CHITON
You will need: tape measure, rectangle of cloth, scissors, pins, chalk, needle, thread, 12 metal buttons (with loops), cord.

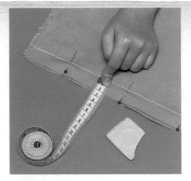

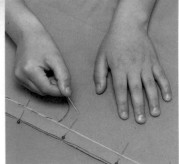

1 Ask a friend to measure your width from wrist to wrist, double this figure. Measure your length from shoulder to ankle. Cut your cloth to these figures.

2 Fold the fabric in half widthwise. Pin the two sides together. Draw a chalk line along the fabric, ¾ in. away from the edge of the fabric.

3 Sew along the chalk line. Then turn the material inside out, so the seam is on the inside. Refold the fabric so the seam is at the back.

POWDER POT

Greek women used face powder and other cosmetics and kept them in ceramic pots called pyxis. This one was was made in Athens in about 450 B.C. The painted decoration shows women spinning and weaving.

TEXTILE TRADE

Clothes in ancient Greece were usually made from wool and linen. The Greeks exported their wool, which was admired for its superior quality. Cotton and silk were imported to make clothes. But only wealthy Greeks could afford clothes made from these materials.

cotton

raw wool

linen

Clothes were handmade in ancient Greece. Enough material would be woven to fit the person they were being made for exactly, to avoid waste.

spiral band

BURIAL JEWELRY

Some pieces of jewelry, like the ones pictured here, were made especially for burial. Very thin sheet gold was beaten into belts and wreaths. Important people like the Kings and Queens of Macedonia were buried in crowns of gold leaves.

belt

wreath

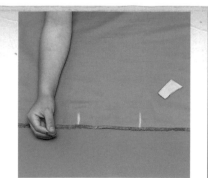

4 Make a gap big enough for your head to fit in, at one of the open ends of the fabric. Mark where the gap is going to be and pin the fabric together there.

5 From the head gap mark a point every 2 in. to the end of the fabric. Pin together the front and back along these points. Your arms will fit through here.

6 At each pin, sew on a button to hold the two sides of material together. To secure the button, sew through the loop several times and knot it.

7 Cut a length of cord to fit around your waist with a little bit spare to tie. Tie this cord around your waist and bunch the material up, over the cord.

163

Gods and Goddesses

THE ANCIENT GREEKS BELIEVED that their gods looked like human beings and felt human emotions that led them to quarrel and fall in love. People also thought that the gods had magical powers and were immortal (meaning that they could live forever). With these powers, the gods could become invisible or disguise themselves and even turn people into animals. The gods were thought to influence all parts of human life and were kept busy with requests for help, from curing illness to ensuring a victory in war. In order to keep on the good side of the gods, individuals made sacrifices, left offerings and said prayers to them. Communities financed the building of temples, such as the Parthenon, paid for priests to take care of and organized festivals all in honor of the gods.

WINGED MESSENGER
Hermes was the god of eloquence and good luck. He was known for his mischievous and adventure-seeking nature. Zeus made him a messenger to the gods, to try and keep him occupied and out of trouble.

KING OF THE GODS
Zeus ruled over earth and heaven from Mount Olympus, (a real place on the border of Macedonia). He was thought to be a fair god who upheld order and justice. He punished wrongdoers by throwing thunderbolts at them.

WILD GODDESS
Artemis was the goddess of wild places and animals, hunting and the moon. She was a skilful archer, whose arrows caused death and plagues. The power to heal was another of her attributes.

PARTHENON
You will need: two pieces of white card stock 24½ x 15 in., ruler, black felt-tip pen, shoebox, scissors, blue, red and cream paint, paintbrush, white glue, piece of red corrugated cardboard (approximately 15 x 11 in.), masking tape, craft knife, 64-in. of balsa wood.

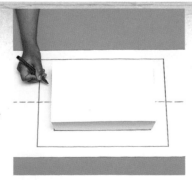

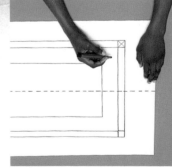

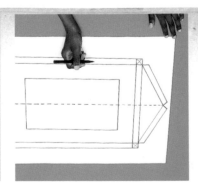

1 Draw a horizontal line across the center of the card stock. Place the shoebox in the middle. Draw around it. Draw a second box 2½ in. away from this.

2 Draw a third box ¾ in. away from the second. Extend the lines of the second box to meet the third, to form four tabs, one in each corner.

3 To make the ends of the roof, draw half a diamond shape along the edge of the second box. Add on two rectangular tabs ½ in. deep.

164

SYMBOLS
Each god and goddess was thought to be responsible for particular aspects of daily life. Each was represented by a symbol. Wheat symbolized Demeter, goddess of living things. Dionysus, god of the vine and wine, was appropriately represented by grapes.

wheat   grapes

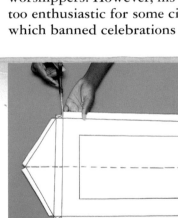

LOVE AND PROTECTION
Aphrodite was the goddess of love and beauty. Her vanity was instrumental in causing one of the biggest campaigns in Greek folklore, the Trojan War. Aphrodite promised to win Paris (son of the king of Troy) the love of the most beautiful mortal woman in the world—Helen. In return, Paris was to name Aphrodite as the most beautiful of all the goddesses. However, Helen was already married to the king of Sparta. When she left him to join Paris, the Greeks declared war on Troy. A bloodthirsty war followed in which heroes and gods clashed.

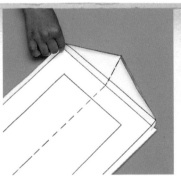

GRAPES OF JOY
The god Dionysus was admired for his sense of fun. As god of fertility, the vine and wine, he was popular with both male and female worshippers. However, his followers were too enthusiastic for some city-states, which banned celebrations in his name.

A POWERFUL FAMILY
Hera was the wife of Zeus and goddess of marriage. She was revered by women as the protector of their married lives. Her own marriage was marked by conflicts between herself and her husband. Her jealousy of rivals for her unfaithful husband's affections led her to persecute them. She was also jealous of Heracles, who was Zeus' son by a mortal woman. Hera sent snakes to kill Heracles when he was a baby. Fortunately for Heracles, he had inherited his father's strength and killed the snakes before they harmed him.

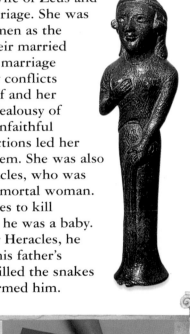

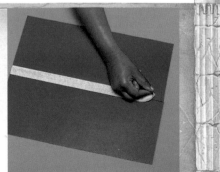

4 Repeat step 3 for the other end of the roof. Cut out both ends of the roof and cut into the four corner tabs. Get your painting equipment ready.

5 Turn the roof piece over. Draw and then paint the above design on to each end piece. Paint a blue, ½-in. margin along each side. Let dry.

6 Turn the card over. Fold up all the sides of the second box. Fold in each corner tab and glue to its adjoining side. Fold down the rectangular tabs.

7 Cut the piece of red corrugated cardboard in half. Stick them together with tape, along the unridged side. Turn them over and fold along the middle.

Temples and Festivals

FESTIVALS TO HONOR THE GODS were important public occasions in ancient Greece. At the heart of each festival was a temple. At festival time, people flocked to the cities from the countryside. The greatest festivals were occasions of splendor and celebration. They involved processions, music, sports, prayers, animal sacrifices and offerings of food, all of which took place at the temple. The earliest Greek temples were built of wood, and none have survived. Later, temples built from stone echoed the simplicity of tree trunks in their columns and beams. The finest temples were made from marble. They were often decorated with brightly painted friezes, showing mythical stories of gods, goddesses and heroes. No expense was spared because temples were thought to be the gods' earthly homes. Each temple housed a statue of the god to which it was dedicated. The statues were usually elaborate and occasionally made from precious materials such as gold and ivory.

A WOMAN'S ROLE
This vase in the shape of a woman's head was made about 600 B.C., probably for a temple dedicated to Apollo. Religion was one of the few areas of life outside the home in which women were allowed to take an active part. They served as priestesses in some cults and were often thought to have the gift of seeing into the future.

GRAND ENTRANCE
The monumental gateways to the temple complex on top of the Acropolis were called the Propylaea. The temple beside it honored Athena who is shown as Nike, goddess of victory.

8 Glue the ends of the corrugated cardboard to the folded up edges of the painted card stock. Let dry. This piece forms the roof of your temple.

9 Draw around the shoebox, on the second piece of card stock. Draw another box 3 in. away. Cut it out, leaving a ½-in. border. This is the temple base.

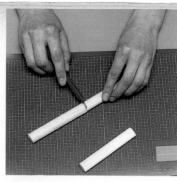

10 Ask an adult to help you with this step. Cut out 32 columns from balsa wood. Each must be 2 in. in height. Paint them cream and let dry.

11 Mark eight points along each edge of the second box by drawing around a column piece. Draw them an equal distance from each other.

A BIRTHDAY PARADE

A parade of horsemen, chariots and people leading sacrificial animals all formed part of the procession of the annual Panathenaic festival. It was held once a year, in Athens, to celebrate the goddess Athena's birthday. Every fourth year, the occasion involved an even more elaborate ceremony, which lasted for six days. During the festivities, the statue of Athena was presented with a new robe.

A TEMPLE FOR THREE GODS

The Erectheum was built on the Acropolis, looking down on Athens 325 ft below. Unusually for a Greek temple, it housed the worship of more than one god: the legendary king Erectheus, Athena, guardian goddess of the city of Athens, and Poseidon, god of the sea. The columns in the shape of women are called caryatids.

BUILDING MATERIALS

Big buildings were often put up near a quarry or navigable water. Limestone was the most commonly used stone, and pine and cypress the most common woods. Costly marble and cedar were reserved for temples and palaces.

marble   *limestone*

pine

THE LION'S MOUTH

This gaping lion is actually a waterspout from an Athenian temple built in about 570 B.C. Although rainfall in Greece is low, waterspouts were necessary to allow storm water to drain off buildings with flat roofs. The lion was chosen as a symbol of strength and power.

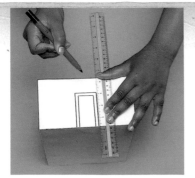

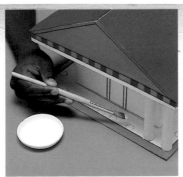

12 Draw a door on one short end of the shoebox. Glue the roof onto the top of the shoebox. Paint the ½-in. border on the temple base, blue.

13 Glue the columns into place, between the roof and the base. Dab glue on to their ends. Position them on the circles marked out in step 11.

The magnificent Parthenon temple housed a 50-ft high statue of Athena that was made of gold and ivory.

Death and the Underworld

PEOPLE IN ANCIENT GREECE lived only about half as long as people in the West do today. It was common for sickly children to die in infancy. Large numbers of men were killed in battle, women often died in childbirth and epidemics could wipe out whole communities.

Most Greeks believed that after death their souls roamed the Underworld, a cold and gloomy region where the wicked were sent to be punished. In *The Odyssey*, the hero Achilles says, "I'd rather be a common laborer on earth working for a poor man than lord of all the legions of the dead." Very few people, it was thought were good enough to be sent to the Isles of the Blessed. If they were, they could spend eternity amusing themselves with sports and music. People who had led exceptional lives (such as the hero Heracles) were thought destined to become gods and live on Mount Olympus.

When someone died, their body was either buried or cremated. The Greeks believed that only when the body or ashes had been covered with earth, could its spirit leave for the Underworld. Graves contained possessions for use in the afterlife, and women left offerings of food and drink at the graveside to help the spirits.

FRAGRANT FAREWELL
Graves were sometimes marked with lekythoi, white clay flasks holding a perfumed oil that had been used to anoint the body. The lekythoi were usually painted with farewell scenes, funerals or images of the dead.

FOOD FOR THOUGHT
The tradition of leaving food at gravesides began in Mycenaean times. Then people could be buried with their armor, cooking pots and even pets and slaves to accompany them. By 300 B.C., the Greeks were leaving food, such as wine and eggs, at gravesides as nourishment for the dead.

wine

eggs

A DIVE INTO THE UNKNOWN
The figure on the painting above is shown leaping from life into the ocean of death. The pillars were put up by Heracles to mark the end of the known, living world. This diver was found painted on the walls of a tomb.

TUG OF LOVE

This painting from a vase shows Persephone with Hades, her husband and ruler of the Underworld. Hades dragged Persephone from earth down to the Underworld. Her distraught mother, the goddess Demeter, neglected the crops to search for her. Zeus intervened and decided that Persephone would spend six months of every year with her mother and the other six with Hades. Whenever her daughter returned in spring, Demeter would look after the crops. However, Demeter grew sad each time her daughter went back to the Underworld, and winter would set in.

LAST JOURNEY

The body of a dead person was taken from their home to the grave by mourners bearing tributes. To express their grief, they might cut off their hair, tear at their cheeks with their nails until blood flowed, and wear black robes. If there was a funeral feast at the graveside, the dishes were smashed afterward and left there.

ROYAL TOMB

Women were less likely to be honored by tombstone portraits than men. Philis, seen above, was an exception to this rule, possibly because she was the daughter of a powerful Spartan king. Athens enforced a law against extravagant tombs. No more than 10 men could be employed for any more than three days to build one.

A Trip to the Theater

THE FIRST GREEK DRAMAS were performed at temples in honor of the gods. The stories they told were a mixture of history and myth, and featured the adventures of famous Greeks as well as the exploits of gods and legendary heroes. The all-male cast was backed up by a chorus of singers and dancers, who provided a commentary on the action. Drama became so popular that large open-air theaters were built in major cities and at sacred places such as Delphi and Epidauros. Prizes were awarded to the best dramatists. The three most famous writers of tragedies were Aeschylus, Sophocles and Euripides. They wrote over 300 plays between them, but only a tenth survive. The works of another 150 known writers have all been lost. Greek drama is still performed in theaters today.

SEAT OF HONOR
Most theater-goers sat on stone benches. This carved chair might have been reserved for an important official or a sponsor who had paid the expenses of a public performance.

THEATER
Large theaters like this one at Ephesus on the coast of modern Turkey had excellent acoustics and could hold an audience of over 10,000. The stage, a circle of beaten earth in the center of the theater, was called the orchestra, which means "dancing floor."

BIRD MASK
You will need: balloon, petroleum jelly, papier-mâché (newspaper soaked in 1 part water to 2 parts white glue), black pen, scissors, paint, paintbrush, 2 pieces of ochre card stock (8 x 4 in.), glue stick, compass, two pieces of red card stock (16 x 16 in.), cord.

1 Blow up a balloon to head-size. Cover front and sides in petroleum jelly. Add several layers of papier-mâché. When this is dry, pop the balloon.

2 Ask a friend to mark the position of your eyes and the top of your ears on the mask. Cut out small holes at these points. Paint the mask as shown at the end.

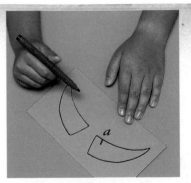

3 Draw and cut out two beak shapes. Repeat for both pieces of ochre card stock. Mark a point ½ in. along the bottom of the beak (the edge marked *a* above).

COMIC TURN

A figurine from the 2nd century B.C. shows a masked comic actor sitting on an altar. He is hiding in a temple to escape punishment. Comedies were much enjoyed, but considered inferior to tragedies.

SUFFERING COMEDY

In this comic scene the actor in the middle plays the part of a centaur called Cheiron. Centaurs were mythical creatures that were half-man and half-horse. Cheiron was the wisest of them all. But he was also seen as a comic figure because he was immortal yet suffered from a fatal wound.

PLAYING PARTS

Greek actors wore masks to represent different characters and emotions. The same actor could play different roles in one drama by changing his mask. All the players were male, but some took female roles. Women were not allowed on the stage, and may even have been barred from joining the audience.

To wear your mask, thread a piece of cord through the holes on each side of the head. Tie them together at the back. This mask is modeled on an original worn by the chorus in Aristophanes' comedy, The Birds.

4 Draw a line from the corner of the top edge (*b*) to this point. Fold back the line. Glue the two pieces together along the top edge. Repeat.

5 Put the compass point in the corner of the red card stock. Draw two arcs, one with a 4-in. radius and one with a 8-in. radius. Cut out as one piece.

6 Cut feather shapes into the top of the red card stock. Draw an arc 2 in. from the bottom. Cut out 14 tabs, as shown. Repeat both steps for the other piece of card stock.

7 Glue the two red pieces together at the top. Glue the tabs down onto the top of the mask. Glue the beak pieces to the mask. Draw on the eyes.

173

Music and Dance

MUSIC AND DANCE WERE BOTH AN important part of Greek life. People sang, played and danced at religious ceremonies. Music was enjoyed for pleasure and entertainment at family celebrations, dramatic performances, feasts and drinking parties. Few written records remain of the notes played, but examples of the instruments do. The most popular instruments were the pipes. They were wind instruments similar to the oboe or clarinet. One pipe on its own was called the *aulos*, two played together were known as *auloi*. The stringed lyre and flute were other popular instruments. The stringed lyre produced solemn and dignified music. It was often played by men of noble birth to accompany a poetry recital. The flute was more usually played by slaves or dancing girls.

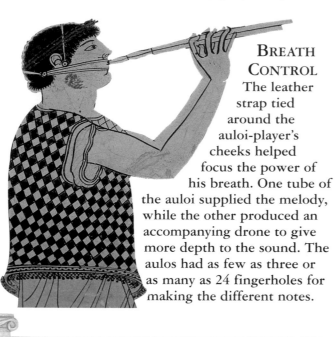

BREATH CONTROL
The leather strap tied around the auloi-player's cheeks helped focus the power of his breath. One tube of the auloi supplied the melody, while the other produced an accompanying drone to give more depth to the sound. The aulos had as few as three or as many as 24 fingerholes for making the different notes.

Greek soldiers complained that lack of music was a hardship of war. Spartan soldiers resolved this problem by blowing tunes on pipes as they marched. Music was believed to have magical powers. Greek legend tells of Orpheus soothing savage beasts by playing his lyre. Another myth tells how Amphion (a son of Zeus) made stones move on their own and built a wall around the city of Thebes, by playing his lyre.

BANG! CRASH!
The bronze figurine above is playing the cymbals. They made a sound similar to castanets. The Greeks used the cymbals to accompany dancing. Other percussion instruments included wooden clappers and hand-held drums, like tambourines.

TIMPANON
You will need: scissors, corrugated cardboard, tape measure, plate, white card stock, compass, pencil, white glue, tape, strips of newspaper, cream paper, red and purple felt-tip pens, ochre card stock, red and yellow ribbons.

1 Cut out a strip of corrugated cardboard 2 in. wide. Wrap it around a dinner plate. Add 2½ in. to the length of this cardboard and cut it off.

2 Put the plate upside down on the white card stock. Draw around it. Draw another circle 1½ in. inside the first. Cut this out to make a ring.

3 Glue the cardboard strip that you made in step 1 to the edge of the cardboard ring you made in step 2. Then tape them together for extra hold.

DIVINE MUSIC

Terpsichore was one of the Nine Muses, or spirits of the arts. She was the spirit of dance and music. Here, Terpsichore plays a harp while her attendants hold the lyre and auloi. Other Muses included Polyhymnia, the spirit of hymns, and Euterpe, the spirit of flute-playing.

PERCUSSION

The timpanon was a tambourine made of animal skin, stretched over a frame. It was tapped to provide rhythmic accompaniment at dances or recitals. Stringed and wind instruments were thought superior because they made appropriate music for solemn or exclusive occasions. Drums, cymbals and clappers were associated with street performers.

ENTERTAINING

In this plate painting a young man plays the auloi while his female companion dances. Professional musicians were often hired to entertain guests at dinner parties. Sometimes the musicians were household slaves.

To play the timpanon, tap on it with your fingers, as the ancient Greeks would have done.

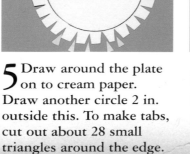

4 Make up some papier mâché solution with 1 part glue to 2 parts water. Soak strips of newspaper in it and cover the cardboard ring with the wet strips.

5 Draw around the plate on to cream paper. Draw another circle 2 in. outside this. To make tabs, cut out about 28 small triangles around the edge.

6 Draw the design shown above on to the paper. Place the paper over the top of the card ring. Dab glue on each tab and stick on to the corrugated cardboard.

7 Cut a strip of ochre card stock big enough to fit around the timpanon. Decorate it as above and glue on. Make 4 bows with the ribbons and glue around the edge.

Arts and Crafts

THE ARTISTS AND CRAFTWORKERS of ancient Greece were admired for the quality of their work. They produced many objects of art including beautiful pottery, fine jewelry and impressive sculptures. Materials they worked with included stone, gold, silver, glass, gemstones and bronze. They also used wood, leather, bone, ivory and horn. Most goods were made on a small scale in workshops surrounding the marketplace (*agora*). A craftsman might work on his own or with the help of his family and a slave or two. In the larger workshops of such cities as Athens, slaves labored to produce bulk orders of popular goods. These might include shields, pottery and metalwork, which were traded around the Mediterranean Sea for a large profit.

BULK PRODUCTION
Above is a terra-cotta mold, and on the right, the casting taken from it. Making a mold was a skilled and time-consuming task. Using a mold made it possible to produce items faster and more cheaply than carving each piece individually.

RAW MATERIALS
Gold was an expensive import and was usually used to make luxury items such as jewelry. Less commonly, it was used to decorate statues and to make gold coins. Clay was used in the production of a wide range of craft goods from vases to statuettes.

clay

gold

PANATHENAIC VASE
You will need: balloon, bowl, white glue, water, newspaper, two rolls of masking tape, black pen, scissors, sheet of paper 16½ x 12 in., card stock, pencil, paintbrush, black and cream paint.

1 Blow up the balloon. Cover it with two layers of papier mâché (paper soaked in one part glue, two parts water). Set aside on one side to dry.

2 Using a roll of masking tape as a guide, draw and cut out two holes at the top and bottom of the balloon. Throw away the burst balloon.

3 Roll the sheet of paper into a tube. Make sure that it will fit through the middle of the roll of masking tape. Secure the tube with tape or glue.

VASE PAINTING

Black-figure vase painting originated in Corinth around 700 B.C. The black-figure style was succeeded by a red-figure style invented in Athens around 525 B.C. The painters were not all anonymous artisans. Many were widely recognized as artists in their own right who signed their works. The export of vases like this became a major source of income for both cities.

HOT WORK

In this scene two blacksmiths are forging metal at a brick furnace. Metal goods were expensive to produce. The furnaces themselves were fueled by charcoal (burnt wood) which was expensive to make because wood was scarce in Greece. In addition, supplies of metal often had to be imported, sometimes from great distances. For example, tin, which was mixed with local copper to make bronze, was brought from southern Spain.

Amphorae like this one were given as prizes at the Panathenaic games. They were decorated with images of sports.

GOLD PECTORAL

This gold pectoral, made on the island of Rhodes in the 7th century B.C., was meant to be worn across the breast. Gold was rare in Greece. It was usually imported at great expense from surrounding areas such as Egypt or Asia Minor.

4 Push the tube through the middle of the balloon. Tape into place. Push a roll of masking tape over the bottom of the paper tube and tape.

5 Tape the second roll of masking tape to the top of the tube. Make sure that both rolls are securely attached at either end of the paper tube.

6 Cut two strips of card stock, 6 in. long. Attach them to either side of the vase, as seen above. Cover the entire vase with papier mâché, and let dry.

7 Using a pencil, copy the pattern seen on the vase in the picture above on your vase. Carefully paint in the pattern and set aside on one side to dry.

Sports and Fitness

FITNESS WAS VALUED as an essential preparation for war. But the Greeks also enjoyed sport for its own sake, and most cities had a public gymnasium, where men gathered to train and to relax. They preferred individual contests to team games, and often celebrated religious festivals by running races to honor the gods. This is how the Olympic Games first began in 776 B.C. It was held every four years and expanded to include long jump, throwing the discus and javelin, boxing, wrestling, chariot races and horse races, as well as poetry and drama competitions. There was also a gruesome fighting sport called *pankration* (total power), a combination of boxing and wrestling in which the only forbidden tactics were eye-gouging and biting. During the Olympics, all wars between cities stopped, so that people could journey safely to the Games. Women were banned from competing or watching the Olympics but they had their own games, also held at Olympia in honor of the goddess Hera.

THE WINNER
A Greek king (on the right) hands a wreath of victory to an Olympic winner. A priest stands by to remind contestants that they are on sacred ground. There were no cash prizes at the Olympics. However, because they brought honor to their cities, winners were sometimes given money on their return home, or even free meals for life.

SPORTING STARS
This vase painting shows a long-jumper holding weights, a discus thrower and two men with javelins. They represent three of the five sports that made up the *pentathlon* ("penta" is Greek for five). The other two were running and wrestling. The pentathlon began with a foot race, which was followed by javelin, throwing, then discus throwing and finally the long jump. The two contestants who scored highest in these events then wrestled one another to decide the overall winner. Most sportsmen were amateurs. There were also many professionals who trained for and competed in a single event.

SPORTING FACILITIES

Much of ancient Olympia, where the first Olympic Games were held, has been uncovered by archaeologists working there since 1829. There were many facilities serving the competitors and spectators. At the center of the complex were two large temples dedicated to Hera and Zeus. Among the buildings surrounding the temples were a hostel, restaurants, a huge gymnasium for training in and a hippodrome for horse and chariot races. Despite its size, Olympia never became a city, because it had no permanent citizens or local government.

DANGEROUS GAME

At the end of a chariot race, an armed man jumped off of the moving vehicle and ran a foot race. This event was eventually dropped from the Games because it often provoked laughter at undignified accidents instead of admiration for the competitors' skill. Chariots frequently overturned with disastrous results. As many as 40 competitors might take part, racing 12 laps of a 1,200-yd circuit. The winner was the owner of the chariot and horses, not the driver.

GOING THE DISTANCE

Long-jumpers carried heavy weights to give them more momentum. The weights also helped them balance. They jumped on a bed of crumbled earth (skamma) raked smooth. This helped them avoid injuries and leave a clear footprint, so that the judges could measure the distance they had covered.

STEP THIS WAY

Competitors taking part in the original Olympic Games entered the stadium through this archway. The grassy embankments surrounding the stadium could seat up to 40,000 spectators.

GETTING READY

An athlete binds his hair with a cloth to keep it out of the way. Most athletes competed naked in the Olympic Games. It was felt that sport glorified male strength and beauty. When women competed against each other in the games to honor Hera, they wore short tunics.

Science and Philosophy

THE GREEKS COULD AFFORD to devote time to studying and thinking because their civilization was both wealthy and secure. They learned astrology from the Babylonians, and mathematics from the Egyptians. They used their scientific knowledge to develop many practical inventions, including water clocks, cogwheels, gearing systems, slot machines and steam engines. However, these devices were not widely used as there were many slave workers to do the jobs.

The word "philosophy" comes from the Greek word philosophus, meaning love of knowledge. The Greeks developed many different branches of philosophy. Three of these were politics (how best to govern), ethics (how to behave well) and cosmology (how the universe worked).

Greek philosophers recognized the value of experimenting. But they could not always see their limitations. Aristotle discovered that evaporation turned salt water into fresh water, and wrongly assumed that wine would turn into water by the same process.

GREAT THINKER
The philosopher Aristotle (384–322 B.C.) is often recognized as the founder of Western science. He pioneered a rational approach to the world, based on observing and recording evidence. For three years, he was the tutor of Alexander the Great.

CLOCK TOWER
The Tower of the Winds in Athens contains a water clock. The original Egyptian invention was a bucket of water with a tiny hole in the bottom. As the water dripped out of it, the water level fell past scored marks on the inside of the bucket, measuring time. The Greeks improved on this design, using the flow of water to work a dial with a moving pointer.

ARCHIMEDES SCREW
You will need: clean, empty plastic bottle, scissors, modeling clay, strong tape, length of clear plastic tube, bowl of water, blue food coloring, empty bowl.

1 Cut off the bottle top. Place the plasticine in the middle of the bottle, about 2 in. from the end. Punch in a hole at this point with the scissors.

2 Cut a strip of tape the same length as the bottle. Tape it to the middle of the bottle. This will give the tube extra grip later on.

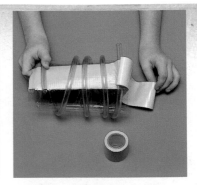

3 Twist the length of tube around the bottle. Go from one end of the bottle to the other. Tape the tube in place over the first piece of tape.

WATER LIFTER

When the Archimedes screw is turned, it lifts water from one level to another. It is named after its inventor, the scientist Archimedes, who lived about 287–211 B.C., in Syracuse, Sicily. It is still in use today.

FATHER OF GEOMETRY

Euclid (about 330–260 B.C.) was a mathematician. He lived in the Greek-Egyptian city of Alexandria. He is known as the father of geometry, which comes from the Greek word for "measuring land." Geometry is the study of points, lines, curves, surfaces and their measurements. His geometry textbook was called *Elements*. It was still widely used in the early part of the 20th century A.D., over 2,000 years after his death. This picture shows the front page of an edition of the book that was printed in London in 1732.

4 Place a few drops of the blue food coloring into the bowl of water. Stir it in so that the color mixes evenly throughout the water.

5 Place one end of the bottle into the bowl of blue water. Make sure that the tube at the opposite end is pointing toward the empty bowl.

6 Twist the bottle around in the blue water. As you do so, you will see the water start traveling up the tube and gradually filling the other bowl.

The invention of the Archimedes screw made it possible for farmers to water their fields with irrigation channels. It saved them from walking back and forth to the river with buckets.

Medical Matters

THE GREEKS BELIEVED THAT ultimately only the gods had the power to heal wounds and cure sickness. But they also developed a scientific approach to medicine. Greek doctors could treat injuries and battle wounds by bandaging and bone-setting. They relied on rest, diet and herbal drugs to cure disease. However, they were powerless against large-scale epidemics, such as the plague. Doctors believed that good health was dependent on the balance between four main body fluids—blood, phlegm and yellow and black bile. If this balance was disturbed, they attempted to restore it by applying heated metal cups to the body to draw out harmful fluids. The sweat this produced convinced them it worked. This mistaken practice continued in Europe until the 17th century.

FATHER OF MEDICINE

Hippocrates founded a medical school around 400 B.C. He taught that observation of symptoms was more important than theory. His students took an oath to use their skills to heal and never to harm.

BODY BALANCE

Bleeding was a common procedure, intended to restore the body's internal balance. This carving shows surgical instruments and cups used for catching blood. Sometimes bleeding may have helped to drain off poisons, but probably only weakened the patient.

HEALING GOD

The Greeks worshiped Asclepius, as the god of healing. He is shown here with a serpent, representing wisdom. Invalids seeking a cure made a visit to his shrine.

LEG OFFERING

You will need: self-drying modeling clay, rolling pin, board, ruler, modeling tool, paintbrush, cream acrylic paint.

1 Divide the clay into two pieces. With the rolling pin, roll out one piece to 6-in. length, 4-in. width and ¾-in. depth. This is the base for the leg.

2 Roll out the second piece of clay. With the modeling tool, carve out a leg and foot shape. It should be big enough to fit on one side of the bottom.

3 Gently place the leg on the right-hand side of the bottom. With the tool, draw a shallow outline around the leg into the bottom. Remove the leg.

THEORY AND PRACTICE

Patients would explain their dreams to doctors, who then prescribed treatment. In this relief, a healing spirit in the shape of a serpent visits a sleeping patient. In the foreground, the physician bandages the wounded arm.

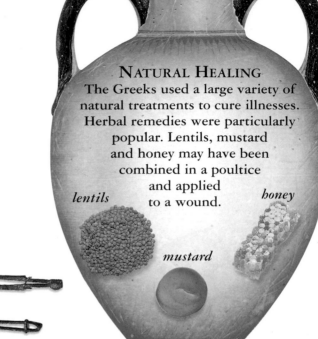

NATURAL HEALING

The Greeks used a large variety of natural treatments to cure illnesses. Herbal remedies were particularly popular. Lentils, mustard and honey may have been combined in a poultice and applied to a wound.

lentils

mustard

honey

TOOL KIT

The Greeks used bronze surgical instruments, including forceps and probes. Surgery was usually a last resort. Even when it was successful, patients often died from the shock and pain, or from infection afterward. Operations on limbs were more successful than those on body cavities such as the chest or stomach.

4 With the tool, score the outline with lines. Carve the ancient Greek message seen in the picture above next to the leg.

5 Mold the leg onto the scored area of the bottom. Use your fingers to press the sides of the leg in place. Carve toes and toenails into the foot.

6 Paint over the entire leg offering with a cream color, to give it an aged look. Let dry overnight. Your leg offering is done.

This model is based on a real one left as an offering of thanks to the god Asclepius by someone whose leg was affected by illness. This was a common practice in ancient Greece.

Travel and Trade

THE MOUNTAINOUS LANDSCAPE of ancient Greece was too rocky for carts or chariots, so most people rode donkeys or walked. Sea travel was simpler—the many islands of the eastern Mediterranean made it possible to sail from one port to another without losing sight of land. Merchant ships were sailed because they were too heavy to be rowed. Greek sailors had no compasses. By day they relied on coastal landmarks and at night they navigated by the stars. However, neither method was reliable. A sudden storm could throw a ship off course or cause it to sink. Merchant ships carried olive oil, wool, wine, silver, fine pottery and slaves. These goods were traded in return for wheat and timber, both of which were scarce in Greece. Other imported products included tin, copper, ivory, gold, silk and cotton.

COINAGE
The gold coin above shows Zeus, ruler of the gods, throwing a thunderbolt. Coins were invented in Lydia (in present-day Turkey) around 635 B.C., and introduced to Greece soon afterward. Before that, the Greeks had used bars of silver and rods of iron as money. Greek coins were also made of silver, bronze and electrum, a mixture of gold and silver.

SEA GOD
Poseidon was the god of the sea, horses and earthquakes. Sailors prayed and made sacrifices to him, hoping for protection against storms, fogs and pirates. He is usually pictured holding a trident, the three-pronged spear used by Greek fishermen. At the trading port of Corinth, the Isthmian Games were held every other year in honor of Poseidon.

HARD CURRENCY
The first coins may have been used to pay mercenary soldiers, rather than for trading or collecting taxes. The earliest coins usually bore a religious symbol or the emblem of a city. Only later did they show the head of a ruler. The coin on the right shows the sea god Poseidon with his trident. The coin on the left bears the rose of Rhodes. Many countries that traded with the Greeks copied their idea of using coins for money.

SHIPPING

The ship on the right is a sail-powered merchantman. The criss-cross lines represent a wooden and rope catwalk stretched over the cargo, which was stored in an uncovered hold. Liquids such as wine and olive oil were transported and sold in long narrow pottery jars called amphorae, which could be neatly stacked in the hold. Merchant ships faced many dangers that could cause the loss of their cargo. Pirates and storms were the worst of these.

WEIGHING GOODS

Most dry goods were sold loose and had to be weighed on a scale such as this one. Officials would oversee the proceedings to ensure that they were fair. They stopped merchants and traders from cheating one another. In Athens, these officials were known as *metronomoi*. It was essential for merchants to familiarize themselves with the various systems of weights and measures used in different countries.

MARKET STALLS

The agora or marketplace was to be found in the center of every Greek town. Market stalls sold a wide range of goods, including meat, vegetables, eggs, cheese and fish. Fish was laid out on marble slabs to keep it cool and fresh.

clams

shrimp

mussels

RIDING

Mountainous countryside made traveling overland difficult in Greece. The few roads that did exist were in poor condition. For most people, walking was the only way to reach a destination. Horses were usually only used by wealthy people to travel on. Donkeys and mules were used by tradesmen to transport large loads. Longer journeys were made by boat.

Fighting Forces

ALL GREEK MEN were expected to fight in their city's army. In Sparta the army was on duty all year round. In other parts of Greece men gave up fighting in autumn to bring in the harvest and make the wine. The only full-time soldiers in these states were the personal bodyguards of a ruler or mercenaries who fought for anyone who paid them. Armies consisted mainly of hoplites (armored infantry), cavalry (soldiers on horseback) and a group of foot soldiers armed with stones and bows and arrows. The

hoplites were the most important fighting force, as they engaged in hand-to-hand combat. The cavalry was less effective in war because riders had no stirrups, which made charging with a lance impossible, as the rider would fall off on contact. They were used for scouting, harassing a beaten enemy and carrying messages.

HARD HELMET
This bronze helmet from Corinth was fashioned to protect the face. It has guards for the cheeks and the bridge of the nose. Iron later replaced bronze as the main metal for weapons.

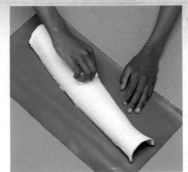

BOWMEN
The Greek army usually employed Scythian archers to fight for them. Archers were useful for fighting in mountainous countryside where they could position themselves above the enemy. Some Greeks soldiers did fight with bows and arrows. They fought in small units known as *psiloi*. But most of the soldiers in these units could only afford simple missile weapons, such as a javelin or slings from which they shot stones.

WARRIOR GREAVES
You will need: plastic wrap, bowl of water, plaster bandages, sheet of paper, paper towels, scissors, cord, gold paint, paintbrush.

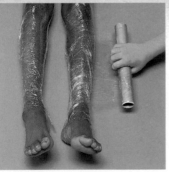

1 Ask a friend to help you with steps 1 to 3. Loosely cover both of your lower legs (from your ankle to the top of your knee) with plastic wrap.

2 Soak each plaster bandage in water. Working from one side of your leg to the other, smooth the bandage over the front of each leg.

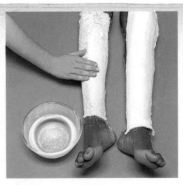

3 Carefully remove each greave. Set them on some paper. Dampen some kitchen paper and use it to smooth the greaves down. Let dry.

A RARE SIGHT IN BATTLE

Chariots were not often used in warfare because they could only be used on flat plains. There were usually two people in the chariot, one to drive it, and the other to fight from the back of it.

FIGHTING FORCES

Tin and copper were used to make bronze, the main material for weapons and armor. Bronze is harder than pure copper and, unlike iron, does not rust. As there was no tin in Greece, it was imported from faraway lands.

copper   tin

HOPLITES

This fighting force was made up of middle-class men who could afford the weaponry. A hoplite's armory consisted of a shield, helmet, spear, sword and greaves. Helmets were made of bronze and were usually crested with horsehair. The body was protected by a bronze cuirass, a one-piece breast- and back-plate, under which the hoplites wore a leather cuirass. Shields were usually round and decorated with a symbol.

4 Trim the edges of the greaves, to make them look neat. Measure four lengths of cord to fit around your leg, below the knee and above the ankle.

5 Turn the greaves onto their front. Lay the cord in place at the point where you want to tie them to your leg. Hold them in place using wet bandages.

6 Let the plaster bandages dry, with the cord in place. Now paint each greave with gold paint. Once they are dry, tie them on.

Greaves were attached to the lower leg to protect it in battle. They were worn by hoplites.

Warfare

WHEN THE GREEKS WENT TO WAR it was usually to engage in raids and sieges of rival city-states. Major battles with foreign powers were rare, but the results could be devastating. Army commanders had to choose their ground with care and rely on the discipline and training of their troops to carry through their overall plan. Once the fighting had started, it was almost impossible to control large masses of men or to change their orders. The death or flight of a few key leaders could cause a whole army to break up in chaos.

The core of a Greek army consisted of heavily armed foot soldiers (hoplites) who fought together in solid blocks called phalanxes. As long as they stayed calm, the soldiers were protected by their bristling spears, overlapping shields and sheer weight of numbers. If they panicked and broke up, it was easy for the enemy to pick off individual hoplites, weighed down by 66 pounds of armor.

HEROES AT PLAY
Achilles and Ajax were legendary Greek heroes of the Trojan war. This vase shows them playing dice. This game was played by soldiers to while away the time or to decide the share-out of loot. The outcome of the game was sometimes interpreted as a symbol of fate and death.

GREEK TRICK
The Greeks ended the siege of Troy by leaving a wooden horse outside the city and pretending to sail away. The Trojans dragged the horse inside, not realizing that it was filled with Greek soldiers. The soldiers crept out of the horse at night and opened the city gates to let their comrades in. Together they overran the city.

CLOSE COMBAT
The Greek soldiers and heroes of Homer's time fought each other in a series of one-on-one duels. In this engraving, Greek and Trojan warriors are fighting hand-to-hand. However, as armies began to use more hoplites, methods of fighting changed to accommodate them. This involved men fighting together in a phalanx.

VICTORY AGAINST THE ODDS

At the battle of Issus in 333 B.C. Alexander the Great (left) led the charge against the Persian king Darius (in the chariot). Darius fled in panic, and his much larger army broke up. The Persian army was made up of many different peoples from all over his vast empire. They spoke different languages and did not trust each other, making control harder. In contrast, Alexander had tight control and much experience fighting with his troops.

SEA FIGHT

In 480 B.C., the battle of Salamis ended a Persian invasion into Greek territory. The Persians had more and faster ships, but the Greeks defeated them by luring them into narrow waters where these advantages were lost. Then the crowded Persian vessels were rammed to pieces by the much heavier Greek ships.

END OF AN EMPIRE

Greece won another decisive victory against Persia in 331 B.C. At the battle of Gaugemala the Persian cavalry outnumbered Alexander's almost five to one and the infantry two to one. Discipline, daring and determination overcame the odds and the Persian army lost the battle. Consequently, the Persian empire finally yielded to Alexander.

Glossary

A

Acropolis A sacred hill overlooking Athens on which temples were built.

agora A marketplace.

alphabet Letters used in writing. The first two letters of the Greek alphabet are alpha and beta, which give us our word alphabet.

amphora A jar with two handles used to store wine or olive oil.

andron The room in a Greek house where men entertained.

Archimedes screw A device for lifting water from one level to another, named after its inventor, the Greek scientist Archimedes.

aristocracy A system of government by wealthy and privileged people.

auloi A pair of musical pipes. One tube supplied the melody, while the other produced a background drone.

B

bleeding A process used by doctors. It was thought to drain off poisons, but often it only weakened the patient.

bronze A metal made by mixing tin with copper. Bronze was used for making armor.

C

Castalian spring A spring at Delphi that gave off vapors. The priestess inhaled them and went into a trance.

cavalry Soldiers on horseback. They were used mainly for scouting ahead and delivering messages.

centaur A mythical beast, half man, half horse.

city-state A center of government. Ancient Greece was made up of about 300 city-states.

D

colony A settlement of people outside their own country. The Greeks founded many colonies around the Mediterranean Sea.

cosmology The study of the workings of the universe.

cuirass A one-piece breast- and back-plate worn by soldiers.

D

Delphi The place the Greeks believed to be the center of the world, and the home of the Oracle.

democracy A system of government by the many. Every citizen has the right to vote and hold public office.

E

electrum A mixture of gold and silver, used for making coins.

ethics A branch of philosophy that considers good conduct and the rules that govern it.

F

flax A plant that yields fibers which are woven into a fabric called linen.

fresco A painting applied to damp plaster and used to decorate walls in the homes of wealthy Greeks.

G

geometry A branch of mathematics concerning measurements of lines, angles and surfaces. It was pioneered by the Greek scientist Euclid. In Greek, it means measuring the land.

gorgon A female monster of such horrific appearance that anyone who looked at her died.

greaves Armor for the legs.

H

helot A slave in Sparta.

K

knucklebones A favorite game of the Greeks. It involved flipping small animal bones from one side of the hand to the other without dropping them.

L

lekythoi White clay flasks used at funerals. They held fragrant oil for anointing the body and were painted with farewell scenes.

Linear A A script used by the Minoans. It remains undeciphered.

M

metic A foreigner resident in Athens. Metics had to pay extra taxes and serve in the military. They were not allowed to own land or marry an Athenian.

metronomoi Athenian officials whose job it was to stop merchants and traders from cheating one another. They oversaw the weighing out of dry goods.

Minoan The first great Greek civilization, and the first in Europe. It flourished on the island of Crete around 2000 B.C.

Minotaur A mythical beast, half man, half bull, that lived in a maze under a palace in Crete. It was slain by the hero Theseus.

monarchy Government by a king or queen.

mosaic A floor made of colored pebbles set in patterns, and found in the houses of wealthy Greeks.

Mount Olympus Home of the Greek gods and goddesses.

muse There were nine muses, or spirits of the arts, including Terpsichore, the spirit of dance and music.

Mycenaean The second great Greek civilization. The Mycenaeans dominated the Greek mainland from around 1600 B.C.

mythology Traditional stories about the exploits of gods and legendary heroes.

O

oligarchy Government by a group of rich and powerful people.

olive The fruit of the olive tree. An important crop in ancient Greece, olives were eaten as an appetizer or pressed to make olive oil. They were also used in medicine.

Olympic Games A sporting competition held every four years at Olympia in honor of the god Zeus. The first Games was held in 776 B.C.

omphalos An egg-shaped stone found at the holy sanctuary at Delphi. Omphalos means navel and this stone was thought to be the center of the world.

Oracle A spirit that could see into the future. The Oracle was believed to live in a cave at Delphi. People paid large sums of money to hear the Oracle's predictions on personal and business matters.

ostracism Every year Athenians could banish an unpopular person from the city for ten years. Voters scratched the name of their choice on a piece of pottery called an ostrakon, so the procedure was called ostracism.

P

Panathenaic festival A yearly procession with sacrifices in honor of Athena, which took place at the Parthenon in Athens.

pankration A gruesome fighting sport that combines boxing and wrestling. (The name pankration means total power.)

Parthenon A temple on the Acropolis in Athens dedicated to the city's goddess, Athena.

pectoral jewelry or armor worn on the breast or chest.

pentathlon Five sports—discus, javelin, running, wrestling and long jump with weights—that formed part of the Olympic Games. (Penta is Greek for five.)

peplos A robe presented to the goddess Athena once every four years at the Panathenaic festival.

phalanx A solid block of hoplites (foot soldiers) in battle.

philosophy A Greek word meaning love of knowledge. Philosophy is the discipline of thinking about the meaning of life.

polis A Greek city-state.

politics The art and science of government (from polis, city-state).

priest Someone who offered prayers and sacrifices on behalf of worshippers at a temple. This was a part-time job, and priests lived among the ordinary people. Some priests inherited their job, others were elected to it. Others still paid for the privilege of being a priest.

Propylaea The monumental gateways to the temple complex on top of the Acropolis.

pyxis A box used for storing face powder or other cosmetics.

Pythia The priestess who officiated at Delphi. She inhaled vapors from the Castalian spring to put her into a trance so that the Oracle could speak through her.

S

slaves People who were not free, but owned by their masters. Some were treated badly, others were treated well and given good jobs.

T

terra-cotta A composition of baked clay and sand used to make statues, figurines and pottery.

timpanon A tambourine made with animal skin.

tragedy A play that ends in disaster. It usually concerns a good and noble person with a fatal flaw in his character that ultimately causes his downfall.

tunic A loose robe worn as everyday clothing by Greek men and women. It was usually fastened at the shoulder with a brooch or pin.

U

underworld A mysterious place to which the spirits of the dead were believed to travel after burial.

W

water clock A bucket full of water with a hole in the bottom. The flow of water worked a dial, which told the time.

wet nurse A woman employed to breastfeed babies.

THE ROMAN
EMPIRE

PHILIP STEELE

CONSULTANT: JENNY HALL, MUSEUM OF LONDON

Almost 2,000 years ago, the powerful Roman Empire ruled the western world. Legions of soldiers marched through country after country, conquering the primitive peoples they came across. They introduced fine wine, central heating, decent roads, and exquisite artworks to northern Europe. But within 400 years, the Empire was falling to pieces. Rome, the city at its heart, was attacked and destroyed by invaders, and the last Roman emperor was deposed. The story of the Roman Empire is one of slaves and gladiators, remarkable feats of engineering such as viaducts and theaters, and a meteoric rise in power unprecedented in human history.

The Story of Rome

THE CITY OF ROME today is a bustling place, full of traffic and crowds. But if you could travel back in time to 800BC, you would find only a few small villages on peaceful, wooded hillsides along the banks of the river Tiber. According to legend, Rome was founded here in 753BC. In the centuries that followed, the Romans came to dominate Italy and the Mediterranean. They farmed and traded and fought for new lands. Rome grew to become the center of a vast empire that stretched across Europe into Africa and Asia. The Roman Empire brought a sophisticated way of life to vast numbers of people. Many Roman buildings and artifacts still survive and help show us what life was like in the time of the Roman Empire.

ROMAN ITALY
As the city of Rome prospered, the Romans gradually conquered neighboring tribes. By 250BC they controlled most of Italy. This map shows some of the important towns and cities of that time.

ANCIENT AND MODERN
In Rome today, people live alongside the temples, marketplaces and public buildings of the past. This is the Colosseum, a huge arena called an amphitheater. It was used for staging games and fights, and first opened to the public in AD80.

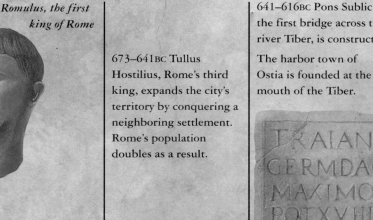

TIMELINE 753BC–276BC

Rome's rise to power was sudden and spectacular. Its eventful history includes bloody battles, eccentric emperors, amazing inventions and remarkable feats of engineering. The Roman Empire prospered for almost 500 years, and still influences the way we live today.

Romulus, the first king of Rome

c. 753BC The city of Rome is founded by Romulus, according to legend.

673–641BC Tullus Hostilius, Rome's third king, expands the city's territory by conquering a neighboring settlement. Rome's population doubles as a result.

641–616BC Pons Sublicius, the first bridge across the river Tiber, is constructed.

The harbor town of Ostia is founded at the mouth of the Tiber.

600BC The Latin language is first written in a script that is still used today.

inscription in Latin, carved in stone

750BC   700BC   650BC   600BC

CLUES TO THE PAST
The coin on this necklace dates from the reign of the Emperor Domitian, AD81–96. Gold does not rot like wood and other materials, so jewelry like this can give us clues about Roman craft methods, changing fashions, trade and even warfare.

ARCHAEOLOGISTS AT WORK
These archaeologists are excavating sections of wallplaster from the site of a Roman house in Britain. Many remains of Roman buildings and artifacts, as well as books and documents, have survived over the years. These all help us build up a picture of what life was like in the Roman Empire.

SECRETS BENEATH THE SEA
Divers have discovered Roman shipwrecks deep under the waters of the Mediterranean Sea. Many have their cargo still intact. These jars were being transported over 2,000 years ago. By examining shipwrecks, archaeologists can learn how Roman boats were built, what they carried and where they traded.

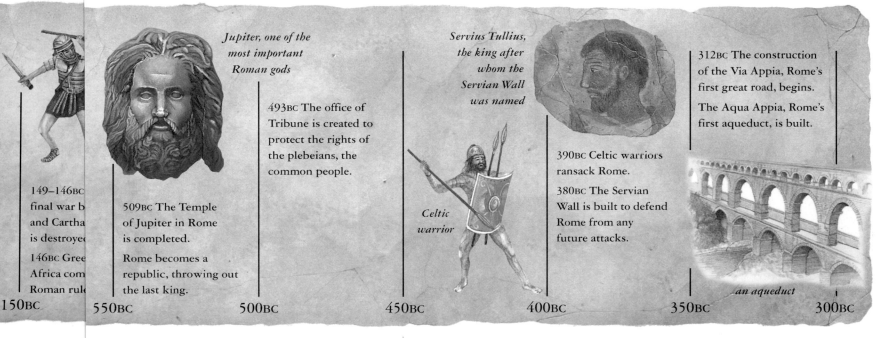

Jupiter, one of the most important Roman gods

Servius Tullius, the king after whom the Servian Wall was named

493BC The office of Tribune is created to protect the rights of the plebeians, the common people.

312BC The construction of the Via Appia, Rome's first great road, begins.

The Aqua Appia, Rome's first aqueduct, is built.

390BC Celtic warriors ransack Rome.

380BC The Servian Wall is built to defend Rome from any future attacks.

149–146BC ... final war b... and Cartha... is destroye...

146BC Gree... Africa com... Roman rul...

509BC The Temple of Jupiter in Rome is completed.

Rome becomes a republic, throwing out the last king.

Celtic warrior

an aqueduct

150BC   550BC   500BC   450BC   400BC   350BC   300BC

The Roman World

THE PEOPLE who made Roman history came from many different backgrounds. The names of the famous survive on monuments and in books. There were consuls and emperors, successful generals and powerful politicians, great writers and historians. However, it was thousands of ordinary people who really kept the Roman Empire going—merchants, soldiers of the legions, tax collectors, servants, farmers, potters, and others like them.

Many of the most famous names of that time were not Romans at all. There was the Carthaginian general, Hannibal, Rome's deadliest enemy. There were also Celtic chieftains and queens, such as Vercingetorix, Caractacus and Boudicca.

AUGUSTUS (63BC–AD14)
Augustus, born Octavian, was the great-nephew and adopted son of Julius Caesar. After Caesar's death, he took control of the army. He became ruler of the Roman world after defeating Mark Antony at the Battle of Actium in 31BC. In 27BC, he became Rome's first emperor and was given the title Augustus.

ROMULUS AND REMUS
According to legend, Romulus was the founder and first king of Rome. The legend tells how he and his twin brother Remus were abandoned as babies. They were saved by a she-wolf, who looked after them until they were found by a shepherd.

CICERO (106–43BC)
Cicero is remembered as Rome's greatest orator, or speaker. Many of his letters and speeches still survive. He was a writer, poet, politician, lawyer and philosopher. He was elected consul of Rome in 63BC, but he had many enemies and was murdered in 43BC.

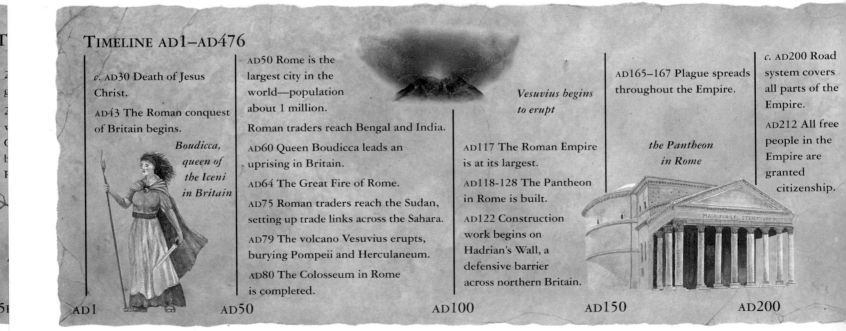

TIMELINE AD1–AD476

c. AD30 Death of Jesus Christ.

AD43 The Roman conquest of Britain begins.

Boudicca, queen of the Iceni in Britain

AD50 Rome is the largest city in the world—population about 1 million.

Roman traders reach Bengal and India.

AD60 Queen Boudicca leads an uprising in Britain.

AD64 The Great Fire of Rome.

AD75 Roman traders reach the Sudan, setting up trade links across the Sahara.

AD79 The volcano Vesuvius erupts, burying Pompeii and Herculaneum.

AD80 The Colosseum in Rome is completed.

Vesuvius begins to erupt

AD117 The Roman Empire is at its largest.

AD118-128 The Pantheon in Rome is built.

AD122 Construction work begins on Hadrian's Wall, a defensive barrier across northern Britain.

AD165–167 Plague spreads throughout the Empire.

the Pantheon in Rome

c. AD200 Road system covers all parts of the Empire.

AD212 All free people in the Empire are granted citizenship.

AD1   AD50   AD100   AD150   AD200

HADRIAN (AD76–138)

Hadrian became emperor in AD117 and spent many years traveling around the Empire. He had many splendid buildings constructed, as well as a defensive barrier across northern Britain, now known as Hadrian's Wall.

NERO (AD37–68) AND AGRIPPINA

Nero became emperor on the death of his adoptive father Claudius, in AD54. A cruel ruler, he was blamed for a great fire that destroyed much of Rome in AD64. Agrippina, his mother, was a powerful influence on him. She was suspected of poisoning two of her three husbands, and was eventually killed on her son's orders.

CLEOPATRA (68–30BC)

An Egyptian queen of Greek descent, Cleopatra had a son by Julius Caesar. She then fell in love with Mark Antony, a close follower of Caesar. They joined forces against Rome, but after a crushing defeat at Actium in 31BC, they both committed suicide. Egypt then became part of the Roman Empire.

JULIUS CAESAR (100–44BC)

Caesar was a talented and popular general and politician. He led Roman armies in an eight-year campaign to conquer Gaul (present-day France) in 50BC. In 49BC, he used his victorious troops to seize power and declare himself dictator for life. Five years later he was stabbed to death in the Senate by fellow politicians.

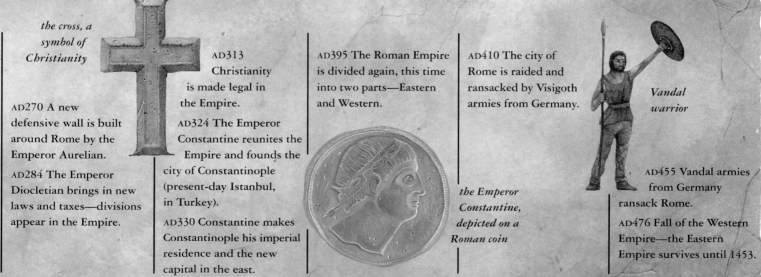

the cross, a symbol of Christianity

AD270 A new defensive wall is built around Rome by the Emperor Aurelian.

AD284 The Emperor Diocletian brings in new laws and taxes—divisions appear in the Empire.

AD313 Christianity is made legal in the Empire.

AD324 The Emperor Constantine reunites the Empire and founds the city of Constantinople (present-day Istanbul, in Turkey).

AD330 Constantine makes Constantinople his imperial residence and the new capital in the east.

AD395 The Roman Empire is divided again, this time into two parts—Eastern and Western.

AD410 The city of Rome is raided and ransacked by Visigoth armies from Germany.

the Emperor Constantine, depicted on a Roman coin

Vandal warrior

AD455 Vandal armies from Germany ransack Rome.

AD476 Fall of the Western Empire—the Eastern Empire survives until 1453.

AD250   AD300   AD350   AD400   AD450

199

Rulers of Rome

IN THE EARLY DAYS, the city of Rome was ruled by kings. The first Roman king was said to be Romulus, the founder of the city in 753BC. The last king, a hated tyrant called Tarquinius the Proud, was thrown out in 509BC. The Romans then set up a republic. An assembly of powerful and wealthy citizens, the Senate, chose two consuls to lead them each year. By 493BC, the common people had their own representatives, too—the tribunes. In times of crisis, rulers could take on emergency powers and become dictators. The first Roman emperor, Augustus, was appointed by the Senate in 27BC. The emperors were given great powers and were even worshipped as gods. Some lived simply and ruled well, but others were violent, cruel men. They were surrounded by flatterers, and yet they lived in constant fear of plotters and murderers.

TRIUMPHAL PROCESSION
When a Roman general won a great victory, he was honored with a military parade called a triumph. Cheering crowds lined the streets as the grand procession passed by. If a general was successful and popular, the way to power was often open to him. Probably the most famous Roman ruler of all, Julius Caesar, came to power after a series of brilliant military conquests.

STATE SACRIFICE
Roman emperors had religious as well as political duties. As *pontifex maximus,* or high priest, an emperor would make sacrifices as offerings to the gods at important festivals.

figs

DEADLY FRUIT
Who killed Augustus, the first Roman emperor, in AD14? It is hard to say. It might have been a natural death... but then again, it might have been caused by his wife Livia. She was said to have coated the figs in his garden with a deadly poison. Roman emperors were much feared, but they were surrounded by enemies and could trust no one, least of all their own families.

PRAETORIAN GUARDS
The Praetorian Guards were the emperor's personal bodyguards. They wore special uniforms and were well paid. The guards were the only armed soldiers allowed within the city of Rome and so became very powerful. They also intervened in politics—assassinating the Emperor Caligula and electing his successor, Claudius.

In Rome, wreaths made from leaves of the laurel tree were worn by emperors, victorious soldiers and athletes. The wreath was a badge of honor. The Romans copied the idea from the ancient Greeks.

WREATH OF HONOR
You will need: tape measure, garden wire, pliers, scissors, clear tape, green ribbon, laurel leaves (real or fake).

1 Measure around your head with the tape measure. Cut some wire the same length, so the wreath will fit you. Bend the wire as shown and tape the ribbon around it.

2 Start to tape the leaves by their stems onto the wire, as shown above. Work your way around to the middle of the wire, fanning out the leaves as you go.

3 Then reverse the direction of the leaves and work your way around the rest of the wire. Fit the finished wreath around your head. Hail, Caesar!

Roman Society

ROMAN SOCIETY was never very fair. At first, a group of rich and powerful noble families, called the patricians, controlled the city and the Senate. Anyone who wanted their voice heard had to persuade a senator to speak on their behalf. Over the centuries the common citizens, known as plebeians, became more powerful until, by 287BC, they shared equally in government. Eventually, in the days of the Empire, even people of humble birth could become emperor, provided they were wealthy or had the support of the army. Emperors always feared riots by the common people of Rome, so they tried to keep the people happy with handouts of free food and lavish entertainments. Roman women had little power outside the family and could not vote. However, many were successful in business or had an important influence on political events. Slaves had very few rights, though Roman society depended on slave labor. Prisoners of war were bought and sold as slaves and many were treated cruelly, making slave revolts common.

A ROMAN CONSUL
This is a statue of a Roman consul, or leader of the Senate, in the days of the republic. At first, only the noble, and often wealthy, ruling class could be senators. However, under the emperors, the power and influence of the Senate slowly grew less and less.

LIFE AS A SLAVE
The everyday running of the Empire depended on slavery. This mosaic shows a young slave boy carrying fruit. In about AD100, a wealthy family might have had as many as 500 slaves. Some families treated their slaves well, and slaves who gave good service might earn their freedom. However, many more led miserable lives, toiling in the mines or laboring in the fields.

SLAVE TAG
This bronze disc was probably worn around the neck of a slave, like a dog-tag. The Latin words on it say: "Hold me, in case I run away, and return me to my master Viventius on the estate of Callistus." Slaves had few rights and could be branded on the forehead or leg as the property of their owners.

COLLECTING TAXES

This stone carving probably shows people paying their annual taxes. Officials counted the population of the Empire and registered them for paying tax. Money from taxes paid for the army and the government. However, many of the tax collectors took bribes, and even emperors seized public money to add to their private fortunes.

ARISTOCRATS

This Italian painting from the 1700s imagines how a noble Roman lady might dress after bathing. Wealthy people had personal slaves to help them bathe, dress and fix their hair. Household slaves were sometimes almost part of the family, and their children might be brought up and educated with their owner's children.

Country Life

THE FIRST ROMANS mostly lived by farming. Even when Rome had become a big city, Roman poets still liked to sing the praises of the countryside. In reality, country life was quite hard. Oxen were used for ploughing. Grain crops were harvested with a sickle, and flour was often ground by hand. Water had to be fetched by hand from the farm's well or a nearby spring.

Many farms were very small. They were often run by retired soldiers, who would raise chickens and geese and perhaps a cow or pig. They would also keep bees and grow olives and a few vegetables.

Other farms in Italy and across the Empire were large estates set up to provide incomes for their wealthy landowners. These estates might have their own olive presses, reaping machines and stores for drying grain. An estate was often laid out around a large, luxurious house or villa. Other villas were grand country houses owned by rich and powerful Romans.

A COUNTRY ESTATE
Life on a country estate was always busy, as this mosaic of a Roman villa in Tunisia, North Africa, shows. North African country estates supplied Rome with vast amounts of grain, fruit and vegetables. The good soil, combined with hot summers and rain in winter, made farming easy.

HADRIAN'S VILLA
One of the grandest country houses of all was built for the Emperor Hadrian between AD124 and 133. Parts of the villa still stand today, as this view of one of its lakeside walks shows. The luxurious villa itself stood on a hilltop, with Rome just visible in the distance. Built on land that belonged to Hadrian's family, the villa had pavilions and pools, terraces, banquet halls, theaters and libraries. All around the villa were parks filled with trees, such as laurels, planes and pines, exotic shrubs and formal flowerbeds. Hadrian designed the villa as a vacation palace where he could escape from the cares of government, but he died just four years after it was completed.

HUNTING WILD BOAR

Hunting scenes often decorated the walls of country villas. The hunt was a favorite pastime for young noblemen or army officers visiting the countryside. A wild boar, like the one shown in this mosaic, was one of the most dangerous animals of all when it charged.

FOOD FOR ROME

Rome needed huge amounts of food for all its people. Vegetables, such as leeks, celery, cabbage, beans and peas, were grown at market gardens around the city. Grain crops included wheat, barley, oats and rye. Grapes were made into wine and, as there was no sugar, honey was used to sweeten foods.

grapes

wheat

honey

GROVES OF OLIVE TREES

Olives were, and still are, an important crop in the lands around the Mediterranean. They were grown on small farms as well as on large estates. The oil was pressed and stored in large pottery jars. It was used for cooking or burned in oil lamps.

PLOUGHING THE LAND

This ploughman from Roman Britain is using a heavy wooden plough drawn by oxen. Large areas of Europe were still covered with thick forests in the days of the Roman Empire. Gradually farmers cleared land to plough, and farmland and orchards spread across the countryside.

Town and City

MANY OF THE TOWNS in Italy and the lands surrounding the Mediterranean Sea were already old and well established when the Romans invaded. Under Roman rule these towns prospered and grew. In other parts of Europe, where people had never lived in a big town, the Roman invaders built impressive new cities.

Roman towns had straight, paved roads planned on a grid pattern. Some were broad streets with pavements. Others were alleys just wide enough for a donkey. Most streets were busy with noisy crowds, street merchants, carts and rowdy bars. The streets divided the buildings into blocks called *insulae*, which means islands. The homes of wealthy families were spacious and comfortable. Poorer Romans often lived in apartment blocks that were badly built, crowded and in constant danger of burning down.

Fresh water was brought into towns through a system of channels called an aqueduct. The water was piped to fountains, public baths and to the homes of the wealthy.

THE STREETS OF POMPEII
On August 24, AD79, the volcano Vesuvius erupted violently, burying the Roman town of Pompeii in ash and lava. Work began in 1748 to excavate the ancient town, and its streets, shops and houses have slowly been revealed. In this excavated street, the deep ruts in the road made by cart wheels are clearly visible. Streets were often filled with mud and filth, so stepping-stones were laid for pedestrians to cross.

AN AQUEDUCT BRIDGE

You will need: ruler, pencil, scissors, thick and thin cardboard, white glue, paintbrush, masking tape, modeling clay, plaster of Paris, acrylic paints, water bowl.

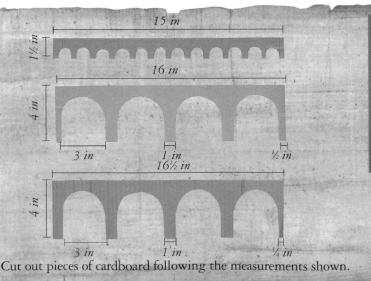

15 in

1½ in

16 in

4 in

3 in   1 in   ½ in
16½ in

4 in

3 in   1 in   ¼ in

Cut out pieces of cardboard following the measurements shown.

1 Draw and cut out the shapes of the arches from the thick cardboard. You need to cut out a pair for each level of the aqueduct— top, middle and bottom.

AQUEDUCTS

Water was carried into Roman towns and cities through a system of channels and pipes called aqueducts. Most of these were underground. Sometimes they were supported on high arches, such as this one, which still stands today in France. The water came from fresh springs, streams and lakes.

HERCULANEUM

The volcanic eruption that buried Pompeii caused a mud flow that buried a nearby coastal town, Herculaneum. Here, too, archaeologists have discovered houses, public baths, shops and workshops side by side on the city's streets. This view shows how crowded parts of the town were, with narrow paved streets separating the buildings.

CITY PLAN

This aerial view of Pompeii clearly shows how Roman streets were laid out on a grid pattern.

Forum baths

Stabian baths

amphitheater

sports ground

N

large theater

market

Forum

Capitol

| 0 | 200 | 400m |
| 0 | 200 | 400yds |

Aqueducts were built at a slight slope to ensure a steady flow of water. Arched bridges carried them across river valleys. The water flowed along a channel at the top of the bridge.

2 Cut strips of cardboard in three widths—1½ in, 1 in and ¾ in. These are for the insides of the arches. Use glue and tape to attach the 1½ in strips to the bottom.

3 Glue on the other side of the bottom level. Attach it with tape. Cut a top section from cardboard and glue and tape this on. Make the two other levels in the same way.

4 Roll the modeling clay into buttresses and wrap with cardboard. Attach these to the three central arches of the bottom level. These will support the aqueduct bridge.

5 Glue the levels together. Cover the model with plaster of Paris and mark on a brick pattern. Let dry. Paint the arches gray. Paint a blue channel of 'water' on top.

House and Garden

ONLY WEALTHY ROMANS could afford to live in a private house. A typical town house was designed to look inward, with the rooms arranged around a central courtyard and a walled garden. Outside walls had few windows and these were small and shuttered. The front door opened onto a short passage leading into an airy courtyard called an *atrium*. Front rooms on either side of the passage were usually used as bedrooms. Sometimes they were used as workshops or shops, having shutters that opened out onto the street.

The center of the atrium was open to the sky. Below this opening was a pool, set into the floor, to collect rainwater. Around the atrium were more bedrooms and the kitchen. If you were a guest or had important business you would be shown into the *tablinium*. The dining room, or *triclinium*, was often the grandest room of all. The very rich sometimes also had a summer dining room, which looked onto the garden.

Houses were made of locally available building materials. These might include stone, mud bricks, cement and timber. Roofs were made of clay tiles.

garden

bedroom

tablinium (living room and office)

LOCKS AND KEYS
This was the key to the door of a Roman house. Pushed in through a keyhole, the prongs at the end of the key fitted into holes in the bolt in the lock. The key could then be used to slide the bolt along and unlock the door.

INSIDE A ROMAN HOME
The outside of a wealthy Roman's town house was usually quite plain, but inside it was highly decorated with elaborate wall paintings and intricate mosaics. The rooms were sparsely furnished, with couches or beds, small side tables, benches and folding stools. There were few windows, but high ceilings and wide doors made the most of the light from the open atrium and the garden.

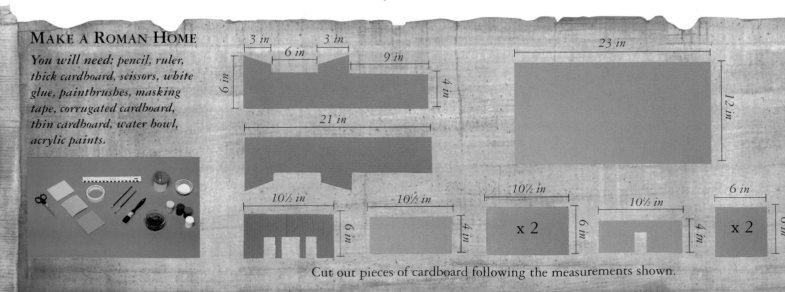

MAKE A ROMAN HOME
You will need: pencil, ruler, thick cardboard, scissors, white glue, paintbrushes, masking tape, corrugated cardboard, thin cardboard, water bowl, acrylic paints.

3 in   6 in   3 in   9 in   4 in

6 in   21 in   23 in   12 in

10½ in   10½ in   10½ in   10½ in   6 in

6 in   4 in   x 2   6 in   4 in   x 2   6 in

Cut out pieces of cardboard following the measurements shown.

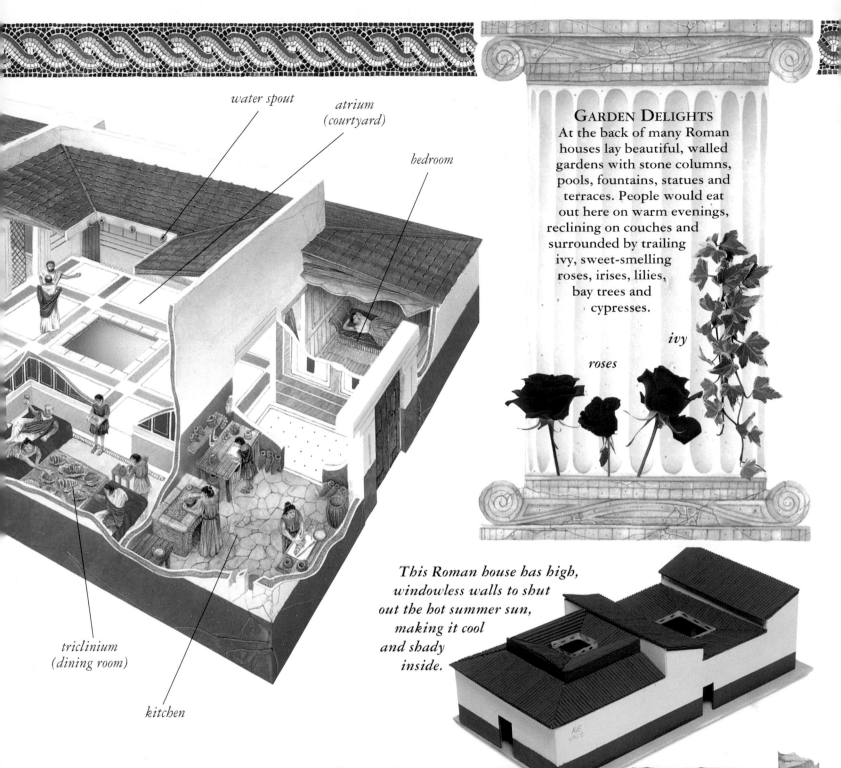

water spout

atrium (courtyard)

bedroom

triclinium (dining room)

kitchen

GARDEN DELIGHTS
At the back of many Roman houses lay beautiful, walled gardens with stone columns, pools, fountains, statues and terraces. People would eat out here on warm evenings, reclining on couches and surrounded by trailing ivy, sweet-smelling roses, irises, lilies, bay trees and cypresses.

ivy

roses

This Roman house has high, windowless walls to shut out the hot summer sun, making it cool and shady inside.

1 Cut out the pieces of thick cardboard. Edge each piece with glue. Press the pieces together and reinforce with tape, as shown. You have now made the walls of your house.

2 Measure your model and cut out pieces of corrugated cardboard for the roofs. Stick them together with glue, as shown above. Paint the roofs red.

3 Rainwater running down the sloped atrium roof was directed into a pool below by gutters and water spouts. Make gutters from strips of thin cardboard, with holes as spouts.

4 Paint the house walls as shown, using masking tape to get a straight line. Glue on the roofs. Why not finish off your Roman house with some authentic graffiti!

209

Home Comforts

ROMAN HOUSES were less cluttered with furniture than our own. People kept their clothes in cupboards and wooden chests rather than in closets or drawers. Wooden or metal stools were used more than chairs. Couches were the most important piece of furniture, used for resting, eating and receiving visitors. Roman furniture was often simple, but rich people could afford fine, hand-crafted tables or benches made from wood, marble or bronze. Dining tables were very low, because wealthy Romans ate their evening meal lying on couches. Beds were often made of wood, with slats or ropes to support the mattress and pillows, which were stuffed with wool or straw.

Lighting in both rich and poor homes came from many small, flickering oil lamps made from clay or bronze. Heating came from charcoal burned in open braziers. The most luxurious houses were warmed by underfloor central heating, especially in colder parts of the Empire.

INTERIOR DECORATION
The walls, ceilings and floors of Roman houses were covered with paintings, mosaics and molded plaster reliefs. Elaborate scenes were painted directly onto the walls, while bright patterns in tiles and mosaics decorated the floor.

UNDERFLOOR HEATING
A furnace, burning wood or charcoal, heated the air beneath the floor. The hot air circulated around pillars of brick or tile that supported the floor. It also flowed up inside the walls through special channels. This kept the whole room warm. Slaves would keep the furnace stoked up.

mosaic-covered floor warmed from below

outside furnace with stokehole at front

A HYPOCAUST
Roman underfloor heating is called a hypocaust. These are the remains of the hypocaust at the palace of Fishbourne in England. Only wealthy Romans could afford this early form of central heating, and many only had it in the dining room.

hot air from the furnace flows under the floor and up inside the walls

HOUSEHOLD SHRINE

The *lararium*, or household shrine, was a small private altar containing images of the family's ancestors. It was usually situated in the *atrium* at the center of the house. Every day the family would honor their ancestors by burning incense at the shrine.

DINNER IS SERVED

These are guests at a banquet in Roman Germany. Only country folk, foreigners and slaves ate sitting upright at the table. Tables and chairs were usually made of wood and might be carved or painted. There were also woven wicker armchairs. Wealthy Romans ate lying on couches around a central low table.

LAMPLIGHT

Roman homes glowed with the soft light of candles and oil lamps. Lamps were made of pottery or bronze, like this one. They came in many different designs, but they all had a central well containing olive oil. The oil was soaked up by a wick, which provided a steady flame. Sometimes lamps would be grouped together or hung from a tall lampstand.

A LUXURY TO LIE ON

This beautifully decorated bed is made from wood inlaid with ivory and semi-precious stones. It dates back to about 50BC, and was discovered in the remains of a villa in Italy. The villa had been buried under ash from a volcanic eruption. Beds, or couches for sleeping on, were much higher than ours are today and people needed steps or a stool to get up on them.

In the Kitchen

W HEN A LARGE MEAL was being prepared, slaves would have to carry water and fresh kindling for the fire into the kitchen. As the fires were lit, the room would become quite smoky because there was no chimney. Soon the coals would be glowing red hot and pots would be boiling on trivets and griddles on the raised brick stove. Food was boiled, fried, grilled and stewed. Larger kitchens might include stone ovens for baking bread or spits for roasting meat. A few even had piped hot water.

The kitchens of wealthy Romans were well equipped with all kinds of bronze pots, pans, strainers and ladles. Pottery storage jars held wine, olive oil and sauces. Herbs, vegetables and cuts of meat hung from hooks in the roof. There were no airtight containers, and no fridges or freezers to keep food fresh. Food had to be preserved in oil or by drying, smoking, salting or pickling.

mortar

VALUABLE GLASS
This glass bottle or pitcher was made about 1,900 years ago. Precious liquids or expensive perfumes were sold in bottles like this throughout the Empire. When a bottle was empty, it was far too valuable to throw away, so it was often reused to store food such as honey in the kitchen.

MORTAR AND PESTLE
The Romans liked spicy food. Roman cooks used a mortar and pestle to grind up foods, such as nuts, herbs and spices, into a paste. Both pieces were usually made of a very tough pottery or stone. The rough inside of the mortar was made of coarse grit to help grind the food.

pestle

A ROMAN KITCHEN

You will need: pencil, ruler, cardboard, scissors, paintbrush, white glue, masking tape, water bowl, acrylic paints, red felt tip pen, plaster of Paris, balsa wood, sandpaper, self-drying clay, work board, modeling tool.

1 Cut out the walls and floor of the kitchen from cardboard, as shown. Glue the edges and press them together. Reinforce the walls with pieces of masking tape.

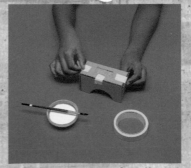

2 Paint the floor gray. When dry, use the ruler and pencil to draw on stone flags. Paint the walls yellow, edged with blue. When dry, use the felt tip pen to draw stripes.

3 Cut out pieces of cardboard to make a stove about ¾ in long, 2 in wide and 1½ in high. Glue the pieces together and reinforce with masking tape, as shown above.

READY FOR THE COOK

Herbs brought fresh from the garden included cilantro, oregano, rue, mint, thyme and parsley. Food was spiced with pepper, caraway, aniseed, mustard seeds and saffron. On the table there might be eggs, grapes, figs and nuts. Much of our knowledge of Roman cooking comes from recipes collected by a Roman gourmet called Apicius nearly 2,000 years ago.

saffron

thyme

mint

quails' eggs

BAKING PAN

This bronze tray was probably used as a mold for baking honey cakes, buns or pastries. The long handle makes it easier to remove from a hot oven. It may also have been used to cook eggs.

STRAINER

This bronze strainer was used by Roman cooks to strain sauces. It was made using the same design as a saucepan, but its bowl has been pierced with an intricate pattern. The hole in the handle was used to hang it from a hook on the wall.

SAUCEPAN

Like many Roman kitchen utensils, this saucepan is made from bronze. Bronze contains copper, which can give food a very strange flavor—the inside of the saucepan has been coated with silver to prevent this from happening.

Foods in a Roman kitchen were stored in baskets, bowls or sacks. Wine, oil and sauces were stored in pottery jars called amphorae.

4 Coat the stove with plaster of Paris. Let dry. Then, use sandpaper to rub it smooth. Make a grate from two strips of cardboard and four pieces of balsa wood, glued together.

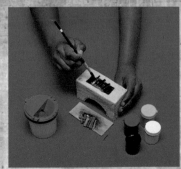

5 Use the acrylic paints to color the stove and the grate, as shown above. Use small pieces of balsa wood to make a pile of wood fuel to store underneath the stove.

6 Make a table and shelves from balsa wood, as shown. Glue them together, and bind with masking tape. Let them dry before painting the pieces brown.

7 Use the clay to form pots, pans, bowls, storage jars, perhaps even a frying pan or an egg poacher. Let the utensils dry before painting them a suitable color.

Food and Drink

FOR POOR ROMANS, a meal was often little more than a hurried bowl of porridge or a crust of bread washed down with sour wine. Many town-dwellers lived in homes without kitchens. They ate take-out meals bought at the many food stalls and bars in town. Even for wealthier people, breakfast might be just a quick snack of bread, honey and olives. Lunch, too, was a light meal, perhaps of eggs or cold meats and fruit. The main meal of the day was *cena*, or dinner. This evening meal might start with shellfish or a salad, followed by a main course of roast meat, such as pork, veal, chicken or goose, with vegetables. It finished with a dessert course of fruit or honey cakes.

More lavish banquets might include fattened dormice, songbirds, flamingos' tongues or a custard made from calves' brains and rose hips! Food was heavily spiced and was often served with a fish sauce called *garum*. Wine was usually mixed with water and sometimes flavored with honey or spices. Guests could take home any tasty morsels that were left over.

SERVING SLAVES
This mosaic shows a slave called Paregorius helping to prepare his master's table for a banquet. On his head he is carrying a tray with plates of food. During a banquet, dishes were brought in a few at a time and set down on a small table. All the food was cooked and served by slaves.

HONEYED DATES

You will need: cutting board, dates, small knife, walnuts, pecans, almonds, hazelnuts, mortar and pestle, salt, 1 cup of honey, frying pan, wooden spoon, a few fresh mint leaves.

1 On the cutting board, slit open the dates with the knife. Remove the pit inside. Be sure not to cut the dates completely in half and be careful with the knife.

2 Put aside the hazelnuts. Chop up the rest of the nuts. Use a mortar and pestle to grind them into smaller pieces. Stuff a small amount into the middle of each date.

3 Pour some of the salt onto the cutting board and lightly roll each date in it. Make sure the dates are coated all over, but do not use too much salt.

CUPS
Pottery cups like this one were used for drinking wine. Many drinking cups had handles and were often highly decorated. Metal cups could make wine taste unpleasant, so colored glass cups and pottery cups were more popular.

THE FAMILY SILVER
These silver spoons were used by a wealthy family in Roman Britain. Food was usually eaten with the fingers, but spoons were used for sauces. At banquets, Romans liked to bring out their best silver tableware as a sign of status.

AT A BANQUET
This wall painting shows a typical Roman banquet. Guests usually sat three to a couch. After the meal they were entertained with poetry readings and music, or jokes and jugglers. Dress and table manners were very important at a banquet. Arguments and bad language were not allowed, but it was fine to spit, belch or even eat until you were sick!

4 Over a low heat, melt the honey in the frying pan. Lightly fry the dates for five minutes, turning them with a wooden spoon. Be careful while using the stove.

5 Arrange the stuffed dates in a shallow dish. Sprinkle on the whole hazelnuts, some chopped nuts and a few leaves of fresh mint. Now they are ready to serve to your friends.

The Romans loved sweet dishes made from nuts and dates imported from North Africa. They also used dates to make sauces for savory dishes such as fish and roast duck.

Getting Dressed

MOST ROMAN CLOTHES were made of wool that had been spun and woven by hand at home or in a workshop. Flax was grown in Egypt to make linen, while cotton from India and silk from China were rare and expensive imports. The most common style of clothing was a simple tunic, which was practical for people who led active lives, such as workers, slaves and children. Important men also wore a white robe called a toga. This was a 6-yard length of cloth with a curved edge, wrapped around the body and draped over the shoulder. It was heavy and uncomfortable to wear, but looked very impressive. Women wore a long dress called a *stola*, over an under-tunic. Often they also wore a *palla*—a large shawl that could be arranged in various ways. Girls wore white until they were married, after which they often wore dresses dyed in bright colors.

ROMAN FOOTWEAR
This sandal (*left*) and child's shoe (*far left*) were found in York, in Britain. Most Romans wore open leather sandals. There were many different designs, and some had nailed soles to make them harder wearing. Shoes and boots were worn in the colder parts of the Empire.

DRESSING FOR DIONYSUS
Wall paintings in the homes of wealthy Romans hold many clues about the way people dressed in the Roman world. This scene was found in the Villa of the Mysteries, in Pompeii. It shows young women being prepared as ceremonial brides for Dionysus, the god of wine.

WEAR A TOGA
You will need: old white sheet, tape measure, scissors for cutting cloth and tape, double-sided tape, purple ribbon, long T-shirt, cord.

1 Ask a friend to help you with the toga. Wealthy Romans had slaves to help them put on their togas. Fold the sheet in half along its length. Cut the ends to make rounded corners at each end, as shown. Use double-sided tape to stick the ribbon along the long edge. Put on a long, white T-shirt tied at the waist with cord.

2 This is a simple way to put on a toga. Get your friend to hold the long, straight edge of fabric behind you. Drape about a quarter of the toga over your left arm and shoulder.

WORKERS' CLOTHES

Not all Romans wore flowing robes. This man is probably a farm worker from Roman Germany. He wears strips of cloth around his legs and a hooded leather cloak to protect him from the cold, wet weather. Hooded cloaks like this were exported from Gaul (present-day France) and Britain.

DRESSED TO IMPRESS

This stone carving shows the family of the Emperor Augustus, dressed for an important state occasion. The women are all shown wearing a *stola*, with a *palla* draped around their shoulders or head. The men and boys are shown in togas. A toga could be worn by all free Roman citizens, but only the wealthy upper classes wore it. This was because it took time—and a helping hand—to put on a toga. Once you had it on, it was also quite awkward to move in!

3 Bring the rest of the toga around to the front, passing it under your right arm. Hook the toga up by tucking a few folds of material securely into the cord around your waist.

4 Now your friend can help you fold the rest of the toga neatly over your left arm, as shown above. If you prefer, you could drape it all over your left shoulder.

Boys from wealthy families wore togas edged with a thin purple stripe until they reached the age of 16. They then wore plain togas. A toga with a broad purple stripe was worn by Roman senators. Purple dye was expensive, so the color was only worn by high-ranking citizens.

Fashion and Beauty

A ROMAN LADY would spend most of the morning surrounded by her female slaves. Some would bring her a mirror made of bronze or silver and jars of perfumed oils or ointments. Another slave would comb out her hair—and could expect a spiteful jab with a hairpin if she pulled at a tangle.

Most rich women wanted to look pale—after all, only women who had to work outdoors became sunburned. So chalk, or even a poisonous powder made from white lead, was rubbed into the face. Face packs were made of bread and milk. One remedy for spots and pimples included bird droppings! Lipsticks and blusher were made of red ocher or the sediment from red wine. Eyeshadow was made of ash and saffron. Women's hair was curled, braided or pinned up, according to the latest fashion.

PORTRAIT OF A LADY
This is a portrait of a lady who lived in the Roman province of Egypt. Her earrings and necklace are made of emeralds, garnets and pearls set in gold. They are a sign of her wealth, as they would have been very expensive. Her hair has been curled, and lampblack or soot may have been used to darken her eyelashes and eyebrows.

CARVED COMB
This comb is carved from ivory and is inscribed in Latin with the words "Modestina farewell." Combs of silver and ivory were used to decorate the intricate hairstyles favored by many Roman women. The poor used wooden or bone combs, though more out of need than fashion.

SCENT BOTTLES
These lovely perfume bottles belonged to a Roman lady. The round one is made of hand-blown, gold-banded glass. The other is carved from onyx, a precious stone with layers of different colors.

A GOLDEN HEADDRESS
You will need: tape measure, plain cardboard, pencil, scissors, white glue, paintbrush, string, plastic beads, gold foil wrappers, tape or paper clip.

1 Measure around your head with the tape measure. Draw the shape of the tiara to the same length on cardboard. Also draw outlines for various sizes of leaf shape, as shown.

2 Carefully cut out the tiara outline from the cardboard. Also cut out the leaf shapes. Then cut out the center of each one so that they look a bit like arches.

3 Use the white glue and a paintbrush to paste the shapes securely onto the front of the tiara. These will be part of an elegant pattern for your tiara.

CROWNING GLORY

This lady's elaborately curled hair is almost certainly a wig. Hairpieces and wigs were always popular with wealthy Roman women—a bride would wear at least six layers of artificial hair at her wedding. Wigs of black hair were usually imported from Asia, while blond or red hair came from northern Europe.

MEN'S CHANGING HAIRSTYLES

Roman men were just as concerned with their appearance as women. They usually wore their hair short, either combed forward or curled. They were mostly clean shaven, but beards became fashionable during the reign of the Emperor Hadrian, AD117–138.

A FINE DISPLAY

This picture shows a ceremonial dance at the Temple of the Sun in Rome. Both the men and women are wearing golden headdresses decorated with precious jewels and gold filigree. Lavish displays like this were reserved for grand public occasions to show off the wealth and power of the Empire.

RINGS ON THEIR FINGERS

Both men and women wore jewelry, especially rings. Rich people would wear rings like these, usually made of gold or silver. Emeralds, pearls and amber were also used in rings. The less wealthy would wear rings of bronze.

4 Cut lengths of string and glue them around the inside edges of the shapes. Glue plastic beads at the top of each arch, so that they look like precious stones.

5 Collect gold foil candy wrappers and glue them onto the tiara. Use the end of the paintbrush to carefully poke the foil into all the corners around the beads.

The finished tiara can be held together at the back by tape or a paper clip. Roman ladies liked to wear tiaras made of gold, with jewels in their hair.

Lessons and Learning

MOST CHILDREN in the Roman Empire never went to school. They learned a trade from their parents or found out about sums by trading on a market stall. Boys might be trained to fight with swords or to ride horses, in preparation for joining the army. Girls would be taught how to run the home, in preparation for marriage.

Wealthy families did provide an education for their sons and sometimes for their daughters, too. They were usually taught at home by a private tutor, but there were also small schools. Tutors and schoolmasters would teach children arithmetic, and how to read and write in both Latin and Greek. Clever pupils might also learn public speaking skills, poetry and history. Girls often had music lessons at home, on a harp-like instrument called a lyre.

INKPOTS AND PENS
Pen and ink were used to write on scrolls made from papyrus (a kind of reed) or thin sheets of wood. Ink was often made from soot or lampblack, mixed with water. It was kept in inkpots such as these. Inkpots were made from glass, pottery or metal. Pens were made from bone, reeds or bronze.

WRITING IN WAX
This painting shows a couple from Pompeii. The man holds a parchment scroll. His wife is probably going through their household accounts. She holds a wax-covered writing tablet and a stylus to scratch words into the wax. A stylus had a pointed end for writing and a flat end for erasing.

A WRITING TABLET

You will need: sheets and sticks of balsa wood, craft knife, ruler, white glue, paintbrush, brown acrylic paint, water bowl, modeling clay, work board, rolling pin, modeling tool, skewer, purple thread, pencil (to be used as a stylus), gold paint.

1 Use the craft knife to cut the balsa sheet into two rectangles 4 in x 9 in. The sticks of balsa should be cut into four lengths 9 in long and four lengths 4 in long.

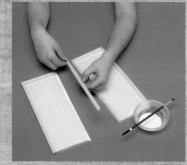

2 Glue the sticks around the edges of each sheet as shown. These form a shallow hollow into which you can press the "wax." Paint the two frames a rich brown color.

3 Roll out the modeling clay on a board and place a balsa frame on top. Use the modeling tool to cut around the outside of the frame. Repeat this step.

TEACHER AND PUPILS

This stone sculpture from Roman Germany shows a teacher seated between two of his pupils. They are reading their lessons from papyrus scrolls. Children had to learn poetry and other writings by heart. Any bad behavior or mistakes were punished with a beating.

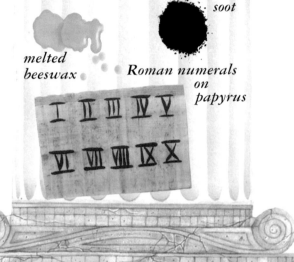

WRITING IT DOWN

Various materials were used for writing. Melted beeswax was poured into wooden trays to make writing tablets. Letters were scratched into the wax, which could be used again and again. Powdered soot was mixed with water and other ingredients to make ink for writing on papyrus, parchment or wood.

soot

melted beeswax

Roman numerals on papyrus

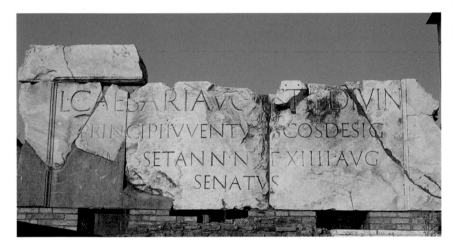

LETTERS IN STONE

Temples, monuments and public buildings were covered in Latin inscriptions, such as this one. Each letter was beautifully chiseled by a stonemason. These words are carved in marble and were made to mark the 14th birthday of Lucius Caesar, the grandson of the Emperor Augustus.

4 Cut off about ½ in all around the edge of each modeling clay rectangle. This helps to make sure that the modeling clay will fit inside the balsa wood frame.

5 Carefully press the clay into each side—this represents the wax. Use the skewer to poke two holes through the inside edge of each frame, as shown.

6 Join the two frames together by threading purple thread through each pair of holes and tying it securely together. You have now made your tablet.

Paint the pencil gold to make it look as if it is made of metal. Use it like a stylus to scratch words on your tablet. Why not try writing in Latin? You could write CIVIS ROMANVS SVM, which means "I am a Roman citizen."

In the Forum

Every large Roman town had a forum—a market square with public buildings around it. This was where people gathered to do business and exchange friendly gossip. In the morning, while the lady of the house had her hair done and her children struggled with their lessons, her husband would walk over to the forum.

In the forum's central square, crowds thronged around market stalls. Sometimes a public fight might break out, as inspectors of weights and measures accused some trader of cheating his customers. Around the square were shops, imposing monuments, marble statues and temples to the gods. The walls of buildings were often scrawled with graffiti made up of political messages, personal insults or declarations of love. On one side of the forum was the basilica, a large building used as the town hall, a court of law and public meeting place. Some of the crowds may have been members of the *curia* or town council, or one of the trade guilds who had their halls there.

Downtown Pompeii
The ruins at Pompeii include these remains of a row of columns. They were part of a two-story colonnade that once took up three sides of the forum. Rows of shops and market stalls were set up behind the colonnade at ground level.

Temples and Prosperity
The forum of every town had splendid temples to the many gods and goddesses of ancient Rome. There were also temples for famous Romans. The grand columns of this temple still remain in the forum at Rome. Today, a Christian church stands behind it. The temple was built in honor of Antoninus Pius, one of Rome's wisest emperors, and his wife Faustina.

MAKING MONEY
Money changers and bankers gathered to make deals and discuss business in the forum. Here, too, tax collectors raised money for the town council—taxes were charged on all goods that passed through the town.

FAST FOOD
As people hurried to work or chatted with friends, they might pick up a snack at a food stall or a street vendor. Pastries filled with spicy meats made popular snacks. On market day, the forum would also be busy with traders and farmers setting up stalls in the central square.

THE BASILICA
This is the Basilica of Maxentius in Rome. A basilica was a huge building used as a cross between a town hall and a court of law. It usually had a very high roof, supported by rows of columns. The columns divided the building into a central area with two side aisles. People came here to work, do business or simply chat with friends.

Shopping—Roman Style

I N MOST LARGE TOWNS, shops spread out from the forum and along the main streets. Shops were usually small, family-run businesses. At the start of the working day, shutters or blinds would be taken from the shop front and goods put on display. Noise would soon fill the air as bakers, butchers, fishmongers, fruit and vegetable sellers all began crying out that their produce was the best and cheapest. Cuts of meat might be hung from a pole, while ready-cooked food, grains or oils would be sold from pots set into a stone counter. Other shops sold pottery lamps or bronze lanterns, kitchen pots and pans or knives, while some traders repaired shoes or laundered cloth. Hammering and banging coming from the workshops at the back added to the clamor of a busy main street.

ROMAN MONEY
The same currency was used throughout the Roman Empire. Coins were made of gold, silver and bronze. Shoppers kept their money in purses made of cloth or leather or in wooden boxes.

HOW'S BUSINESS?
This carving shows merchants discussing prices and profits while an assistant brings out goods from the stockroom. Most Roman shops were single rooms, with stores or workshops at the back.

GOING TO MARKET
This is a view of Trajan's Market, a multistory group of shops set into a hillside in Rome. Most Roman towns had covered halls or central markets like this, where shops were rented out to traders.

A ROMAN DELICATESSEN
About 1,700 years ago this was the place to buy good food in Ostia, the seaport nearest Rome. Bars, inns and cafés had stone counters that were often decorated with colored marble. At lunchtime, bars like this would be busy with customers enjoying a meal.

A BUTCHER'S SHOP
A Roman butcher uses a cleaver to prepare chops while a customer waits for her order. Butchers' shops have changed very little over the ages—pork, lamb and beef were sold, and sausages were popular, too. On the right hangs a steelyard, a metal bar with a pan like a scale, for weighing the meat.

DISHING IT UP
These are the remains of a shop that sold food. Set into the marble counter are big pottery containers, called *dolia*. These were used for displaying and serving up food, such as beans and lentils. They were also used for keeping jars of wine cool on hot summer days. The containers could be covered with wooden or stone lids to keep out the flies.

Pictures and Statues

THE ROMANS loved to decorate their homes and public places with paintings and statues. Mosaics were pictures made using *tesserae*—cubes of stone, pottery or glass—which were pressed into soft cement. Mosaic pictures might show hunting scenes, the harvest or Roman gods. Geometric patterns were popular and often used as borders.

Wall paintings, or murals, often showed garden scenes, birds and animals or heroes and goddesses. They were painted onto wooden panels or directly onto the wall. Roman artists loved to trick the eye by painting false columns, archways and shelves. The Romans were skilled sculptors, using stone, marble and bronze. They imitated the ancient Greeks in putting up marble statues in public places and gardens. These might be of gods and goddesses or emperors and generals.

A COUNTRY SCENE
This man and wild boar are part of a mosaic made in Roman North Africa. Making a mosaic was quite tricky—a lot like doing a jigsaw puzzle. Even so, skilled artists could create lifelike scenes from chips of colored glass, pottery and stone.

SCULPTURE
Statues of metal or stone were often placed in gardens. This bronze figure is in the remains of a house in Pompeii. It is of a faun, a god of the countryside.

FLOOR MOSAICS
Birds, animals, plants and country scenes were popular subjects for mosaics. These parrots are part of a much larger, and quite elaborate, floor mosaic from a Roman house.

MAKE A MOSAIC

You will need: rough paper, pencil, ruler, scissors, large sheet of cardboard, self-drying clay, rolling pin, work board, modeling knife, acrylic paints, paintbrush, water bowl, varnish and brush (optional), plaster of Paris, spreader, muslin rag.

1 Sketch out your mosaic design on rough paper. A design like this one is good to start with. Cut the cardboard so it measures 10 in x 4 in. Copy the design onto it.

2 Roll out the clay on the board. Use the ruler to measure out small squares on the clay. Cut them out with the modeling knife. Let dry. These will be your tesserae.

3 Paint the pieces in batches of different colors, as shown above. When the paint is dry, you can coat them with clear varnish for extra strength and shine. Let dry.

MOSAIC MATERIALS

Mosaics were often made inside frames, in workshops, and then transported to where they were to be used. Sometimes, the tesserae were brought to the site and fitted on the spot by the workers. The floor of an average room in a Roman town house might need over 100,000 pieces.

tesserae

pot shards

MUSICIANS AND DANCERS

This dramatic painting is on the wall of an excavated villa in Pompeii. It is one in a series of paintings that show the secret rites, or mysteries, honoring the god Dionysus.

REAL OR FAKE?

Roman artists liked to make painted objects appear real enough to touch. This bowl of fruit on a shelf is typical of this style of painting. It was found on the wall of a villa that belonged to a wealthy Roman landowner.

4 Spread the plaster of Paris onto the cardboard, a small part at a time. While it is still wet, press in your tesserae following the design, as shown. Use your sketch as a guide.

5 When the mosaic is dry, use the muslin rag to polish up the surface. Any other soft, dry cloth would also be suitable. Now your mosaic is ready for display.

The Romans liked to have mosaics in their homes. Wealthy people often had elaborate mosaics in their courtyards and dining rooms, as these were rooms that visitors would see.

Doctors and Medicine

SOME ROMANS lived to a ripe old age, but most died before they reached the age of 50. Archaeologists have found out a lot about health and disease in Roman times by examining skeletons that have survived. They can tell, for example, how old a person was when they died and their general state of health during their life. Ancient writings also provide information about Roman medical knowledge.

Roman doctors knew very little science. They healed the sick through a mixture of common sense, trust in the gods and magic. Most cures and treatments had come to Rome from the doctors of ancient Greece. The Greeks and Romans also shared the same god of healing, Aesculapius. There were doctors in most parts of the Empire, as well as midwives, dentists and eye specialists. Surgeons operated on wounds received in battle, on broken bones and even skulls. The only pain killers were made from poppy juice—an operation must have been a terrible ordeal.

GODDESS OF HEALTH
Greeks and Romans honored the daughter of the god Aesculapius as a goddess of health. She was called Hygieia. The word hygienic, which comes from her name, is still used today to mean free of germs.

A CHEMIST'S SHOP
This pharmacy, or chemist's shop, is run by a woman. This was quite unusual for Roman times, as women were rarely given positions of responsibility. Roman pharmacists collected herbs and often mixed them for doctors.

MEDICINE BOX
Boxes like this one would have been used by Roman doctors to store various drugs. Many of the treatments used by doctors were herbal, and not always pleasant to take.

MEDICAL INSTRUMENTS
The Romans used a variety of surgical and other instruments. These are made in bronze and include a scalpel, forceps and a spatula for mixing and applying various ointments.

TAKING THE CURE

These are the ruins of a medical clinic in Asia Minor (present-day Turkey). It was built around AD150, in honor of Aesculapius, the god of healing. Clinics like this one were known as therapy buildings. People would come to them seeking cures for all kinds of ailments.

BATHING THE BABY

This stone carving from Rome shows a newborn baby being bathed. The Romans were well aware of the importance of regular bathing in clean water. However, childbirth itself was dangerous for both mother and baby. Despite the dangers, the Romans liked to have large families, and many women died giving birth.

HERBAL MEDICINE

Doctors and traveling healers sold all kinds of potions and ointments. Many were made from herbs such as rosemary, sage and fennel. Other natural remedies included garlic, mustard and cabbage. Many of the remedies would have done little good, but some of them did have the power to heal.

garlic

sage

rosemary

Keeping Clean

tepidarium (warm room)

THE ROMANS may not have all enjoyed good health, but they did like to keep clean. There were public toilets, flushed with constantly flowing water, and people regularly visited public baths. Most towns, even military bases on the frontiers of the Empire, had public bath houses.

The baths were more than just places to wash in. Bathers would meet their friends and spend the afternoon gossiping, in between dips in the bathing pools. Others would exercise, play ball games or just relax. Businessmen even held meetings at the baths. Men and women used separate rooms or visited the bath house at different times. Slaves would bring bath towels and wooden-soled sandals. Bathers needed the sandals because many of the rooms had hot floors heated by a system of underfloor heating.

OIL FLASK AND STRIGILS
Romans used olive oil instead of soap. They would rub themselves with oil and scrape it off with a curved metal tool called a strigil. The oil would be kept in a small flask, like this one, which has two strigils chained to it.

warm air ducts in walls

BATHING AT BATH
This is a view of the Roman baths in the town of Bath, in Britain. The Romans built the baths there because of the natural hot spring, which bubbled up from the rocks at temperatures of up to 122°F. Rich in health-giving minerals, it attracted visitors from far and wide. This large lead-lined pool was used for swimming. In Roman times, it was covered by a roof.

frigidarium (cold room)

caldarium (hot room)

hot air from furnace

furnace

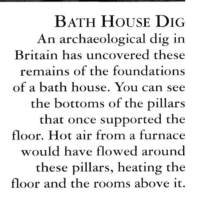

BATH HOUSE DIG
An archaeological dig in Britain has uncovered these remains of the foundations of a bath house. You can see the bottoms of the pillars that once supported the floor. Hot air from a furnace would have flowed around these pillars, heating the floor and the rooms above it.

THE BATHS
The public baths included exercise areas, changing rooms, a sauna and various pools. The rooms and water were heated by hot air from one or more underground furnaces. The *frigidarium*, or cold room, usually had an unheated pool for bathers to take an icy plunge and was often partly open-air. It led onto a warmer area, the *tepidarium*. In the warmth, bathers would rub themselves with oil, then scrape off any dirt or grime. When they were clean, they were ready to take a dip in the pool. The steamy *caldarium*, or hot room, was nearest to a furnace. Here, bathers could soak or sweat to their hearts' content.

PUBLIC TOILETS
The remains of public toilets like these have been found in many parts of the Empire. People used sponges on sticks to clean themselves. They could rinse the sponges in a channel of flowing water in front of them. Another channel of water, under the stone seats, carried away the waste.

Sport and Combat

MOST ROMANS preferred watching sport rather than taking part themselves. There were some, however, who enjoyed athletics and keeping fit. They took their exercise at the public baths and at the sports ground or *palaestra*. Men would compete at wrestling, long jump and swimming. Women would work out with weights.

Boxing matches and chariot races were always well attended. The races took place on a long, oval racetrack, called a circus. The crowds would watch with such excitement that violent riots often followed. Charioteers and their teams became big stars. Roman crowds also enjoyed watching displays of cruelty. Bloody battles between gladiators and fights among wild animals took place in a special oval arena, called an amphitheater. Roman entertainments became more spectacular and bloodthirsty as time passed. They would even flood the arenas of amphitheaters for mock sea battles.

A COLOSSEUM
This is the colosseum in the Roman city of El Djem, in Tunisia. A colosseum was a kind of amphitheater. Arenas such as this were built all over the Empire. The largest and most famous is the Colosseum in Rome.

DEATH OR MERCY?
Gladiators usually fought to the death, but a wounded gladiator could appeal for mercy. The excited crowd would look for the emperor's signal. A thumbs-up meant his life was spared. A thumbs-down meant he must die.

COME ON YOU REDS!
Charioteers belonged to teams and wore their team's colors when they raced. Some also wore protective leather helmets, like the one in this mosaic. In Rome, there were four teams—the Reds, Blues, Whites and Greens. Each team had faithful fans, and charioteers were every bit as popular as football stars are today.

A DAY AT THE RACES
This terra-cotta carving records an exciting moment at the races. Chariot racing was a passion for most Romans. Chariots were usually pulled by four horses, though just two or as many as six could be used. Accidents and foul play were common as the chariots thundered around the track.

THE CHAMP
Boxing was a deadly sport. Fighters, like this boxer, wore studded thongs instead of padded boxing gloves. Severe injuries, and even brain damage, were probably quite common.

THE GREEK IDEAL
The Romans admired all things Greek, including their love of athletics. This painted Greek vase dates from about 333BC and shows long-distance runners. However, Roman crowds were not interested in athletic contests in the Greek style, such as the Olympic Games.

Music and Drama

MUSIC AND SONGS were an important part of Roman life. Music was played at banquets, at weddings and funerals, at the theater, in the home and at fights between gladiators and other public events. The Romans played a variety of musical instruments, including double flutes, panpipes, lyres, cymbals, rattles and tambourines. These had already been well known in either Egypt or Greece. The Romans also had trumpets and horns, and water-powered organs.

Going to the theater was a popular Roman pastime. The whole idea of drama came from Greece, so Greek comedies and tragedies were often performed. Roman writers produced plays in a similar style, as well as comic sketches and dances. The stage used the stone front of a building as a backdrop. Rising banks of stone or wooden seats curved around it in a half circle.

MUSIC LESSONS
Girls from wealthy families often had music lessons at home. This wall painting shows a girl being taught to play the *cithara*, a type of lyre. The Romans adopted this harp-like instrument from the Greeks.

THE ENTERTAINERS
This mosaic from Pompeii shows a group of actors in a scene from a Greek play. Actors were always men, playing the parts of women whenever necessary. The role of actors in a play was shown by the colors of their costume and their masks. The piper in this mosaic is wearing the white mask of a female character.

MAKE A MASK

You will need: self-drying clay, work board, rolling pin, large bowl, modeling knife, acrylic paints, paintbrush, water bowl, scissors, cord, pencil, green paper or cardboard, gardening wire, some colored beads.

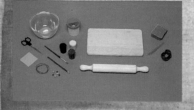

1 Put the clay on the board. Roll it out into a sheet that is bigger than the large bowl you are using. Drape it over the bowl and shape it, as shown above.

2 Trim off the edges and cut out eye holes and a mouth. Roll out the clay you trimmed off and cut out a mouth and nose piece, as shown above. Make a small ball of clay, too.

3 Mold the nose onto the mask. Press the small ball of clay into the chin and put the mouth piece over it, as shown. Make a hole on each side of the mask, for the cord.

MUSICIANS

Some of the musicians in this procession are playing the *cornu*, a large curved horn. It was played at religious festivals and funerals, at public games, and by the Roman army.

ACTORS' MASKS

Roman actors wore masks and wigs to show the type of character they were playing. This detail of a mosaic from Rome shows the kind of elaborate masks they wore.

DRAMA IN THE OPEN AIR

Roman theaters were usually open to the sky. These are the ruins of the larger of the two theaters in Pompeii. It could seat up to 50,000 people. It had no roof, but could be covered by an awning to protect the audience from the hot summer sun.

4 When the clay is dry, paint the mask in bright colors. You can paint it like this one, shown above, or you could make up your own design. Let the paint dry.

5 Cut two lengths of cord. Thread them through the holes in the sides of the mask, as shown. Secure with a knot. Tie the cord around your head when you wear the mask.

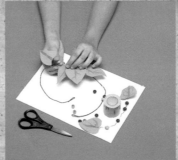

6 Draw, cut out and paint leaf shapes. Thread them onto a length of wire, as shown. Thread beads between some of the leaves. Wind the wire around the top of the mask.

Actors' masks had large mouths for them to speak through. The actual masks were probably made of shaped and stiffened linen.

235

Fun and Games

ROMAN CHILDREN played games such as hide-and-seek, marbles and hopscotch, which are still popular today. Young children played with dolls and little figures of people and animals. These were made of wood, clay or bronze. A child from a wealthy family might be given a child-size chariot, to be pulled along by a goat.

Roman men and women loved playing board games. There were simple games, similar to tic-tac-toe, and more complicated games, a lot like chess or checkers. In some games, players had to race toward the finish. Dice were thrown to decide how many squares they could move at a time. They played with markers made of bone, glass or clay.

The Romans were great gamblers. They would place bets on a chariot race or a cockfight or on throwing dice. Gambling became such a problem that games of chance were officially banned—except during the winter festival of Saturnalia, when most rules were relaxed. However, the rattle of dice could still be heard in most taverns and public baths.

Two women play the popular game of knucklebones, or *astragali*. The idea was to throw the knucklebones in the air and catch as many of them as possible on the back of your hand. The number you caught was your score.

KNUCKLEBONES
Most Romans used the ankle bones of sheep to play knucklebones. These had six sides and were also used as dice—each side had a different value. Wealthy Romans might use knucklebones made of glass, bronze or onyx, like these.

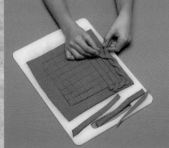

MARBLES
Roman children played with these marbles many centuries ago. Two are glass and one is made of pottery. Marbles were either rolled together or onto marked game-boards. They were also thrown into pottery vases. Nuts, such as hazelnuts and walnuts, were often used like marbles.

MAKE A ROMAN GAME

You will need: self-drying clay, rolling pin, cutting board, modeling knife, ruler, glass tiles for making mosaics, two beads (in the same colors as your tiles).

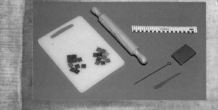

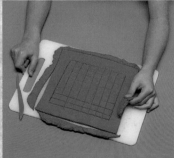

1 Roll out the clay and trim it to about 10 in square. Use the ruler and knife to mark out a grid, 8 squares across and down, leaving a border around the edge.

2 Decorate the border using the clay you trimmed off, as shown above. Let dry. Each player chooses a color and has 16 tiles and a bead—this is the *dux* or leader.

3 Players take turns putting their tiles on any squares, two at a time. The *dux* is put on last. Players now take turns moving a tile one square forward, backward or sideways.

JUST ROLLING ALONG

Children from poor families had few toys and had to work from a young age. However, even poor children found time to play, and made do with whatever was at hand. This boy is rolling wheels in front of him as he runs.

YOUR THROW!

This mosaic from Roman North Africa shows three men playing dice games in a tavern. The Romans loved to gamble and would bet on anything, including the roll of the dice. Large amounts could be won or lost when the dice stopped rolling.

MARKERS

These gaming markers are made of bone and ivory. As well as using quite plain, round ones, the Romans liked to use markers carved in intricate shapes. Here you can see a ram's head, a hare and a lobster. The large round marker has two women carved on it.

DICE

Dice games were played by the poor and the rich. These dice have survived over the centuries. The largest is made of greenstone, the next is made of rock crystal, and the smallest is agate. The silver dice in the form of squatting figures were probably used by wealthy Romans.

4 If you sandwich your opponent's tile between two of yours, it is captured and removed. You then get an extra turn. The *dux* is captured in the same way as any tile.

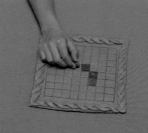

5 The *dux* can also jump over a tile to an empty square, as shown. If your opponent's tile is then trapped between your *dux* and one of your tiles, it is captured.

During the game, you must move a tile or dux if it is possible to do so—even if it means being captured. The winner is the first player to capture all of the other player's tiles and dux.

Religions and Festivals

THE ROMANS believed in many different gods and goddesses. Some of them were the same as the gods of ancient Greece, but with different names. Jupiter, the sky god, was the most powerful of all. Venus was the goddess of love, Mars was the god of war, Ceres the god of the harvest, Saturn the god of farmers, and Mercury of merchants. Household gods protected the home. Splendid temples were built in honor of the gods. The Pantheon, in Rome, is the largest and most famous. Special festivals for the gods were held during the year, with processions, music, offerings and animal sacrifices. The festivals were often public holidays. The mid-winter festival of Saturnalia, in honor of Saturn, lasted up to seven days.

As the Empire grew, many Romans adopted the religions of other peoples, such as the Egyptians and the Persians.

JUPITER
Jupiter was the chief god of the Romans. He was the all-powerful god of the sky. The Romans believed he showed his anger by hurling a thunderbolt to the ground.

THE PANTHEON
The Pantheon in Rome was a temple to all the gods. It was built between AD118 and 128. Its mosaic floor, interior columns and high dome still remain exactly as they were built.

DIANA THE HUNTRESS
Diana was the goddess of hunting and the Moon. In this detail from a floor mosaic, she is shown poised with a bow and arrow, ready for the hunt. Roman gods were often the same as the Greek ones, but were given different names. Diana's Greek name was Artemis.

A TEMPLE TO THE GODS

You will need: thick stiff cardboard, thin cardboard, old newspaper, scissors, balloon, white glue, ruler, pencils, masking tape, drinking straws, acrylic paints, paintbrush, water bowl, plasticine.

dome base — 7 in

portico — 2 in, 2 in, 5 in, 8½ in

roof — 6 in, 1 in

roof — 1 in, 3 in, 3 in, ½ in, ½ in, 5 in

base — 7 in, 3½ in, 3 in, 5 in, 5½ in, 6 in, 1 in

Cut out pieces of cardboard following the measurements shown.

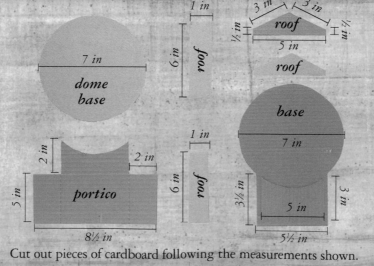

1 Blow up the balloon. Cover it in strips of newspaper pasted on with glue. Keep pasting until you have a thick layer. Leave to dry. Then burst the balloon and cut out a dome.

238

PRIESTS OF ISIS

The Egyptian mother-goddess Isis had many followers throughout the Roman Empire. This painting shows priests and worshippers of Isis taking part in a water purification ceremony. The ceremony would have been performed every afternoon.

BLESS THIS HOUSE

This is a bronze statue of a *lar* or household god. Originally gods of the countryside, the *lares* were believed to look after the family and the home. Every Roman home had a shrine to the *lares*. The family, including the children, would make daily offerings to the gods.

MITHRAS THE BULL-SLAYER

Mithras was the Persian god of light. He is shown here, in a marble relief from a temple, slaying a bull. This bull's blood was believed to have brought life to the earth. The cult of Mithras spread through the whole Empire, and was particularly popular with Roman soldiers. However, only men were allowed to worship Mithras.

The Pantheon was built of brick and then covered in stone and marble. Its huge dome, with a diameter of over 43 yards, was the largest ever constructed until the 1900s.

2 Put the dome on its card base and draw its outline. Cut out the center of the base to make a halo shape. Make a hole in the top of the dome. Bind the pieces together, as shown.

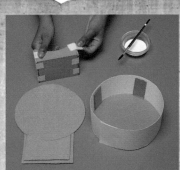

3 Glue together the base pieces. Cut a piece of thin cardboard long enough to go around the base circle. This will be the circular wall. Use tape to hold the portico in shape.

4 Cut some straws into eight pieces, each 2 in long. These will be the columns for the entrance colonnade. Glue together the roof for the entrance. Secure with tape.

5 Glue together the larger pieces, as shown. Position each straw column with a small piece of plasticine at its base. Glue on the entrance roof. Paint your model.

Family Occasions

THE FAMILY was very important to Romans. The father was the all-powerful head of the family, which included everyone in the household—wife, children, slaves and even close relatives. In the early days of Rome, a father had the power of life and death over his children. However, Roman fathers were rarely harsh and children were much loved by both parents.

Childhood was fairly short. Parents would arrange for a girl to be betrothed at the age of 12, and a boy at 14. Marriages took place a few years later. Brides usually wore a white dress and a yellow cloak, with an orange veil and a wreath of sweetly scented flowers. A sacrifice would be made to the gods, and everyone would wish the couple well. That evening, a procession with flaming torches and flute music would lead the newlyweds to their home.

Funerals also featured music and processions. By Roman law, burials and cremations had to take place outside the city walls.

HAPPY FAMILIES
This Roman tombstone from Germany shows a family gathered together for a meal. From the Latin inscription on it, we know that it was put up by a soldier of the legions, in memory of his dead wife. He lovingly describes her as the "sweetest and purest" of women.

MOTHER AND BABY
A mother tenderly places her baby in the cradle. When children were born, they were laid at the feet of their father. If he accepted the child into the family, he would pick it up. In wealthy families, a birth was a great joy, but for poorer families it just meant another mouth to feed. Romans named a girl on the 8th day after the birth, and a boy on the 9th day. The child was given a *bulla*, a charm to ward off evil spirits.

TOGETHERNESS
When a couple became engaged, they would exchange gifts as a symbol of their devotion to each other. A ring like this one might have been given by a man to his future bride. The clasped hands symbolize marriage. Gold pendants with similar patterns were also popular.

MOURNING THE DEAD

A wealthy Roman has died and his family has gone into mourning. Laments are played on flutes as they prepare his body for the funeral procession. The Romans believed that the dead went to Hades, the Underworld, which lay beyond the river of the dead. A coin was placed in the corpse's mouth, to pay the ferryman. Food and drink for the journey were buried with the body.

TILL DEATH US DO PART

A Roman marriage ceremony was a lot like a present-day Christian wedding. The couple would exchange vows and clasp hands to symbolize their union. Here, the groom is holding the marriage contract, which would have been drawn up before the ceremony. Not everyone found happiness, however, and divorce was quite common.

WEDDING FLOWERS

Roman brides wore a veil on their wedding day. This was often crowned with a wreath of flowers. In the early days of the Empire, verbena and sweet marjoram were a popular combination. Later fashions included orange blossom and myrtle, whose fragrant flowers were sacred to Venus, the goddess of love.

orange blossom

verbena

Soldiers of the Legions

THE ARMY OF THE EARLY EMPIRE was divided into 28 groups called legions. Each of these numbered about 5,500 soldiers. The legion included mounted troops and foot-soldiers. They were organized into cohorts of about 500 men, and centuries of about 80 men—even though centuries means "hundreds." Each legion was led into battle by soldiers carrying standards. These were decorated poles that represented the honor and bravery of the legion.

The first Roman soldiers were called up from the wealthier families in times of war. These conscripts had to supply their own weapons. In later years, the Roman army became paid professionals, with legionaries recruited from all citizens. During the period of the Empire, many foreign troops also fought for Rome as auxiliary soldiers.

Army life was tough and discipline was severe. After a long march carrying heavy kits, tents, tools and weapons, the weary soldiers would have to dig camp defenses. A sentry who deserted his post would be beaten to death.

AT WAR
Trajan's Column in Rome is decorated with scenes from the Dacian wars. These were fought in the region of present-day Romania. Scenes like these can tell us much about Roman soldiers, the weapons they used, their enemies and their allies.

A LEGIONARY
This bronze statue of a legionary is about 1,800 years old. He is wearing a crested parade helmet and the overlapping bronze armor of the period. Legionaries underwent strict training and were brutally disciplined. They were tough soldiers and quite a force to be reckoned with.

ON HORSEBACK
Roman foot-soldiers were backed up by mounted troops, or cavalry. They were divided into groups of 500 to 1,000, called *alae*. The cavalry were among the highest paid of Roman soldiers.

RAISING THE STANDARD

The Emperor Constantine addresses his troops, probably congratulating them on a victory. They are carrying standards, emblems of each legion. Standards were decorated with gold eagles, hands, wreaths and banners called *vexilla*. They were symbols of the honor and bravery of the legion and had to be protected at all costs.

A ROMAN FORT

The Roman army built forts of wood or stone all over the Empire. This fort is in southern Britain. It was built to defend the coast against attacks by Saxon raiders from northern Europe. Today, its surrounding area is called Porchester. The name comes from a combination of the word port and *caster*, the Latin word for fort.

HADRIAN'S WALL

This is part of Hadrian's Wall, which marks the most northerly border of the Roman Empire. It stretches for 75 miles across northern England, almost from coast to coast. It was built as a defensive barrier between AD122 and 128, at the command of the Emperor Hadrian.

Weapons and Armor

ROMAN SOLDIERS were well equipped. A legionary was armed with a dagger, called a *pugio*, and a short iron sword, called a *gladius*, which was used for stabbing and slashing. He carried a javelin, or *pilum*, made of iron and wood. In the early days, a foot-soldier's armor was a mail shirt, worn over a short, thick tunic. Officers wore a cuirass, a bronze casing that protected the chest and back. By about AD35, the mail shirt was being replaced by plate armor made of iron. The metal sections were joined by hooks or by leather straps. Officers wore varying crests to show their rank. Early shields were oval, and later ones were oblong with curved edges. They were made of layers of wood glued together, covered in leather and linen. A metal boss, or cover, over the central handle could be used to hit an enemy who got too close.

ROMAN SOLDIERS
Artists over the ages have been inspired by the battles of the Roman legions. They imagined how fully armed Roman soldiers might have looked. This picture shows a young officer giving orders.

HEAD GEAR
Helmets were designed to protect the sides of the head and the neck. This cavalry helmet is made of bronze and iron. It would have been worn by an auxiliary, a foreign soldier fighting for Rome sometime after AD43. Officers wore crests on their helmets, so that their men could see them during battle.

ROMAN ARMOR

You will need: tape measure, sheets of silver cardboard (one or two, depending on how big you are), scissors, pencil, white glue, paintbrush, 2 yards length of cord, compass.

1 Measure yourself around your chest. Cut out three strips of cardboard, 2 in wide and long enough to go around you. Cut out thin strips to stick these three together.

2 Lay the wide strips flat and glue them together with the thin strips, as shown above. The Romans would have used leather straps to hold the wide metal pieces together.

3 When the glue is dry, bend the ends together, silver side out. Make a hole in the end of each strip and thread the cord through, as shown above.

TORTOISE TACTICS

Siege tactics were one of the Roman army's great strengths. When approaching an enemy fortress, a group of soldiers could lock their shields together over their heads and crouch under them. Protected by their shields, they could safely advance toward the enemy. This was known as the tortoise, or *testudo,* formation. During a siege, catapults were used to hurl iron bolts and large stones over fortress walls.

DEADLY WEAPONS

These iron spearheads were found on the site of an old Roman fort near Bath, in Britain. The wooden shafts they were on rotted long ago. Roman soldiers carried both light and heavy spears. The lighter ones were used for throwing, and the heavier ones were for thrusting at close range.

SWORDS

Both short and long swords would have been kept in a scabbard. This spectacular scabbard was owned by an officer who served the Emperor Tiberius. It may have been given to him by the Emperor himself. It is elaborately decorated in gold and silver.

4 Cut a square of cardboard as wide as your shoulders. Use the compass to draw a 3-in diameter circle in the center. Cut the square in half and cut out the half circles.

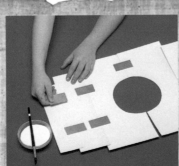

5 Use strips of cardboard to glue the shoulder halves together, leaving a neck hole. Cut out four more strips, two a little shorter than the others. Attach them in the same way.

Put the shoulder piece over your head and tie the chest section around yourself. Now you are a legionary ready to do battle with the enemies of Rome. Metal strip armor was invented during the reign of the Emperor Tiberius, AD14-37. Originally, the various parts were hinged and were joined either by hooks or by buckles and straps.

Ships and Sailors

THE ROMANS USED SHIPS for trade, transport and warfare. Roman warships were slim, fast vessels called galleys. They were powered by oarsmen who sat below deck. A standard Roman war galley had 270 oarsmen. It also had a large, square sail that was used for more speed when the wind was favorable.

All kinds of goods, from wool and pottery to marble and grain, had to be moved around the Empire. Most goods, especially heavy cargoes of food or building materials, were moved by water. Merchant ships were deeper, heavier and slower than galleys. They had big, flapping sails and longer oars to make steering easier. Barges were used on rivers.

CONTAINERS
Oil and wine were often shipped in large pottery jars called *amphorae*. Here, an amphora is being carried from one ship to another. The amphorae were usually stacked in the ship's hold, with layers of brushwood as padding.

AT THE DOCKS
This wall painting from the port of Ostia shows a merchant ship being loaded. Heavy sacks of grain are being carried on board. You can see the two large steering oars at the stern, or rear, of the ship.

The Romans built lighthouses on treacherous coasts—stone towers topped by big lanterns or blazing beacons. Pirates, uncharted waters and the weather also made sea travel dangerous.

ROLLING ON THE RIVER
Wine and other liquids were sometimes stored in barrels. These were transported by river barges, like the one in this carving. Barrels of wine would be hauled from the vineyards of Germany or southern France to the nearest seaport.

MAKE AN AMPHORA
You will need: sheet of thin cardboard, ruler, two pencils, scissors, corrugated cardboard—two circles of 4 in and 8 in in diameter, two strips of 16 in x 12 in and another large piece, masking tape, white glue, old newspaper, paintbrush, reddish-brown acrylic paint, water bowl.

1 Cut two pieces of cardboard—2 in and 15 in in depth. Tape the short piece to the circle. Curl the long piece to make the neck. Make two holes in the side and tape it to the large circle.

2 Roll up the strips of corrugated cardboard. Bend them, as shown, attaching one end to the hole in the neck and the other to the cardboard. Set in place with glue and tape.

3 Cut a piece of cardboard, 6 square in. Roll it into a cylinder shape. Cut four lines, 4 in long, at one end, so it can be tapered into a point, as shown. Bind with tape.

SAILING OFF TO BATTLE

This painting imagines the impressive spectacle of a Roman war galley leaving harbor on its way to battle. Galleys were powered by rows of oarsmen, who sat on benches below deck. The helmsman, who controlled the galley's steering, shouted orders down to them. This galley has three banks, or layers, of oars. An underwater battering ram stuck out from the bow, or front, of war galleys. During a sea battle, the mast was lowered and the galley would try to ram the enemy ship. With the ram stuck in its side, Roman soldiers could easily board the enemy ship to finish the fight man to man.

An amphora like this one might have been used to carry wine, oil or fish sauce. Its long, pointed end would be stuck into layers of brushwood for support during transport.

4 To give the amphora a more solid base, roll up a cone of corrugated cardboard and stick it around the tapered end. Push a pencil into the end, as shown. Tape in position.

5 Stick the neck onto the main body. Cover the whole piece with strips of newspaper brushed on with glue. Let dry. Repeat until you have built up a thick layer.

6 When the paper is dry, paint the amphora. Roman amphorae were made of clay, so use a reddish-brown paint to make yours look like it is clay. Let dry.

247

Builders of the Empire

THE ROMANS were great builders and engineers. As the legions conquered foreign lands, they built new roads to carry their supplies and messengers. The roads were very straight, stretching across hundreds of miles. They were built with a slight hump in the middle so that rainwater drained off to the sides. Some were paved with stone and others were covered with gravel or stone chippings. Roman engineers also used their skills to bring water supplies to their cities by building aqueducts.

The Romans constructed great domes, arched bridges and grand public buildings all across the Empire. Local supplies of stone and timber were used. Stone was an important Roman building material, but had to be quarried and transported to sites. The Romans were the first to develop concrete, which was cheaper and stronger than stone.

The rule of the Romans came to an end in western Europe over 1,500 years ago. Yet reminders of their skills and organization are still visible today.

ROMAN ROADS
A typical Roman road, stretching into the distance as far as the eye can see. It runs through the coastal town of Ostia, in Italy. It was the 1800s before anyone in Europe could build roads to match those of ancient Rome.

MUSCLE POWER
This stone carving shows how Romans used big wooden cranes to lift heavy building materials. The crane is powered by a huge treadwheel. Slaves walk around and around in the wheel, making it turn. The turning wheel pulls on the rope, which is tied around the heavy block of stone, raising it off the ground.

MAKE A GROMA
You will need: large piece of cardboard, scissors, ruler, pencil, square of cardboard, white glue, masking tape, balsa wood pole, plasticine, silver foil, string, large sewing needle, acrylic paints, paintbrush, water bowl, broom handle.

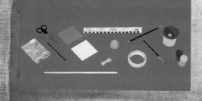

1 Cut out three pieces of cardboard—two 8 in x 2½ in, one 16 in x 2½ in. Cut another piece, 6 in x 5 in, for the handle. Then cut them into shape, as shown above.

2 Measure to the center of the long piece. Use a pencil to make a slot here, between the layers of cardboard. The slot is for the balsa wood pole.

3 Slide the pole into the slot and tape the cardboard pieces in a cross. Use the cardboard square to make sure the four arms of the groma are at right angles. Glue in place.

BUILDING MATERIALS

The Romans used a variety of stones for building. Local quarries were the most common source. Limestone and a volcanic rock called tufa were used in Pompeii. Slate was used for roofing in parts of Britain. Fine marble, used for temples and other public buildings, was available in the Carrara region of Italy, as it still is today. However, it was also imported from overseas.

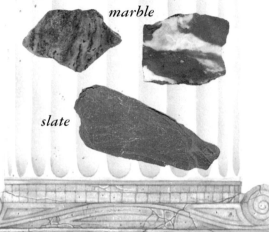

marble

slate

SURVIVING THE CENTURIES

This Roman bridge crosses the River Guadalquivir at Córdoba in Spain. The Romans had no bulldozers or power tools, and yet their buildings and monuments have survived thousands of years.

WALLS OF ROME

The city of Rome's defenses were built at many stages throughout its history. These walls were raised during the reign of the Emperor Marcus Aurelius, AD121–180. Known as the Aurelian Walls, they are still in good condition today.

Slot the arms onto the balsa wood pole. Use the plumb lines as a guide to make sure the pole is vertical. The arms can then be used to line up objects in the distance. Romans used a groma to measure right angles and to make sure roads were straight.

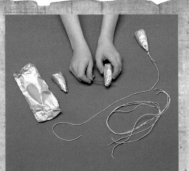

4 Roll the plasticine into four small cones and cover them with foil. Thread string through the tops, as shown. These are the groma's plumb lines, or vertical guides.

5 Tie the plumb lines to each arm, as shown. They must all hang at the same length—8 in will do. If the plasticine is too heavy, use wet newspaper rolled up in the foil.

6 Split the top of the handle piece, and wrap it around the balsa wood pole. Glue it in place, as shown. Do the same on the other end with the broom handle. Paint the groma.

Glossary

A

amphitheater An oval, open-air arena surrounded by seats. It was invented by the Romans for public shows such as gladiators fighting to the death and battles between wild animals.

amphora (plural: amphorae) A pottery storage jar, often shaped like a tall vase with handles and a pointed base. Amphorae came in all shapes and sizes—tall and slim, fat and round.

anvil A block used by smiths for shaping hot metals.

aqueduct

aqueduct An artificial channel for carrying water over a long distance. Aqueducts were usually underground or were supported on arched bridges.

arena The dirt floor area in an amphitheater where games and combats took place.

atrium The hallway or courtyard in a Roman house. The center of the atrium was open to the sky.

auxiliaries Soldiers recruited from non-Roman citizens.

B

basilica A building in the forum of a Roman city, used as law courts and a town hall.

blacksmith A craftsman who makes or repairs iron goods.

brazier A bronze container filled with hot coals, used for heating rooms.

C

catapult A large wooden structure used during a siege to fire stones and iron bolts at the enemy.

chariot

century A unit of the Roman army, numbering from 80 to 100 soldiers.

chariot A lightweight cart drawn by horses. Chariots were used in warfare or for racing.

circus An oval track used for chariot races.

citizen A free person with the right to vote.

civilization A society that has made advances in the arts, science and technology, law or government.

cohort A division of the Roman army, at times numbering about 500 soldiers.

conscript Someone who is called up by the government to serve in the army.

consul One of the two leaders of the Roman republic, elected each year.

cremation The burning of dead bodies.

Consul

cuirass Armor that protects the upper part of the body.

curia The council in ancient Roman cities.

D

dictator A ruler with total power.

E

emperor The ruler of an empire.

empire A large number of different lands ruled over by a single person or government.

estate A large amount of land, houses and farms, usually owned by a single person or group.

F

flax A plant whose stems are used to make a cloth called linen. Its blue flowers can be used to make a dye, and its seeds are crushed to produce linseed oil.

forceps Surgical instruments shaped like pincers or tongs.

forum The town center or downtown area of a Roman city.

G

galley A warship powered by oars.

gladiator A professional fighter, a slave or a criminal who fought to the death for public entertainment.

graffiti Words or pictures scrawled or scratched in public places, particularly on walls.

grid pattern A criss-cross pattern of straight lines at right angles. It was used to divide a town into blocks and straight streets.

groma An instrument used by Roman surveyors. They used it to measure right angles and to make sure roads were straight.

gruel A soup of cereal and water, such as porridge.

guild A society that protected the interests of people working within a trade.

J

javelin A throwing spear.

K

kiln An industrial oven, or a furnace.

kindling Twigs, woodchips or other material used to start a fire.

L

legion A section of the Roman army made up only

of Roman Citizens. Non-Roman citizens could not be legionaries.

litter A form of transport in which a seat or platform is carried by bearers.

lyre One of various harp-like instruments played in ancient Greece and Rome.

M

mail Chain armor, made up of interlocking iron rings.

midwife Someone who helps a woman to give birth.

mosaic

mosaic A picture made up from many small squares or cubes of glass, stone or pottery, set in soft concrete.

myrrh A kind of resin from shrubs, used to make perfume and medicine.

O

ocher An earthy iron ore used as pigment. It is usually red or yellow.

P

palla A large shawl that could be arranged in various ways.

panpipes A musical instrument made up of a series of pipes of different lengths.

papyrus A reed that grows on the River Nile. It is used to make a kind of paper.

patrician A member of one of the old, wealthy and powerful families in ancient Rome.

plate armor Fitted body armor made of linked sheets of solid metal.

plebeian A member of the (free) common people of ancient Rome.

preserve To treat food so that it does not spoil or go bad.

R

ram A large, pointed beam extending from the hull, or front, of an ancient warship. It was used to ram into the side of an enemy ship, making it easeir to board.

republic A state that is governed by an assembly of its citizens rather than by a king.

S

sacrifice The killing of a living thing in honor of the gods.

Samian ware A type of glazed, red-clay pottery that was popular throughout the Roman Empire.

Samian pot

Saturnalia A winter festival held in honor of the god Saturn.

Senate The law-making assembly of ancient Rome.

sickle A tool with a curved blade used to cut grass or grain crops.

society All the classes of people living in a particular community or country.

standard A banner used by armies to rally their troops in battle or carried in parades.

stola A long dress worn by Roman women. It was worn over a tunic.

oil flask and strigils

strigil A metal scraper used for cleaning the body.

stylus A pointed tool, such as the one used to scratch words onto a wax tablet.

survey To map out and measure the land. Land is surveyed before the construction of a building or a road, or any other structure.

T

tablinium The formal reception room and study in a Roman house.

terra-cotta Baked, unglazed, orange-red clay.

toga A white woolen robe, worn by the upper classes in ancient Rome.

tortoise or testudo A method of covering a group of soldiers with shields to protect them from missiles.

treadwheel A wooden wheel turned by the feet of people, used to power mills or other machinery.

tribune One of the officials elected to represent the interests of the common people in ancient Rome. Tribune was also a rank in the Roman army.

triclinium Dining room. Its name comes from the Roman tradition of having an arrangement of three (tri) couches to lie on while dining.

trident

trident A three-pronged spear used by fishermen and gladiators.

trivet A metal stand placed over a flame to support a cooking pot.

tunic A simple, shirt-like garment.

tutor A personal teacher.

V

villa A Roman country house, often decorated with mosaics and wall paintings. Villas were usually part of an argicultural estate.

Index

255

Acknowledgments

ANNESS PUBLISHING would like to thank the following children for modelling for this book: Mohammed Asfar, Emily Askew, Anthony Bainbridge, Leon R. Banton, Afsana Begum, Donna Marie Bradley, Lucilla Braune, Ha Chu, Charlene Da Cova, Paula Dent, Frankie Timothy Junior Elliot, Lana Green, Aileen Greiner, Rikky Charles Healey, Francesca Hill, Aslom Hussain, Roxanne John, Alex Lindblom-Smith, Amarni McKenzie, Imran Miah, Daniel Ofori, Vanessa Ofori, Edward Parker, Rajiv M. Pattani, Mai-Anh Peterson, Emily Preddie, Susan Quirke, Eva Rivera/Razbadavskite, Brendan Scott, Claudia Martins Silva, Clleon Smith, Roxanne Smith, Nicky Stafford, Mark Stefford, Simon Thexton, Shereen Thomas, Saif Uddowlla, Ha Vinh, Peter Watson, Kirsty Wells and Harriet Woollard. Gratitude also to their parents, and to Hampden Gurney and Walnut Tree Walk Schools.

PICTURE CREDITS

b=bottom, t-top, c=centre, l=left, r=right

Lesley and Roy Adkins Picture Library: 195cr, 203t, 221bl, 225b, 226l, 227b, 239tl; B and C Alexander: 18tl, 20t, 34bl, 46l, 47tl, 47tr, 49t, 53br, 55tl, 68r; Heather Angel: 33 bc; The Ancient Art and Architecture Collection Ltd: 13tl, 19t, 43tr, 45tl, 50l, 51b, 57cl, 66r, 67tl, 74b, 79tc, 80t, 80b, 81bc, 81tr, 82r, 82/83, 84br, 86, 87bl, 88l, 88r, 89tl, 90t, 91cl, 91br, 92b, 100l, 102r, 103tl, 106t, 107t, 108b, 109bc, 110l, 110r, 111b, 112r, 113r, 114br, 115tl, 115tr, 115b, 116t, 117t, 120r, 121tr, 122tr, 56b, 125l, 126l, 127r, 135tr, 138cr, 139br, 141cl, 142cr, 145tl, 148tl, 151br, 151bl, 152tl, 152cl, 154cr, 155br, 157tr, 157cl, 160tr, 162tl, 162cl, 163c, 165cr, 168cr, 169cl, 170tl, 174tr, 176cl, 177tr, 179br, 182cl, 184bl, 185cl, 186tr, 188tl, 198b, 198l, 199tl, 199tc, 201tl, 204b, 211tr, 211cl, 211cr, 214/215, 217r, 221bl, 222b, 223tr, 223br, 229t, 230b, 237tr, 238bl, 236tr, 236bl, 238tr, 241tl, 245bl; A-Z Botanical Collection Ltd: 247br; The Bridgeman Art Library: 12l, 22b, 23tr, 23br, 24l, 32l, 49c, 59br, 66l, 67cr, 69bl, 135cr, 146bl, 150br, 159t, 162tr, 164cl, 164tr, 171r, 203b; The British Museum: 20c, 37tr, 87tr, 89br 83t, 90b, 98l, 98r, 100r, 105bc, 106bl, 108t, 109tr, 113l, 122br, 123l, 123br, 125r, 142tl, 142bl, 161cl, 165cl, 169tl, 212r, 213tr, 213cr, 213bl, 218c, 218r, 220l, 230c, 236bl, 236br, 236br, 237b, 241b, 247bc; Peter Clayton: 43cr, 57tl, 57tr, 58bl, 59tl, 59cl, 85t, 85b, 89bl, 105bl, 105br, 106br, 114t, 114bl, 121tl, 121bl, 122l, 123tr, 145bl, 149br, 154tl, 160cl, 161tr, 181tr, 183tl, 183cl, 208l, 215cr, 224tl; Bruce Coleman: 33t, 35br, 43bl, 48t, 68l; Colorific: 69t; Sylvia Corday: 23tl, 30cr; C M Dixon: 13tr, 16l, 22l, 25tl, 26l, 28r, 31tl, 32r, 33t, 33b, 35t, 37tl, 38b, 41tr, 41c, 42t, 42bl, 42br, 44l, 44r, 45tr, 46r, 48cr, 50r, 52bl, 54l, 56l, 56r, 58r, 58br, 61cr, 62r, 64r,

64b, 65bl, 65br, 78b, 79b, 84t, 87tl, 78tr, 91tr, 101t, 104, 105t, 109tl, 117b, 118l, 118r, 120l, 129t, 134c, 138c, 139tr, 139cl, 140c, 141tl, 141cr, 143c, 146tr, 146br, 147tr, 147cl, 147br, 149cl, 149bl, 150cl, 153tr, 154bl, 155tl, 156tl, 157tl, 157cr, 158tr, 158c, 159cl, 163tr, 166tl, 168tl, 169tr, 173tl, 175cl, 180tr, 180cl, 184cr, 184br, 185bl, 186cl, 187tr, 189br, 200l, 202bl, 204t, 205bl, 207tl, 207cr, 210bl, 214bl, 215tr, 215br, 216l, 216r, 217l, 219tl, 219tc, 219tr, 220r, 222/223, 223bl, 224tr, 224b, 225t, 225c, 226br, 228cl, 228tr, 229bl, 232t, 233tl, 233cl, 233bl, 235t, 235c, 236tr, 237tl, 238tl, 238br, 251tl, 243tr, 243b, 244l, 245tr, 246tr, 246bl, 246br, 248l, 248r, 250t, 251c; Ecoscene: 52t, 39tr; E T Archive: 17t, 67tr; Mary Evans Picture Library: 18b, 21tl, 25tr, 34br, 43tl, 94r, 94l, 102l, 138tl, 139tl, 140tl, 143b, 144tr, 164c, 171bl, 173tr, 178tr, 181cl, 182tl, 182cr, 184cl, 187cl, 188bl, 189tr, 189cl, 199bl, 199br, 200r, 210tr, 219bl, 232b, 242br, 244r, 247t; FLPA: 19cl, 37br, 59cr; Werner Forman Archive: 47bc, 55c, 62l, 211bl, 241t; Fortean Picture Library: 53t, 54r, 60c; Geoscience Features Picture Library: 249tr; Griffith Institute, Ashmolean Museum: 74t, 97t, 97b; Sonia Halliday Photographs: 150tl, 151tr, 205tl, 226tr, 251l; Robert Harding 5cl, 19b, 21b, 23bl, 31cl, 39tl, 39br, 61tl, 61tr, 143t, 188br; Michael Holford Photographs: 84bl, 99bl, 56t, 129b, 256cr, 360tl, 361tl, 365tr, 366cr, 149tr 171tl, 173cl, 174cl, 175tl, 178bl, 179cr, 180tr, 195tr, 202tr, 202br, 206, 212l, 218l, 219br, 228bl, 228br, 233br, 234bl, 239tr, 239bl, 241bl, 242bl, 249tl, 250br; Simon James: 231tr, 231br; Manchester Museum: 99tl; Museum of London: 35bl; Museum of Sweden: 33c; Michael Nicholson: 141tr, 144c, 145tr, 148bl, 167tl, 167cl, 167bl, 172tr, 172cl, 179tl, 179cl, 179bl; Bob Partridge and the Ancient Egypt Picture Library: 89tr, 92t, 119t, 119br; Courtesy of the Petrie Museum of Egyptian Archaeology, University College London: Planet Earth Pictures Ltd: 195b; 111c; Radiotimes Hulton Picture Library: 116b; Tony Stone Images: 194/195; Visual Arts Library: 227tr, 236/237; Zefa: 75t, 78tl, 79tl, 79tr, 81tl, 82l, 83b, 92l, 93tl, 93b, 96, 96/97, 97c, 99tr, 101b, 103tr, 103cr, 103b, 110/111, 112l, 126r, 127l, 198r, 205br, 235b.